STUDENT ACTIVISM AND CURRICULAR CHANGE
IN HIGHER EDUCATION

The Mobilization Series on Social Movements, Protest, and Culture

Series Editor

Professor Hank Johnston
San Diego State University, USA

Published in conjunction with *Mobilization: An International Quarterly*, the premier research journal in the field, this series disseminates high quality new research and scholarship in the fields of social movements, protest, and contentious politics. The series is interdisciplinary in focus and publishes monographs and collections of essays by new and established scholars.

Other titles of interest from Ashgate

Culture, Social Movements, and Protest
Edited by Hank Johnston

The Policing of Transnational Protest
Edited by Donatella della Porta, Abby Peterson and Herbert Reiter

Student Activism and Curricular Change in Higher Education

MIKAILA MARIEL LEMONIK ARTHUR
Rhode Island College, USA

ASHGATE

Published by
Ashgate Publishing Limited
Wey Court East
Union Road
Farnham
Surrey, GU9 7PT
England

Ashgate Publishing Company
Suite 420
101 Cherry Street
Burlington
VT 05401-4405
USA

www.ashgate.com

British Library Cataloguing in Publication Data
Lemonik Arthur, Mikaila.
Student activism and curricular change in higher education. – (Mobilization series on social movements, protest, and culture)
1. Curriculum change – United States – Case studies. 2. Universities and colleges – Curricula – United States. 3. Student movements – United States – Case studies. 4. Women's studies – United States. 5. Asian Americans – Study and teaching (Higher) – United States. 6. Gay and lesbian studies – United States. 7. Education, Higher – Aims and objectives – United States. 8. Education, Higher – Social aspects – United States.
I. Title II. Series
378.1'99'0973-dc22

Library of Congress Cataloging-in-Publication Data
Arthur, Mikaila Lemonik.
Student activism and curricular change in higher education / by Mikaila Lemonik Arthur.
  p. cm. — (Mobilization series on social movements, protest, and culture)
Includes bibliographical references and index.
ISBN 978-1-4094-0934-2 (hardback : alk. paper) — ISBN 978-1-4094-0935-9 (ebook)
1. Universities and colleges—Curricula—United States—Case studies. 2. Curriculum change—United States—Case studies. 3. Student movements—United States—Case studies. I. Title.
LB2361.5.A78 2011
378.1'990973—dc22

2010035151

ISBN 9781409409342 (hbk)
ISBN 9781409409359 (ebk)

Printed and bound in Great Britain by the
MPG Books Group, UK

Contents

To Sami—for reasons too numerous to explain.

List of Figures and Tables

Figures

Tables

Preface

The journey that became this book started over a decade ago in my undergraduate classes at Mount Holyoke College. I was introduced to the study of Asian American Studies by Karen Cardozo, to the sociological study of social movements by Ken Tucker, the practice of social research by Eleanor Townsley, and the joys of working in the archives by the Mount Holyoke College Archives staff. Ken Tucker, Eleanor Townsley, and Bob Schwartz supervised a senior honors project on 1960s-era student movements and guided me into graduate school. It is the influence of this amazing group of faculty and staff that created the scholar, and the teacher, that I am today. I didn't know then that all of those experiences would turn into a decade of work on a project like this, but that's what happened, as a paper I wrote in Ken Tucker's social movements course on the Asian American movement transformed into a dissertation on social movements and curricular change.

That dissertation was written while I was a graduate student at New York University. Mitchell Stevens, Jeff Manza, Amy Binder, Patrick Carroll, Robert Max Jackson, Ed Lehman, Chris Rhomberg, Dean Savage, David Slocum, and David Greenberg all provided advice, comments, and feedback that helped shape this project. Mildred Schwartz was always there to lend a caring ear and provided some of the most valuable advice that any graduate student could want. My dissertation committee, Jeff Goodwin, Caroline Persell, and Edwin Amenta have left their indelible impression on my research. A National Science Foundation Doctoral Dissertation Improvement Grant (#0622299) made this research possible and fellowship funding from New York University kept food on the table and the lights on at night. Audiences at New York University, the Marist College Conference on Women & Society, the annual meetings of the American Sociological Association and the Eastern Sociological Society, Fairleigh Dickinson University, Hamilton College, Bates College, Washington College, and Cornell University heard versions of the arguments presented here and helped strengthen the final manuscript.

While the pseudonymous nature of the case studies included in this book prevents me from thanking by name the hundreds of staff (especially the archivists), faculty, administrators, and former students at these six colleges and universities for their time and participation in this project. They were willing to share their own recollections of curricular change on their campuses, whether over a cup of tea at a local coffee shop or across a crackling international phone connection. They provided time, resources, and the data that made this book possible. Of course, more importantly, they participated in curricular change in the first place. It is their inventiveness and persistence that resulted in the creation of the programs I studied, and for that they deserve much more than appreciation.

Colleagues across the field of sociology have provided moral support and essential feedback at various stages of this process. I would particularly like to thank Danielle Bessett, Emily Rauscher, Michael McQuairre, Michael Friedson, Josipa Roksa, Neal Caren, Libby Wheatley, Owen Whooley, Kate Pfieffer, and Monika Krause, though I am sure there are valuable contributions I have forgotten to mention from countless others. Friends outside of sociology, especially Silvia Poggioni, Alexis Greer, and Kyong-Sook Boo, have been essential allies in the writing process. Gilda Zwerman shepherded me through the process of creating a book proposal, and Hank Johnston and Claire Jarvis saw the merit in my work and invited me to create this book with Ashgate. The Rhode Island College Department of Sociology has been an amazingly hospitable place to finish this project. My colleagues have been enthusiastic about my work and have given me the space and (somehow) the time necessary to craft this manuscript, while my students provide me with a sense of fulfillment and purpose that makes long days of writing tolerable and reminds me why college curricula matter in the first place. To whatever extent the arguments presented in this book are clear, it is because I spend my days explaining complex ideas to undergraduates, and they always help me refine that skill.

My family has been a source of strength and inspiration throughout this writing. My grandparents, Edythe Arthur Haines, Irving Lemonik, and Anne Lemonik, have always encouraged me to reach for the stars. My sister, Sami Lemonik-Arthur, inspires me with her dedication to her own work, which takes the form of beautiful objects you can see and hold instead of these words on limp sheets of paper. My parents, Baila Lemonik and Dwight Arthur, have put up with my absences when I needed to be writing and have always been there to remind me how much everything else in life matters.

Finally, there is Benjamin Ledsham. I don't know how much this book has served as a disruption to our lives together, but you have certainly made it easier by putting food on the table, printing out things for me to read, and being the only face I see after a long day of writing. The decade I have spent on this project would have been immeasurably lonely without you, and I cannot imagine what the end result would have looked like. Thank you for always being there. My love for you goes to the moon and back, and yours has made this book go further, too.

Mikaila Mariel Lemonik Arthur
June 23, 2010

PART I
Introduction

Chapter 1
The Promise (and the Threat)
of Curricular Change

On May 3, 1999, Junaid Rana and ten other students were led away from a University of Texas Austin administrative office building in handcuffs. Rana had helped draft a proposal for Asian American studies at UT Austin the prior year and had served as one of two student members on a search committee charged with hiring a director of the fledgling program. Students had been pushing for an Asian American studies program since at least 1992 by forming committees, creating proposals, and lobbying the university administration (Kennedy 2000b). In 1998, they had started to feel like they were getting somewhere. But during the spring semester, the search effort had rapidly deteriorated. Bitter disappointment followed in the wake of the search committee's inability to hire a director and the weeks of fruitless meetings. Finally, the announcement that the interim Dean of Liberal Arts decided to reject the leading candidate for the position triggered a sit-in and Rana's arrest for criminal trespass. Was this the end of the effort to bring Asian American Studies to the University of Texas?

Rana's arrest record and those of the other students were expunged after they all performed community service and avoided getting arrested again for a period of time. In response to the sit-in, the administration agreed to establish an Asian American Studies advisory council with both students and faculty as members, a speakers series, the hiring of a one-year visiting faculty member, and a new search for a permanent director and tenure track professor. A series of interim directors and faculty hires were appointed beginning shortly thereafter. Junaid Rana went on to earn an assistant professorship in Asian American studies at the University of Illinois Urbana-Champaign. By 2005, the Center for Asian American Studies at UT Austin (officially founded in 2000) offered an undergraduate major; an honors program; an established group of core and affiliated faculty as well as lecturers and instructors; and about 20 academic courses a year (Kennedy 2000a).

The events at the University of Texas illustrate a successful initiative on the part of students to effect curricular change. Much of the same support exists at Wesleyan University for a program in queer studies[1]. Since approximately 1991,

---

1   Throughout this book, I refer to my third case as "queer studies." This is despite the prevalence and perhaps even dominance of other names for the discipline, such as lesbian and gay studies, LGBT studies, and sexuality studies. There are a few reasons for this choice. First, "queer studies" is both specific (it excludes those programs focused on sexology rather than the transformative nature of non-heterosexual identities and practices) and

students had been pushing the administration to develop such a program and to hire more faculty to teach courses focusing on issues of sexuality. Students were not even able to convince the university to retain the faculty they had already hired—noted queer theorist Judith Butler began her career at Wesleyan and was turned down for a permanent position. Students at Wesleyan even had formal faculty support—the American Studies program had submitted a formal request to hire a faculty member with expertise in queer studies for at least four years. In 2001, after students organized a "kiss-in" during an event for prospective undergraduates to demand increased access to courses in queer studies, the hiring of a tenure-track faculty member to offer these courses, and the development of a major within five years (Silbergeld 2001), the administration agreed to fund a queer studies faculty member in American Studies, which now allows students to develop queer studies concentrations within the department. But as of this writing, students at Wesleyan still can neither major in queer studies nor have a queer studies minor recorded on their transcripts.

Why were the students at the University of Texas Austin so much more able to reach their goals than the students at Wesleyan? And why does the process of curricular expansion that enabled the development of the Asian American studies program at the University of Texas remain so contentious? This book seeks to answer these questions by drawing on case studies of six colleges and universities in the United States and focusing on the emergence of curricular programs in women's studies, Asian American studies, and queer studies.

Contentious Politics at College

As the stories of Asian American studies at the University of Texas Austin and queer studies at Wesleyan College highlight, individuals often seek to change the organizations that they are part of by engaging in contentious politics. The term "contentious politics" refers to a broad range of activities beyond but also including social movements that involve public, episodic contestation around issues that affect the interests of the claimants and/or their targets (McAdam, Tarrow, and Tilly 2001; Morrill, Zald, and Rao 2003). This concept is more expansive than the concept of a social movement because most definitions of social movements

broad (it includes a wide variety of identities and practices that are not easily encompassed by other terms or sets of terms). Second, the term queer has typically been used in a way that suggests a specific radical intellectual orientation to sexual identities and practices, and this kind of perspective is dominant in driving the emergence of queer studies as a discrete field of its own. Third, it highlights the linkages between queer studies as a discipline and that which came before it, particularly the development of queer theory in English and cultural studies. While some find the term unsuitable for their own variety of reasons (it is reclaimed from a slur, it suggests difference instead of similarity, etc.) it is the term which most clearly encapsulates the intellectual project of the discipline I am exploring here.

require that movements consist of those who are outside of "politics as usual" or do not have access to institutionalized forms of political action (Snow, Soule, and Kriesi 2004), while the concept of contentious politics does not require this outsider status.

Because of the high likelihood that at least some individuals involved in any given episode of contentious politics within a college or university are positioned as insiders, much of contemporary social movements scholarship has precluded consideration of these episodes of contention as social movements. However, insiders can indeed be part of social movement activism (see, for instance, Katzenstein 1998; Santoro and McGuire 1997; Wilde 2004). These insiders are typically those who can and do participate in "politics as usual" while simultaneously facing structural exclusion from decision-making processes (Grossman 2005), as students might, or being rendered invisible by the cultural politics of the organization (Slaughter 1997). Where insiders are marginalized in these ways, they can and do turn to activism and indeed to social movements as they attempt to create the change they desire. Though some of the campaigns covered in this book clearly involve social movement organizations and others might be further along the spectrum towards contentious organizational politics, I will refer to all of the contentious campaigns as social movements. Regardless of whether the individuals participating positioned themselves as insiders or outsiders, these contentious campaigns occurred when change could not be or was not won through the conventional decision-making process, and thus participants turned to alternative forms of action as they sought to change their organization.

While contentious politics and social movements within colleges and universities have never been limited to student movements, they are the most widely known example. Student movements have always had a presence in higher education (Boren 2001) and in curricular debates, particularly in the late 1960s and the early 1970s when the curricular changes studied here emerged (Degroot 1998; Foster and Long 1970; Glazer 1970; Levitt 1984; Lipset 1967). Scholars have often suggested that student movements may be more likely than other types of movements to arise, perhaps because students are more "available" to protest (Lipset 1967, 1976), because students are less mature and more "irrational" (Smelser 1963), or perhaps because students (as relatively privileged members of society) have access to more of the resources necessary for organizing and sustaining movements (Jenkins 1983; McCarthy and Zald 1977, 2002; Zald and McCarthy 1979). Movements targeting educational institutions are quite common—of 4,656 protest events between 1968 and 1975 that were reported in the *New York Times*, 24 percent targeted educational institutions (Van Dyke, Soule, and Taylor 2004), while between 1960 and 1990, 18 percent did (Walker, Martin, and McCarthy 2008).

However, scholars studying student movements have often discounted the role of political context and opportunities leading to movement emergence and have ignored the study of movement impacts. More contemporary social movement theories have emerged that are grounded in an understanding of the role of political contexts and opportunities and attempt to understand how movement impacts come about (Amenta, Caren, Fetner et al. 2002; Amenta and Young 1999a; Goodwin and Jasper 1999; Kriesi 2004). But these models have generally specified their propositions as applying specifically to social movements who name states as the targets of their activism and have not considered the dynamics of social movements that target organizations (Arthur 2008). As Mary Katzenstein (1998) writes, organizations are the nexuses for conflicts over status and resources in the contemporary political world; in addition, much of the impact of social movements is about influencing organizational practices (Rao 2009), and thus movements in the organizational sphere deserve a politically-oriented framework for understanding their outcomes. Indeed, "it is rather easier to change the world than to change the university" (Glazer 1970: 193).

In addition, few commentators on movements within colleges and universities have seriously considered the role that non-student members of college and university communities may play in contentious politics. Many instances of contentious politics involve the coordinated action of students, faculty, and or staff. Each group has access to a different set of resources and faces a different set of costs from their involvement in contentious politics. While it may be true that only a few faculty members are involved in any given episode of contentious politics (Bayer 1972), that does not mean we should discount their role entirely (Riesman 1973). The important thing to recognize here is that faculty involvement in a curricular change campaign does not preclude the possibility that contentious politics are at work. Not all faculty members have the same access to and not all changes are adopted through the regular shared governance procedures—some require contention to be adopted.

Understanding Social Movements

If we assume that social movements are responsible for changes in colleges and universities, we are arguing that change happens inside educational institutions due to the pressure created by activists' articulated demands and their participation in organized and perhaps disruptive contention. This contention then functions as a "bargaining chip" (Burstein, Einwohner, and Hollander 1995) that causes those in power to believe it would be easier to approve new courses and programs than to continue facing activism and protest. There are, of course, a number of different models that aim to explain how and when social movements are able to reach their goals.

Classical social movement theorists did not devote much attention to understanding the outcomes of social movements. Indeed, early commentators saw social movements as irrational attempts to engage in social and political change that were unlikely to succeed (Smelser 1963). Perhaps the most traditional model for explaining student movements is the resource mobilization perspective (Jenkins 1983; McCarthy and Zald 1977, 2002; Zald and McCarthy 1979). The resource mobilization perspective proposes that those movements that have access to a sufficient quantity of resources (usually defined in terms of money and time) will be those most able to accomplish their goals. The resource mobilization model would thus predict that colleges and universities which adopted new programs experienced organized student movements with access to significant financial resources, human resources, time, and/or allies or "conscience constituencies" (those who will not be beneficiaries of the movement but who nevertheless actively support it [Jenkins 1983]). However, though student movements do vary in terms of how much money and time they have (students working their way through college differ from students attending elite schools debt-free), the differences in financial and time resources among student movements is less significant than the differences in other types of resources, particularly what Edwards and McCarthy call "human resources"—"labor, experience, skills, and expertise [and] leadership" (2004:127). This means the resource mobilization perspective is less likely to explain the differences between student movements than it is to be useful in other domains.

A second perspective is that of frame theory. The frame theory model suggests that movements which choose frames that resonate with their constituency and which clearly specify the appropriate ameliorative action (Benford and Snow 2000; Cress and Snow 2000; Snow, Rochford, Worden et al. 1986) will be most able to have an impact on their targets. These frames include diagnostic frames, which explain what a problem is and where it comes from; prognostic frames, which propose a solution to the problem; and motivational frames, which encourage individuals to become involved in activism. Framing models often fail to provide a mechanism by which the "successful" framing strategy is in fact translated into "success," however. Perhaps a way to approach this question would be by understanding the factor that leads to movement impacts as instead the "strategic capacity" (Ganz 2000) that leaves a movement able to create and utilize appropriate frames. The frame theory perspective would thus propose that colleges and universities would be more likely to enact curricular change when they experienced movements that developed the strategic capacity to create and deploy frames that resonated with the campus community and which left the administration feeling that program creation was the only way to respond.

The third set of explanations is rooted in a political understanding of social movements, including political opportunity theory and political mediation theory. The political opportunity model suggests that movements will be able to have an impact when the political structure is open to the demands of the movement and when it has the capacity to implement them (Kitschelt 1986; Meyer 1993; Meyer and Minkoff 2004). The political mediation model builds further on this framework to say that it is not only that the political context of a movement matters, but rather that movements must align their organizational form and strategic choices to that political context (Amenta and Caren 2004; Amenta, Caren, and Olasky 2005). Even more than framing and resource mobilization models, political models were developed to apply to states—particularly democratic states. Therefore, the assumptions about what an open and supportive political context might be are rooted in understandings of the way that states operate, focusing on the role of political parties and the nature of governmental bureaucracy. However, these political models can be used to build predictions about when curricular change campaigns are likely to make an impact on colleges and universities. The political mediation model would predict that the organizational context varies from organization to organization and that in order to create new programs, student movements must choose organizational forms and strategies that fit these contexts. In general, we would hypothesize that in supportive contexts (those where colleges and universities are open to interdisciplinary work, are not experiencing significant outside constraints, and believe in the role of students in influencing the direction of the curriculum), social movements would be able to demand and achieve new programs through institutionalized action like creating course proposals and signing petitions as part of an informal campaign coordinated by existing or loosely affiliated student organizations. However, in unsupportive contexts (those where colleges and universities have reason to be hostile to the particular curricular change in question, where budgets are extremely tight, or where students have traditionally not played much role in determining the direction of the curriculum), social movements would need to engage in concerted and assertive action such as holding demonstrations and calling on allies to put pressure on the administration as part of a strategy that would include creating new organizations or coalitions specifically for the purpose of demanding curricular change.

Social Movement Outcomes

When social movement scholars began to address movement impacts, many developed fairly simple formulations that relied on few variables (such as strategy, opportunity, repression, and bureaucracy) to explain outcomes in terms of a binary success-failure framework (Gamson 1990; Jenkins 1983; Tarrow 1998). But movement outcomes are much more complex than simply success and failure. Movements can have impacts that create real change in their targets but fall well short of their intended goals (for instance, a movement could intend to reconstruct the curriculum of an entire university to make it more inclusive of women's perspectives and pedagogical needs, but end up gaining only a well-funded minor in women's studies). They can also have unintended consequences, or even consequences that they see as negative (for instance, a movement could intend to create a minor in queer studies but end up creating a film and lecture series as well as the eradication of a special-interest housing program for queer students). Perspectives on social movement outcomes that only look at success and failure, therefore, fall well short of a complete understanding of what movements do. In order to develop this more expansive understanding of social movement impacts, we can turn to the collective goods framework (Amenta and Young 1999b). The collective goods framework abandons the notion that social movement impacts can only be understood in terms of movements' own perceptions of success or failure.

Instead, we can consider the various impacts—intentional or unintentional, small or large—that have stemmed from movement activism.

The collective goods framework is an important part of the advance offered by political models of social movements. While political context and political mediation approaches provide significant advances in terms of understanding when movements are most able to have an impact, there are two significant limitations facing these perspectives. First, their focus on when impacts happen precludes significant attention to *how* these impacts are produced. Movement impacts could occur directly due to the influence of the movement, indirectly by influencing the opinion of decision-makers and the general public, or simultaneously through direct and indirect influence (Guigini and Yamasaki 2009). Guigini and Yamasaki found that social movements on their own are neither necessary nor sufficient to create policy change. Instead, where public opinion and political allies (in the ideological rather than the structural sense) are already favorable to social movement goals, the social movement is largely unnecessary in creating the desired change. Where public opinion and political allies are *not* already favorable, the role of social movement activism is to create the change in the opinions of both the general public and of decision-makers such that the desired change will ultimately stem from these forces (Guigini and Yamasaki 2009).

Second, political context and political mediation models, as noted above, are designed to explain the outcomes of social movements that target the state. Scholarship on the outcomes of movements targeting organizations, while a growing presence (Binder 2002; Eisenstein 1996; Grossman 2005; Katzenstein 1998; Meyerson 2001; Raeburn 2004; Rao 2009; Van Dyke et al. 2004), has not yet developed a comparable theoretical model to explain what such movements do and do not accomplish. Armstrong and Bernstein (2008) have taken a major step in the right direction with their multi-institutional politics perspective on social movements. They understand that social movement activism can—and indeed often must—include insiders and that movements target a wide variety of non-state institutions. However, Armstrong and Bernstein's model is focused on movements that target institutional fields rather than on movements that target individual formal organizations[2]. Furthermore, their model focuses on why

---

2   Organizational studies scholars argue that institutions are broad fields of social action (such as education or religion) while organizations are specific configurations of rules and relationships (such as a specific school or a specific religious denomination). However, sociologists debate the specific meanings that each should have. For instance, Kelly Moore writes that organizations constitute institutions (Moore 1999); neoinstitutional theorists in contrast see institutions as individual entities and use the term "organizational fields" in much the way Moore uses the term institutions (DiMaggio and Powell 1983). Similarly, the *Blackwell Encyclopedia of Sociology* defines an institution as "the fixing of stereotyped social interactions in the form of rules" including large or small organizations (Henning 2007), and defines organizations as "any purposeful arrangement of social activity that implies active control over human relationships ordered for particular ends" (Hunt 2007). Though in conventional English we often refer to colleges and universities as

movements develop and why they make particular strategic choices; it is less interested in explaining how movements are able to have an impact. This book, then, develops a model—the organizational mediation model—to explain when and how social movements that target organizations are able to have an impact. It does so by exploring the dynamics of a series of campaigns for curricular change within colleges and universities.

Why Curricular Change Matters

Colleges and universities serve as "site[s] where legitimate knowledge is created, transmitted, and sanctified" (Stevens, Armstrong, and Arum 2006:17), they define which "knowledge is authoritative" (Meyer, Ramirez, Frank et al. 2005:30) based on cultural principles, and they serve to arbitrate what knowledge is necessary and/or useful (Clark 1996; Gumport and Snydman 2002; Hefferlin 1969; Maher 1993; Meyer et al. 2005; Rudolph 1989). This function of universities in governing and regulating knowledge also includes structuring the status of different sorts of knowledge (Gumport 2000), determining what knowledge people should be familiar with as members of modern society (Hefferlin 1969), and credentialing and regulating access to professions (Meyer 1977). Colleges and universities provide the credentials which individuals need in order to be accepted into desirable careers—credentials which are becoming only more valued as our economy continues to transition away from manufactured goods and towards service and knowledge as its base. In addition, as ever-higher percentages of students go on to college, colleges and universities have come to serve important socializing functions for a broader swath of young people. We look to colleges and universities to teach students how to write and speak formally, how to work in teams with others, how to manage an independent life, and most relevant for this research, how to cope with diversity.

Yet despite all of the expectations we have of tertiary education and the myriad roles it plays in contemporary society, colleges and universities remain a distinct type of organization. Though critics worry greatly about the blurring borders between colleges and universities and the corporate sector (Kirp 2003; Slaughter and Leslie 2001; Slaughter and Rhoades 2005), and though the higher education news is filled with stories about the penetration of business onto the campus (refer, for instance, to the student loan scandals of 2007), colleges and universities maintain formal autonomy from other social sectors and still act differently from businesses (Stevens et al. 2006). One of the key loci of this difference has to do with governance and decision-making structures.

Analysts of leadership and governance in higher education often point to the difficulties in decision-making on campus. Unlike in the corporate sphere, where

---

"higher education institutions," I have tried to avoid this language in favor of a more careful attention to the differences between organizations and institutions as sociological concepts.

those in upper management are empowered to make decisions in their leadership of the company, colleges and universities can be seen as "organized anarchies" (Cohen and March 1974; Cohen, March, and Olsen 1972). In organized anarchies, goals are inconsistent and problematic, it is difficult for organizational insiders to understand internal processes, learning happens through trial and error, and organizational membership and participation is fluid and shifting. Alternatively, colleges and universities can be seen as "loosely coupled systems" (Weick 1976), or systems where the various parts retain unique and autonomous identities while still being tied to the whole. Such systems reduce costs, make it easier to preserve the system, and allow room for change, but make it much more difficult to get things done. As Cohen and March argue, these organizational characteristics turn decisions into "garbage cans," whereby various problems get conflated with the current decision opportunity, and in fact problems are often not resolved at all. These organizational arrangements, of course, shape the actors and interactions that occur within organizations (Clemens and Cook 1999). The tendency of colleges and universities to take on these characteristics can perhaps be seen most clearly in the rise of the "multiversity," an organizational form growing in preponderance in contemporary higher education in which the organization resembles a federalist government with separate colleges, schools, and institutes, each of which have semi-autonomous governance structures as well as ties to the center, but often conflicts with one another (Baldridge 1971).

Higher education has gone through many other transitions across the last century, moving from an elitist system mostly dominated by white males educated in the classical tradition to a much broader system emphasizing not only the liberal arts but also vocational education (Rudolph 1989). The percentage of college graduates in the United States majoring in a "traditional liberal arts discipline" fell from 38 percent in 1970–71 to only 25 percent by 1994–95 (McPherson and Schapiro 1999:49) and has undoubtedly fallen further in the decade since, while occupational fields now award 60 percent of all college degrees (Brint, Riddle, Turk-Bicakci et al. 2005). Despite these changes, the 1960s and 1970s, according to Brint et al., marked a kind of high-water point in the history of the liberal arts, with a greater importance accorded them than was before (when agriculture and divinity degrees had been quite popular) or after. The liberal arts, considered the traditional core of the arts and sciences education, particularly in elite colleges, have often become little more than general education subjects a student must take in order to graduate. These courses may be defined in terms of providing students across the country with a set of shared knowledge and cultural concepts that help to build a coherent national identity (Readings 1996), or they may be defined in terms of providing students with at least a passing familiarity with different (academic) disciplinary perspectives before or in lieu of a specialized education in one professional or technical field (Brinker 1960). Central here is that, though liberal arts degrees certainly increase the earnings potentials of their holders, the liberal arts are not focused directly on jobs and economic gain but rather on the pursuit of knowledge for its own sake (Brint et al. 2005). Another perspective focuses on the role of the liberal arts to inculcate students with critical thinking skills, a particular type of reasoning that Martha Nussbaum (1997) describes as consisting of critical self-examination, striving for the ideal of being a world citizen, the development of the narrative imagination, and confronting that which makes us uncomfortable.

But the erosion of the liberal arts is not the only change that has occurred in higher education since the 1960s. The numbers of women, people of color, and working-class people participating in higher education have also grown significantly. As the student (and faculty) populations at colleges and universities have become more diverse, so also have these populations become more aware of their own diversity and more interested in ensuring that the curriculum that their colleges and universities offer is relevant to their own diverse personal backgrounds and experiences. Beginning with the mass mobilization of students during the Vietnam War, students at colleges and universities across the nation have pushed their campuses to open their doors to new types of courses and programs that focus on representing the experiences of marginalized groups within the curriculum.

The opening of higher education to interdisciplinary areas of study focused on group identities has been one result of this process of change. While these transitions occurred gradually, many scholars became aware of the opening of their ivory towers in the late 1960s and began to write about the new "democratic" educational order (Hefferlin 1969; Lipset 1967, 1976; Smith 1970). These texts form only a small part of the legacy of scholarly writing about curriculum change, but they point to the fact that the post-1960s diversification of higher education has been fundamental in reshaping the curriculum that students experience today. There are a variety of perspectives on how new disciplines emerge. Many scholars of disciplinary emergence have focused their attention on professional and vocational areas of study and have focused on the roles of markets (Becher and Trowler 1989; Tierny 1989) or other external pressures like the state, demographic shifts, or diffusion processes (DiMaggio and Powell 1983, 1991; Hashem 2002; Powell and DiMaggio 1991). These types of arguments would tend to suggest that visionary leaders create new disciplines to respond to explicit or implicit demands from the environment. But other perspectives focus less on the drive and direction of leadership. Disciplines may instead emerge through contentious politics, be they those of social movements or movement-like processes (Arthur 2009; Frickel 2004; Frickel and Gross 2005) or through what Abbot calls "fractals" that result in the endless subdivision and recombination of knowledge fields (Abbot 2001).

The three areas of study this book explores—women's studies, Asian American studies, and queer studies—exhibit considerable similarities in terms of their developmental roots and current conditions, as will be further discussed in the next chapter. They all first emerged in the same broader historical moment—the late 1960s and early 1970s—after Black studies paved the way for other similar efforts. In fact, these three disciplines have often looked to Black studies as a model for their own emergence, as well as having a complex history of cooperation and contention with Black studies—much as John Skrentny argues movements for "minority rights" used the Civil Rights movement as a model (Skrentny 2002). Moreover, all three interdisciplines concern identities and thus experience similar political conflicts surrounding the meanings and nature of their inclusion in undergraduate education. The dynamics of the emergence of these three areas of study as part of the broader knowledge environment will be considered in the next chapter—but the main focus of this book is on how, when, and why such programs emerge within particular colleges and universities.

Alternative Explanations

As noted above, colleges and universities are organized in such a way as to complicate decision-making processes. And yet, change still occurs. What makes this possible? Keller argues that three main factors are responsible for prompting change in colleges and universities:

> One is a major crisis in finances, enrollments, or quality that mandates quick, decisive, intelligent action. Another is strong pressure from outside, by a governor or legislature, influential alumni, the press, key trustees, or a state higher education agency (if it is reputable and not just political or aggrandizing). The third is a vigorous, farsighted leader, usually the campus president, but sometimes the academic or financial vice-president, and more rarely a chairman of the board of trustees or one or two deans and a few senior faculty members. (Keller 1983:164)

Besides the social movement explanations considered above, scholars of curricular change have proposed three main alternative models for how curricular changes come about, and these roughly correspond to Keller's models. The first of these models suggests that changes occur when they are demanded by market competition for students, funding, or other resources. The second model is grounded in neoinstitutional theory and predicts that organizations subject to similar environmental conditions will come to resemble one another through a process of isomorphism, diffusion, or imitation. A third explanation for curricular change is that it occurs through the initiative and pressure of leader. These leaders may be college and university faculty who believe such changes to be important or who wish to teach in new areas and who therefore utilize the shared governance procedures at their colleges or universities to adopt such changes. Alternatively, these leaders may be visionary administrators who see new innovations as a way to improve the standing of their campuses.

The Market for Students

Models rooted in the notion of a market for students suggest that colleges and universities develop new curricular programs when there is sufficient demand for them within the customer base of potential students or when instituting such programs would enable the college or university to draw on untapped pools of students or other resources (Tierny 1989). Though the specific workings of these markets may be different for different types of colleges and universities, with prestigious and prestige-seeking campuses implementing changes when necessary to increase selectivity and draw while other types of campuses change when students need them to do so (Brewer, Gates, and Goldman 2002), the market model proposes that change occurs in response to economic, demand-based forces of some kind. The particular characteristics of these potential customers may vary, but it is often suggested that universities seeking to satisfy the demands of female consumers will institute women's studies and those seeking to satisfy the demands of racial minorities will institute various ethnic studies programs (Mora-Ninci 1999; Wood 1979).

In other words, curricular change in market models occurs when an innovation is needed in order to attract new customers or forestall the loss of existing ones, or when innovation allows organizations to access new sources of revenue. Researchers have found that universities do often operate in market-like ways; in particular, factors such as cost, geography, prestige, and "fit" are likely to influence prospective students to make market-based decisions on where to spend their tuition dollars (Avery, Clickman, Hoxby et al. 2004; Hoxby 2000). Others suggest that the curricular programs available, particularly in the case of vocationalized areas of study, may be related to the market for prospective students (Becher and Trowler 1989; Slaughter and Leslie 2001).

However, many higher education analysts point to the limitations of viewing universities as market actors. Unlike traditional market-based organizations, universities specialize in producing public goods (Cantor and Courant 1997, 2001). Decision-making is not based on accurate measures of quality, efficiency, or production (Bok 2003; Kirp 2003; Winston 1999). There are also significant external controls, subsidies, and influences that do not operate in traditional free-market economic systems (Kirp 2003; Winston 1999). These limitations to viewing higher education as a market suggest that market forces may play a limited role in effecting curricular change, particularly in terms of non-vocational fields.

Neoinstitutionalism

Decision-making can also happen through processes of diffusion or imitation, particularly when colleges and universities (or parts of them) are interested in adapting to real-world dynamics and when they are densely nested in networks (Spalter-Roth, Fortenberry, and Lovitts 2006). Neoinstitutional explanations for organizational change address this possibility. These explanations come out of the larger literature in organizational change studies and suggest that organizations which are subject to a similar set of external and environmental constraints will alter themselves in ways that lead to a growing homogeneity across a field of similar organizations (DiMaggio and Powell 1983). This process, called "institutional isomorphism," can occur via three pathways: coercive isomorphism, where external agents of control such as the state or regulatory agencies force organizations to undergo change; normative isomorphism, where organizations change occurs as part of bringing an organizations into line with norms of professional practice; and mimetic isomorphism, where organizations respond to environmental uncertainty by copying what other successful organizations are doing in a process of diffusion (DiMaggio and Powell 1983).

Mimetic isomorphism is the most important of these three for understanding processes of curricular change, as regulatory forces and professional associations rarely exert control over whether colleges and universities offer majors or programs in particular curricular areas (coercive or normative isomorphism would be more important in considering other aspects of higher education, such as tenure or financial aid policies). Many of the contextual factors which neoinstitutional theorists believe would increase the likelihood of institutional isomorphism are also factors which characterize colleges and universities, such as being subject to uncertainty, experiencing resource limitations, a high degree of professionalization, frequent interactions with state agencies, and the limited availability of alternative organizational models (DiMaggio and Powell 1991). The neoinstitutional perspective, then, would suggest that colleges and universities change their curricula because other colleges or universities around them—those perceived as successful—have already done so.

However, neoinstitutional models may not always be appropriate for understanding change in colleges and universities. Imitative organizational changes may not last (Hashem 2002), colleges and universities may fail to imitate those peers that observers might expect them to look up to (Kraatz and Zajac 1996), and they may be able to resist isomorphic pressures and choose their own goals and strategies for organizational change (Oliver 1988). While it is clear that in terms of such factors as general organizational structure, colleges and universities in the United States do exhibit a remarkable degree of institutional isomorphism (Meyer et al. 2005), this fact does not mean that all colleges and universities share the same missions, values, or conceptions of what sorts of knowledge belong in the curriculum.

Initiative and Innovation

Many academics would like to point to the dominance of faculty within the campus power structure and suggest then that most new programs, whether disciplines or interdisciplines, emerge because of faculty pressure or the intellectual priorities of the faculty. In particular, this model highlights the tradition of shared governance structures in colleges and universities that delegates substantial authority over curricular matters to the faculty (Cohen and March 1974) and thus argues that faculty members with an interest in a new area use the shared governance process to create programs in line with their interests (Blau 1994). This model suggests that external pressures or students and student movements may play a small auxiliary role but are not particularly important to the ultimate outcome. For instance, Wood (1979) has shown that women's studies program development is most likely at colleges and universities with a rather low percentage of female faculty (where female faculty may feel inspired to do something to increase the visibility of women's issues in the curriculum), but this relationship is not statistically significant. Some advocates of this perspective have even gone so far as to suggest that White men deserve "credit for having created the sensibility and values that see these things [racism, sexism, homphobism (*sic*), heterosexism, ableism, Eurocentrism] as evils in the first place" (Bernstein 1994:214).

If the shared governance explanation is correct, we would find that faculty members who desire curricular change are able to implement it through the regular shared governance process; while controversy may occur among faculty, it need not spread to the rest of the campus. Hashem (2002), however, finds that the faculty do not play a significant role in creating new departments and programs in his study of vocationalized fields in higher education. Clark Kerr makes a similar point:

> … faculty members are properly partners in the enterprise with areas reserved for their exclusive control. Yet when change comes it is rarely at the instigation of this group of partners as a collective body. The group is more likely to accept or reject or comment, than to devise and propose. (1995:75)

Keller (1983) similarly argues that faculty and academic departments are quite resistant to change, and he furthermore sees no role for students. However, student support appears to be necessary for a program to become institutionalized, even if it is not necessary for the first tentative course offerings. If students do not want the program, they will simply not enroll in its courses, unless they are made mandatory. Other researchers have found evidence of the connections between movements for the interdisciplines and activism for broader issues of social justice (Louie and Omatsu 2001; Schmitz, Guy-Sheftall, Butler et al. 2004; Wei 1993; Wood 1979). Hefferlin notes that even in a random sample of faculty and administrators conducted in the 1960s, faculty (1969) perceived that student activism's greatest impact on the college or university comes in terms of curriculum reform.

Other scholars argue that administrative leaders are likely to be the source of change (Hefferlin 1969), especially when they are visionary "charismatic leaders" (Etzioni 1975), perhaps of the type described by Karabel (2005). However, in the "organizational anarchy" (Cohen et al. 1972) of a college or university, administrators themselves are often constrained in their decision-making authority. Administrative leadership models such as Keller's tend not to explain how or why administrators come to the decision that organizational change such as curricular revision is necessary, particularly given Cohen and March's contention that presidents tend not to concern themselves with curricular issues because they believe that it is the role of faculty in the shared governance process to deal with this issue (Cohen and March 1974). Perhaps they are more likely to do so when facing the market-based or neoinstitutional pressures discussed above.

Contentious Politics and Organizational Change

This book argues that the emergence of programs in women's studies, Asian American studies, and queer studies is best understood by looking at the dynamics of social movements or movement-like activities within colleges and universities. The fact that women's studies, Asian American studies, and queer studies programs are best explained through the study of the movements that produced them does not limit the importance of the other three models—the market, neoinstitutionalism, and individual or small group leadership—for explaining curricular change more broadly. Undoubtedly, some curricular innovations have emerged through each of these three paths, such as academic programs that are clearly linked to vocational outcomes and which are important for maintaining organizational legitimacy and prestige. However, these three explanations do not provide much explanatory power for understanding the emergence of the interdisciplinary, identity-based, and non-vocational programs under consideration here.

Instead, this book will show how episodes of contentious politics arose in campaigns for new curricular programs at six colleges and universities and what these campaigns did (or did not do) that shaped their likelihood of making an impact on their campus. Because the political context approach described above is limited to the state sphere, the book develops a new model—the organizational mediation model—for understanding the dynamics of movements within organizations. This model predicts that movements targeting organizations—such as those demanding new programs in women's studies, Asian American studies, and queer studies from the colleges and universities they are part of—will be most likely to have an impact on the organizations they target when they choose strategies that are well-aligned to the context they inhabit. In particular, the organizational mediation model highlights as key elements of organizational context the importance of administrative openness and flexibility along with the extent to which the organization's mission is favorable to social movement demands; it highlights as key elements of strategic choice the resonance of framing strategies with particular movement constituencies and the degree to which movements utilize assertive versus assimilative and insider versus outsider tactics.

The Plan of the Book

This chapter has introduced a series of models of curricular change that aim to explain why some colleges and universities adopt new programs and majors while others do not. Chapter 2 provides additional background information necessary for understanding the answer to this question. It explores the histories of women's studies, Asian American studies, and queer studies as broader fields of knowledge, situating them within a discussion of disciplinarity, interdisciplinarity, and knowledge construction.

After laying out this groundwork, Part II of the book considers case studies of six individual colleges and universities across the United States. These colleges and universities—Abigail Adams College, Promenade University, Technopark University, Jeffrey University, Sagebrush University, and the College of Assisi—are all referred to with pseudonyms to protect the confidentiality of the individuals I spoke with at each campus. These six campuses are diverse in terms of size, geographical location, prestige, and other factors and exhibit different histories of curricular change campaign and program adoption. Each case study explores the history and current dynamics of the college or university and the current shape of curricular offerings in women's studies, Asian American studies, and queer studies. In cases where curricular change campaigns did exist, the case studies draw on archival materials and interviews with key actors and observers to tell the stories of these campaigns; where campaigns did not exist, archival materials and interviews are used to shed light on reasons why they may not have emerged.

The third section of the book uses these six case studies to develop an explanation of how, when, and why curricular change happens and when and why it does not. In particular, Chapter 9 presents the organizational mediation model, which emphasizes the dynamics of social movements within organizations to explain which curricular change movements were successful and which were not. Chapter 10 concludes the book and explores how these findings may be applicable to future instances of curricular change. Finally, a methodological appendix describes the data collection and analysis strategies utilized in the preparation of this book. This appendix furthermore situates the findings of the case study analysis within a broader statistical and quantitative picture of when and where programs in women's studies, Asian American studies, and queer studies have emerged in North American higher education.

Chapter 2
Interdisciplinary Studies in Context: The Births of Women's Studies, Asian American Studies, and Queer Studies

There are colleges and universities that are first movers or unique innovators—in other words, they adopt curricular programs that are not available elsewhere within the higher education field. For instance, Wilson College and Rocky Mountain College offer majors in equine journalism; students at the University of Wisconsin can major in Scandinavian Studies; and students at Carnegie Mellon University can major in bagpipe or euphonium performance. But most colleges and universities don't strike out on their own. Instead, they offer programs and majors in fields of study that are already recognized as part of the realm of knowledge appropriate for college study. Women's studies, Asian American studies, and queer studies were not always so recognized. Rather, they each had to emerge as available knowledges either outside of the academy or in a few locations within it before most colleges and universities were willing to consider adopting them. This chapter considers the broader context of how each field of knowledge was born and became accepted as part of the knowledge base colleges and universities draw upon when constructing their curricula.

Disciplines and Interdisciplines

Before considering the historical patterns of emergence of women's studies, Asian American studies, and queer studies, it may be useful to outline what disciplines are and how interdisciplinarity is different. Disciplines serve as the basic building blocks of contemporary knowledge and as the fundamental organizational unit of most colleges and universities. They create a common culture, shared language, and community of knowledge (Turner 2000) that serves as the basis for developing academic programs, publication outlets, conferences, and careers. Interdisciplinary scholars may argue that disciplines are "static, rigid, conservative, and averse to innovation," but they also tend to admit that disciplines stand "for tough-mindedness, (necessary) order, and control, all features deemed to be prerequisites of progress and innovation" (Weingart 2000:29).

In fact, one of the simplest ways of understanding the differences between disciplines and interdisciplinarity involves examining the connection between disciplines and careers. Disciplines can be understood as mechanisms for creating restricted employment markets (Calhoun 2006; Turner 2000) by establishing specific credentials that are necessary for entry into the discipline and then developing protected and self-perpetuating markets to fill these jobs. This is accomplished primarily through disciplinary control over the training programs that provide said credentials. For instance, in order to gain employment as a researcher or teacher of economics, the prospective employee generally must complete a doctoral degree in economics within a disciplinary economics program. In contrast, interdisciplines are not directed toward an employment market and generally cannot sustain one. While some interdisciplinary doctoral-granting programs do exist, most individuals who attain employment in interdisciplinary fields have earned their credentials from one or more traditional disciplines (Chan 2005).

While the employment relation may be one of the most fundamental ways of differentiating between disciplines and interdisciplines, there are other differences as well. Interdisciplines are characterized by their own unique dynamics (Small 1999). They are made up of scholars with distinct academic and intellectual backgrounds who work together (Turner 2000) with the capacity to provide knowledge integration and the ability to keep up with rapid change (Weingart 2000). Interdisciplinarity, when it results in the creation of curricular programs, also involves considerably more complexity than disciplinarity. Interdisciplines tend to be organized as programs rather than as departments, and issues such as budgetary autonomy and personnel power have traditionally been reserved for disciplinary departments (Klein 1996; Lattuca 2001).

Of course, there is a gradient between interdisciplinarity and disciplinarity—as particular areas of knowledge move along that gradient, they take on more of the characteristics of a traditional discipline, including establishing credentialing programs and employment markets, forming departments within colleges and universities, and ultimately becoming an institutionalized part of the knowledge and organizational system. This process—the disciplining of interdisciplines—is not the focus of the present study, but the question of institutionalization will be taken up later on.

So where are women's studies, Asian American studies, and queer studies on the interdiscipline-discipline gradient? The answer varies. Though opponents of women's studies remain eager to dismiss its movement toward disciplinary status, it would probably be proper to consider women's studies a discipline today. Women's studies has a professional association and at least seven interdisciplinary journals publishing its scholarship. At least 14 universities offer doctoral degrees in women's studies; while many women's studies faculty jobs still go to candidates trained in traditional disciplines, increasing numbers of job listings do ask for applicants with women's studies backgrounds. Asian American studies occupies a more intermediate territory. Ethnic studies, the larger field of knowledge of which Asian American studies is part, offers doctoral degrees and many of the other trappings of disciplinarity. While Asian American studies does have a professional association and several journals, graduate students in Asian American studies must seek training in ethnic studies or in traditional disciplines (Chan 2005). Finally, queer studies rests most squarely in the interdisciplinary camp. Journals and scholarly organizations in queer studies exist, but they are typically affiliated with traditional disciplines rather than standing on their own. While a handful of universities offer master's programs with queer studies foci, there are no opportunities for graduate training in the field. These differences in institutionalization and disciplinary status make comparisons between women's studies, Asian American studies, and queer studies useful. However, for simplicity's sake, the term 'discipline' will be applied to all three throughout this text except when specific clarifications are needed.

Women's Studies

For hundreds of years—indeed, for as long as the university has existed—the areas of study that comprised higher education did not concern themselves with the issues, experiences, and accomplishments of women. Biology and anatomy took men's bodies as the standard. Psychology and other social sciences focused on the ways in which men interacted with the world. Literature courses taught almost exclusively texts written by men, and historical scholarship focused on the accomplishments of male diplomats and warriors rather than female healers and educators. The absence of women in higher education curricula remained relatively unchallenged even as women gained access to college education in the mid-1800s, first with the opening of all-female colleges like Mount Holyoke College and the admission of women to coeducation at Oberlin College and later with the arrival of coeducation at the land grant universities (the first of which to admit women was the University of Iowa in 1855).

Though the entry of women into higher education did lead to changes in the curriculum—the presence of botany (Levin 2005), modern languages, and home economics have all been traced to women's presence in the academy—women's own experiences remained largely absent. The first course which may have specifically focused on women as an object of study in their own right, a course on the sociology of women, was not offered until 1892 at the University of Kansas (Shircliffe 1996). While the daughters of the wealthy, professional, and merchant classes were making significant inroads into higher education in the early part of the 1900s, women's participation in college and university learning declined by the middle part of the century. But by the 1960s, the number of women enrolled in post-high-school education had begun to climb again (Figure 2.1).

The women attending college at mid-century were not only the daughters of privilege—for the first time, significant numbers of middle and working class women were beginning to enroll in college courses. At the same time, these women entered college in an environment of political action and were educated outside the classroom in the civil rights, anti-war, and free speech movements. Their activities in these movements showed them how to make demands of the universities in which they were enrolled at the same time as they were learning how women's voices were excluded even within progressive causes (Freeman

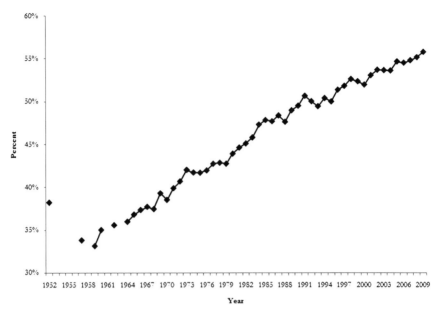

Figure 2.1   Percentage of College Graduates Aged 25–34 Years Old Who Were Female, 1952–2009 (U.S. Census Bureau 2010b)

1973). Thus, women students, faculty, and community members began to believe that a few scattered courses dealing with women's experiences were not enough.

The History of Women's Studies

It is out of this history that the discipline we now know as women's studies emerged. Feminist women at colleges and universities across the country began to organize consciousness-raising groups that went beyond the personal to develop an academic understanding of women's lives and experiences. Young faculty members, graduate students, and even undergraduates organized courses— sometimes for credit, sometimes as part of continuing education or "free university" curricula, and sometimes entirely external to academe—that helped spread this new learning about women to others within their communities. While these women were far from the first feminist activists their communities had seen (Boxer 1982), they did have strong ties to the women's movement, and many early instructors were activist women (Klein 1996). The goals of this new knowledge movement (Arthur 2009) did not originally focus on the development of a new discipline but rather on the emergence of an academy free of sexism. Scholars, students, and activists hoped that their activities would open up disciplinary boundaries so that the experiences of women could infuse the curriculum.

The first course of this kind, a course focusing not only on studying women's experiences but on doing so from a politically informed and feminist perspective, was offered in women's history in 1965 at the Free University of Seattle, an enterprise outside the auspices of accredited academic organizations which was part of the 1960s-era emphasis on radical alternatives to the traditional higher education sphere. By 1969, the year conventionally thought of as the founding point of women's studies as a field of academic inquiry, approximately sixteen formal women's studies courses were being offered in the United States (Klein 1996), along with an unknown number of informal discussion groups and independent study teams. These early courses were explicitly feminist, taught by activist rather than academic women, and were focused on "transforming the disciplines" and on dismantling "the boundary separating knowledge from action, discipline from politics" (Klein 1996:117–18). The first formal women's studies program was developed at San Diego State College (now San Diego State University) in 1971 (Boxer 1998), giving students their first opportunity to gain a degree focusing on women. By 1973, Klein (1996) estimates that approximately 5,000 courses in women's studies were offered in the United States, and by the mid-1970s, between 10 and 33 percent of female students at campuses offering women's studies were enrolling in women's studies coursework (Buhle 2000); 16 colleges and universities offered master's degrees in women's studies by 1976 (Howe 1977). A final measure of the rapid movement of women's studies through the higher education field is the fact that 6 percent of all students who graduated from high school in 1972 and subsequently earned a bachelor's degree earned credits in general women's studies within 8.5 years of high school graduation (Adelman 2004).

Women's studies took another step forward in the mid-1970s, as the students and faculty involved with the fledgling women's studies programs across the U.S. worked to found the first disciplinary association devoted to the study of women, what came to be known as the National Women's Studies Association (NWSA). It was officially launched in 1977, with a vision in its constitution "… of a world free not only from sexism, but also from racism, class-bias, ageism, heterosexual bias— from all the ideologies and institutions that have consciously or unconsciously oppressed and exploited some for the advantage of others" (Boxer 1982: 14). When the NWSA was launched, it counted 276 programs in women's studies as its core constituency.

In 1980, the NWSA published a list of women's studies programs then in existence. While it is likely that some programs were excluded from this list accidentally, it included a total of 327 programs—majors, minors, graduate degrees or certificates, and committees to coordinate women's studies coursework (Hagan and Howe 1980). Indeed, in its first decade, women's studies built its organizational capacity, along with over half of the growth in programs and enrollments that it would see by the end of the century (Buhle 2000). The emergence of women's studies was, however, not limited to the United States. Canadian women's studies developed in a trajectory similar to that in the United States, and students and faculty were working on adding women to the curriculum in Australia beginning in 1973. By 1982, women's studies programs could be found across North and South America as well as in Europe, Australia, New Zealand, Asia, and the Middle East (Crowley 1999; Wotipka, Ramírez, and Martínez 2007).

By 1990, women's studies had become commonplace in American higher education. That year, at least 520 colleges and universities counted women's studies among their programs, with 235 offering majors and 404 offering minors (Klein 1996). These statistics encompass 68 percent of universities, 50 percent of four-year colleges, and over a quarter of two-year colleges, with a total of well over 30,000 individual courses offered. But the expansion of women's studies into an institutionalized force by the 1990s brought with it the beginning of the end of women's studies' radical roots. By the close of the decade, at least twenty women's studies programs had changed their names to portray a focus on studying *gender* rather than *women* (Wiegman 2002). While this change may seem trivial, in fact it has significant consequences for the content of teaching and research that occurs within academic programs. The transition to gender studies and the movement away from radicalism marks an increase in the academic acceptability of these programs (Griffin 2009). For instance, committee members at one college seeking to convert its women's studies program into a gender studies department note that "the study of women therefore remains central to this field, but does not constitute its exclusive or singularly privileged focus" (Renda and the Gender Studies Advisory Group 2005:7). While gender studies is thus still a feminist field which provides a rationale for institutionalizing feminism as a mode of academic inquiry, and while the move from "women" to "gender" provides a way to avoid having to continually struggle for legitimacy, the move to gender studies removes the one place in the curriculum which was entirely about women. Even the introductory course is no longer a course about women's experiences, but rather one in which men and women must be analyzed together, much as they are likely to be across the contemporary curriculum in colleges and universities which are sensitive to gender issues.

Women's Studies Today

Today at San Diego State University (SDSU), the site of the first women's studies program, students minor, major, and earn master's degrees in the SDSU program, which offers about 50 course sections per semester and employs over 20 full-time, teaching emeritae, and affiliated faculty. The SDSU women's studies department awarded 26 degrees in spring 2005 and offered over 1 percent of all university courses in fall 2005 (calculated on a full-time equivalent basis; SDSU offers 176 different degree programs). The story of the women's studies program at SDSU is the story of women's studies as a discipline—it has moved from being a radical rethinking of higher education curricula to an institutionalized center of teaching and research, considered by many elite colleges and universities to be as necessary to preserving the diversity of their liberal arts offerings as are programs like classics and earth sciences.

But the story of institutionalization cannot be told without attention to the obstacles along the way. Women's studies is still attacked by educational traditionalists who claim that it takes away time that should be spend educating students on "the basics" or on delving more deeply into the classical core curriculum, as well as by social conservatives who fear that women's studies coursework will turn their daughters into lesbians and lead to zero population growth (see, for instance, Phyllis Schlafly's *Feminist Fantasies*) or just that it is "dangerously conformist" in political ideology (Damrosch 1995). Others suggest that women's studies disadvantages students by focusing too much attention on activism and too little on academics (Patai and Koertge 2003). While most women's studies programs have been able to weather these challenges, pointing to the strengths of their liberal arts training and the successes of their graduates, a more difficult fight has been to prove their continued relevance. As traditional academic disciplines have become more willing to produce scholarship on women, academic administrators have questioned the need for a separate programmatic structure to coordinate women's studies.

One of the reasons for these difficulties has been women's studies programs' reluctance to seek departmental status for themselves. For many activist women involved in the foundation of the discipline, departmental status and the traditional, hierarchical bureaucracy it entails have seemed antithetical to the inclusive and egalitarian ethos that guided the formation of programs, leading to what Biddy Martin calls "a point of stasis that ... has lost much of its critical and intellectual vigor" (2001:353). Similarly, departmental status has been seen as reducing the interdisciplinarity so prized by women's studies scholars. But programs that have been reluctant to move to departmental status have often suffered from this decision: without departments, women's studies is (more) vulnerable to attacks on its legitimacy as a field of scholarly inquiry, to facing financial hardship when budgets are cut, and to difficulty in shepherding its faculty through the tenure and career advancement processes (O'Connell 2004).

Women's studies also continues to face difficulties in maintaining disciplinary coherence due to the diverse training and backgrounds of its faculty. Though there are at least 14 doctoral programs in women's studies in the United States, as well as additional joint doctoral programs with women's studies and another discipline; at least 30 master's degree programs; and over 70 graduate schools that offer graduate students can earn a transcript notation such as a certificate or graduate minor along with their degrees, the majority of women's studies faculty still arrive in the professoriate with training in a specific disciplinary field. These faculty members may retain primary allegiances to the field of their disciplinary training or may be hired in joint appointments that force them to work doubly hard to fulfill the tenure standards of two different disciplines. Though traditional academic disciplines are much more open to scholarship on women than they were in the 1960s and 1970s, disciplinary boundaries can still serve to reduce the focus on women (O'Connell 2004), and that is why scholars interested in engaging in teaching and research on women continue to turn to women's studies despite the obstacles they may face.

In spite of these continuing struggles, the field of women's studies has grown significantly since its first steps in the mid-1960s. Today, the NWSA claims approximately 600 affiliated programs, and other listings (be they of minors, majors, certificates, or credentials of some other kind) may show as many as 700 or more colleges or universities offering programs. A wide variety of journals as well as caucuses on gender and women within professional associations have developed. And the reach of women's studies is not only broad—it is deep as well. Over nine percent of all students graduating from high school in 1992 who subsequently went on to study for a bachelor's degree earned women's studies credits within 8.5 years of high school graduation, as did 6.1 percent in gender studies. Even more significantly, 12.7 percent of all 1992 high school graduates who went on to earn at least ten credits in college coursework enrolled in courses in women's studies (Adelman 2004).

Though women's studies has become an institutionalized part of the curricular landscape, theory and practice continue to inform one another within the discipline women's studies, much as the earliest scholar-activists planned. This can be seen in the continuing choice of women's studies programs to require or strongly encourage service learning and internships for undergraduate majors. If we conceive of women's studies as a social movement (Arthur 2009), we can perhaps see it as a victim of its own success (Martin 2001; Miller 1999). In other words, women's studies has been so successful at institutionalizing itself within the higher education sphere that it is no longer the radical force it once was. However, scholars of women's studies and feminism (such as Feldman 1982; McMartin 1993; Naples 2002) have come to see women's studies as the "institutionalized arm" of the women's movement. And scholar-activists continue to say that "since 'feminist activity made women's studies possible, women's studies must in turn make feminist activity possible'" (Kay 1978, as cited in Boxer 1982:676).

Asian American Studies

Like women's studies, the origins of Asian American studies are rooted in the growing self-awareness that developed among students newly included in higher education in the 1960s. While people with ancestral roots in the continent of Asia have lived in the United States since Filipino fishermen in the 1750s began settling in the area which would come to be known as Louisiana, severe restrictions on immigration from Asia were imposed until passage of the Immigration Act of 1965 (Chan 1991; Takaki 1989). The provisions of this new law enabled Asian Americans to serve as familial sponsors, bringing relatives from Asia to join them in the U.S. Asian immigration increased dramatically in the years after the law was passed, and by the end of the 1960s, Asian American students were a significant presence in colleges and universities located in areas of Asian immigrant settlement. In addition, the children born to Japanese American parents in the years after internment (Ancheta 1998) were reaching college age by the late 1960s. Homeland politics, American racial classification practices, the internment experience, and immigration laws had combined to inhibit the formation of a group identity of Asian Americanness until after these legal and demographic changes, but by the late 1960s, second and third generation Asian Americans were coming to see themselves as members of one group with common interests (Espiritu 1992).

Just as their numbers (see also Figure 2.2) and collective sense of self were growing, many Asian American college students became involved in the broader struggles for racial equality that were sweeping the nation and were confronted with their own lack of equality, conditioned in large part by the experiences of Japanese Americans who were interned during World War II (Maeda 2009; Takaki 1989). Also like other groups during the 1960s, Asian Americans became involved in popular protest movements against racial inequality and the Vietnam War (Maeda 2009). The anti-War movement had special meaning for some Asian American protesters: some traced their family heritage to Vietnam itself, and others had the experience of being lumped in with the Viet Cong as a purported enemy of the state. For instance, those Asian Americans who had served in the U.S. military often recalled experiences like the following: "...upon entering basic training [this man] was called a gook and made to stand in front of his platoon as an example of 'what the enemy (the Vietnamese) looked like'" (Yoshimura 1971:29).

But the discipline of Asian American studies does not only owe its origins to the experiences of Asian Americans as immigrants. Another significant factor was the history of Black studies upon which Asian American students, scholars,

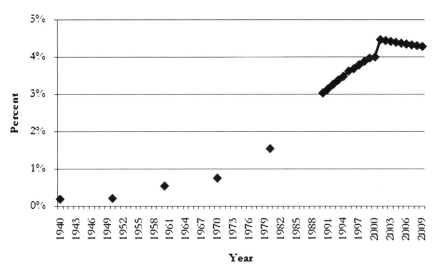

Figure 2.2 **Percentage of the United States Population Identified as Asian (U.S. Census Bureau 2010a)**

and community members could draw. Black studies emerged as a discipline in the wake of the Civil Rights movement and was seen by students, faculty, administrators, and others as a way to ameliorate the feelings of Black students that higher education was not relevant to their experiences and to provide a forum for increasing recruitment and retention of promising Black scholars (Rojas 2007). While individual courses which could be described as teaching in a Black studies framework had been offered for some years, particularly at historically Black colleges and universities (Aldridge and Young 2000), the first formal program in Black studies was created in 1968 at San Francisco State College (Rojas 2007), and universities across the United States rapidly created their own programs within the next few years—at least 50 percent of which were founded in direct response to campus activism. Other groups disadvantaged by the higher education system were inspired by their participation in and observation of the progress of Black studies, and Asian Americans along with Latinos/Chicanos (Mora-Ninci 1999) and Native Americans (Kimura-Walsh 2009) joined forces to create the new discipline of ethnic studies.

The History of Asian American Studies

The history of Asian American studies begins with the history of ethnic studies. However, the story of ethnic studies often ignores the history of Asian American studies (Edelstein 1973), even though this field was a key participant in even the earliest struggles to include the experiences of people of color in the college curriculum. The center of the earliest developments in Asian American studies was the San Francisco Bay Area—the same place where the first Black studies program was developed. Between 1964 and 1970, students organized for ethnic studies at San Francisco State College as well as at the University of California Berkeley and at Stanford University (Asregadoo 2000).

At San Francisco State, a group of students and community members known as the Third World Liberation Front (TWLF) initiated a student strike during the 1969–70 academic year. The strike was a tactic designed to pressure the College into agreeing to 15 demands made by the TWLF, demands which focused on issues such as the development of ethnic studies, open admissions to increase the population of students of color, the hiring of more faculty of color, and the involvement of students in academic governance. The strike kept the College closed for weeks and forced the resignation of its president (Barlow and Shapiro 1971). While the TWLF did not have all of its demands met in the short term, San Francisco State College did found a College of Ethnic Studies, and Asian American studies eventually became the largest department in this organizational unit.

While the earliest programs in Asian American studies were formed on the West Coast, especially in California—UC Berkeley and UC Santa Barbara formed programs at about the same time as San Francisco State (Hu-DeHart 1993)—they rapidly diffused to large universities in the Midwest and in New York, and the first Asian American studies program beyond the West Coast was founded at Bowling

Green State University in Ohio in 1979 (Hu-DeHart 1993). Initially, these programs were usually organized as parts of ethnic studies departments also housing other fields. As in women's studies, instructors were often activists and community organizers, and advisory boards featured students and community members. Early Asian American studies programs explicitly focused on engagement with the community, community action, and community service (Omatsu 2010). The first courses were usually offered under broad titles, like "Asians in America" or "The Asian American Experience," and were interdisciplinary enterprises drawing on literature, history, and the social sciences.

Asian American studies has thus had as its core goal the production of knowledge about the Asian American experience. The scholar-activists of Asian American studies have challenged the notion of the Black-White racial binary and White supremacy in the United States (Ijima 2001) and worked to reclaim the forgotten history and literature of the earliest Asian immigrants. These scholars aimed to raise the self-awareness and ethnic consciousness of Asian American studies; transmit knowledge about the history, culture, and experiences of Asian Americans; develop research, theory, and practice regarding the Asian American experience and rooted in radical frameworks; and provide education and other services designed in a culturally sensitive fashion to Asian American students as well as to communities surrounding colleges and universities (Chan 2005; Nomura and Endo 1989:279). Instructors and researchers often aimed to expand beyond the one-sided treatment of people of color in the curriculum and to explore the impact of historical events (like the internment of the Japanese during World War II) on the psyches of those affected by them. But also like women's studies, Asian American studies has sought to reexamine structures of higher education themselves. In particular, one pedagogical goal has been revising methods of assessment to make them "culturally relevant" (Teraguchi 2002), such as by instituting holistic portfolios or bringing community members into the pedagogical process.

A second wave of Asian American studies development has occurred since the late 1980s. During this period of disciplinary development, new programs emerged, particularly at elite private colleges and universities in the northeastern United States but also in public and private colleges and universities all across the country. Unlike the earlier departments of Asian American studies, these newer programs have often been interdepartmental in structure with less institutionalized legitimacy and are less likely to have community-centered governance. The differences between the early mobilization that began in California and the later waves of activities throughout the U.S. are significant enough to have resulted in somewhat of a rift within the discipline—Asian American studies scholars now talk of the "California model," rooted in an Asian American experience as a multi-generational ethnic group in a multicultural society, and the "East of California model," rooted in an Asian American experience as immigrants or migrants (Sumida 1998). In many of the East of California areas, the development of Asian American studies was one of the earliest organized movements around Asian American issues. Though East of California programs tended to be somewhat less connected to community action and community service than the earlier programs, they were no less assertive or political in their orientation (Lien 2001).

Asian American Studies Today

Ethnic studies programs in general have come to be a common feature in higher education curricula. By 2005, 9 percent of all colleges and universities offered degrees in African American or Black studies (Rojas 2006), for instance, with many more offering minors or concentrations within ethnic studies programs. And 17 percent of all students graduating from high school in 1992 and enrolling in at least ten credits of college took coursework in ethnic studies (Adelman 2004). Over 20 departments, with a geographical focus in California, have formed a National Association of Ethnic Studies, and estimates suggest that in 2002 there were 359 Black studies programs, 144 American Indian/Native American studies programs, and 127 Hispanic/Latino/ Chicano studies programs (Teraguchi 2002), as well as an unknown number with various titles like "multi-ethnic studies," "American racial studies," or "cultural diversity studies."

Many higher education analysts writing in the wake of ethnic studies' emergence thought it would be a transitory phenomenon, that students would "get over it" and see that career-oriented studies were more useful to their futures (Kerr 1995; Smith 1970). This seems surprising in light of contemporary fears that the liberal arts are being eviscerated in favor of professional and vocational studies, but in fact the 1960s and 1970s marked the high point for liberal arts and sciences majors in the United States (Brint et al. 2005). Interdisciplinary programs like ethnic studies offer a marked contrast to these trends. They have also persevered over a period of substantial social change. Asian American studies in particular has watched as Asian American people in the United States have moved from a tiny, localized, and relatively homogeneous population (most early Asian Americans had ethnic ancestry in China, Japan, Korea, or the Philippines) to a large and dispersed one, quite diverse in terms of ethnic background, immigrant status, language, religion, and class.

Though the emergence of Asian American studies was closely tied to other sorts of Asian American political and social activism, the energy directed towards academic causes has remained stronger than some other aspects of the movement (Chiang 2009; Omatsu 2010). Indeed, there are still efforts to bring Asian American studies to new places, particularly in smaller colleges and in areas where few Asian American students have lived or studied until recently. These efforts have sometimes been aided by the trend among colleges and universities to add course requirements focusing on the study of social, racial, or ethnic diversity (Yamane 2001). Asian American studies courses provide an opportunity to fill these requirements, and diversity or multicultural course listings that exclude this group can highlight the absence of Asian American studies on specific campuses. However, a consequence of the move towards multicultural requirements is that Asian American studies programs, like all ethnic studies programs, often struggle with internal debates about their purpose and role within higher education, particularly when they are asked to provide service courses to introduce expanding numbers of often-reluctant White students to multicultural and diversity issues (Chan 2005; Chang 1999).

But the impact of ethnic studies on the curricular landscape has not gone without notice. Responses to ethnic studies have included resistance and repression—some programs are founded only to be shut down or face severe budget cuts limiting their operation. In part, this may be due to the 'last hired, first fired' syndrome, with ethnic studies seen as superfluous to the core mission of the college or university and with untenured or otherwise vulnerable faculty who are easy to dismiss. The students, faculty, and community members who first supported ethnic studies programs, however, are still able to respond in an effort to protect these departments. For instance, at UC Berkeley in 1999, students took over the ethnic studies building and held a successful eight-day hunger strike in response to threats to dismantle the program, which was the first to offer an ethnic studies Ph.D., and absorb its courses and faculty into traditional disciplines (Cook 2001). At the same time as colleges and universities seek to reduce or limit the funding, resources, and institutionalization available to them, ethnic studies programs are critiqued for not being rigorous enough. The truth behind this critique may be due to institutional arrangements that rely on a cafeteria curriculum without permanent faculty or administrative resources (Hu-DeHart 2004).

The reactions to ethnic studies are of course not limited to these conflicts over resources, structure, and budgets. The very missions and content of these programs are subject to ideological and political clashes (Bernstein 1994). Conservative critics like David Horowitz suggest that ethnic studies is a tool of political indoctrination, while neo-liberal critics argue that ethnic studies serves to divide students, create racial tensions on campus, and shackle people of color who would be better served studying "the classics." In 2010, for instance, the state of Arizona passed a law prohibiting the teaching of ethnic studies in public and charter schools because they might "promote ethnic solidarity instead of treating students as individuals" (Santa Cruz 2010). Critics from across the political spectrum take advantage of scandals such as those involving Leonard Jeffries or Ward Churchill—events which do not represent the mainstream of ethnic studies programs—to discredit the discipline as a whole.

In spite of these challenges, Asian American studies remains a feature of the curricular landscape. Though it has been less able to permeate the curriculum than Black studies, there were at least 43 Asian American studies programs in the United States as of 2001 (Lim 2001). Over 50 colleges and universities have officially registered their Asian American studies programs or departments with the Association for Asian American Studies, as have approximately twenty other colleges and universities who have organized courses and in some cases minors or certificates. There are at least three scholarly journals focused entirely on Asian American studies and an Asian American studies professional association as well as caucuses within other professional associations devoted specifically to the discipline. About 20 percent of all Asian American high school students who graduated in 1992 and subsequently enrolled for at least ten college credits completed coursework in ethnic studies within 8.5 years of high school graduation (Adelman 2004). While this figure does not provide the necessary detail to communicate what percentage of these courses were in Asian American studies specifically, it is likely that the majority of Asian American students who do take ethnic studies courses take at least one course focusing on Asian American studies. A more recent study, which considered a sample of eight colleges and universities that is representative of the top tier of colleges and universities nationwide, but which unfortunately conflated Asian American studies with Asian studies, found that 17 percent of all students—and 52 percent of Asian American students—took such coursework, while 4 percent majored and 5 percent minored in the field (Espenshade and Radford 2009).

Queer Studies

Like the disciplines of women's studies and Asian American studies, the first task facing queer studies in its struggle for existence was to legitimate itself as a subject worthy for study in the higher education curriculum. And again like these other disciplines, the late 1960s and early 1970s was an opportune time to undertake this task. The decades preceding the emergence of queer studies had proved revolutionary for the status of gay and lesbian people in North America and Europe. Beginning in 1948 with the publication of Kinsey's *Sexual Behavior in the Human Male*, gay and lesbian activists as well as mainstream academics slowly began to take note of the fact that same-sex desire was not as rare or abnormal as many had previously thought. Throughout the 1960s, beginning perhaps with the 1962 legal change in Illinois which made it the first state to legalize consensual same-sex intimacy, increased gay and lesbian activism and sexual liberation were accompanied by some loosening in the social and legal stigma attached to gay and lesbian lives and identities. By 1966, students were forming organizations devoted to gay and lesbian issues on campus; protesters were gathering outside the Pentagon as well as in Canada, the United Kingdom, and other nations; and court challenges to discrimination against gays and lesbians were gathering steam. For the future of the nascent academic attempt to understand the queer experience, perhaps the most significant change was the removal of homosexuality from the psychiatric profession's list of mental disorders at the end of 1973. After all, if homosexuality was not a disease, perhaps it could be a legitimate area of academic inquiry (Cruikshank 1992). And in fact, 1974 marked the founding of an academic journal entitled *The Journal of Homosexuality*.

The History of Queer Studies

Academic courses dealing with issues of homosexuality did not have to wait until 1974 to come into existence, however. The first academic courses dealing with issues of homosexuality were taught at NYU and Yale in late 1960s (Dynes 1993) and focused on homosexuality in literature. But these courses were isolated attempts to bring gay and lesbian issues into the curriculum. The field known as gay studies (later gay and lesbian studies) did not come into existence until the early 1970s, and what we now know as queer studies had its start in the early 1980s (Bull 1998). Programs were developed early on at colleges and universities ranging from the elite, at schools like Stanford, Berkeley, Yale, Amherst College, and MIT, to the less prestigious like Brooklyn College, California State Stanislaus, and Sonoma State (Cruikshank 1992).

Though courses were already being offered at some colleges and universities, the disciplinary beginnings of queer studies can be traced to a March 1973 meeting of eight people (faculty, graduate students, and professionals outside of the academy) who constituted a rap group on the issues surrounding being gay in the university. They sought to connect their own liberation, the larger gay liberation movement, and the academic setting by creating a formal organization known as the Gay Academic Union (GAU). This organization served as a support group as academics engaged in early attempts at gay and lesbian-focused research and teaching (D'Emilio 1974). The GAU's first conference, held in November 1973 at the City University of New York, drew 300 attendees; by the third conference two years later, 1,000 people were in the audience (Gross 2005).

During the 1970s and 1980s, caucuses on gay and lesbian issues within professional associations began to form—first in the Modern Language Association and the American Library Association, but soon across the disciplinary terrain (Taylor and Raeburn 1995). But it was not until the late 1980s, by which time (in 1984) the GAU had disbanded, and when the disciplinary framework of queer studies was beginning to take shape, that the field took its next leap forward. At San Francisco City College, which had offered courses since 1972, a department offering a major in gay and lesbian studies was formed in 1989. This program, the first and still the only department of gay and lesbian studies in the United States, had as its aims to develop more knowledge about gay and lesbian culture and increase social awareness of gay and lesbian issues. By 1991, SFCC employed Jack Collins in the first full-time tenure track position in gay and lesbian studies. Around the same time, journals offering the opportunity to publish gay and lesbian scholarship (such as the *Journal of the History of Sexuality*) began to proliferate, and the City University of New York chartered the Center for Lesbian and Gay Studies (CLAGS), the first university-based research center on lesbian and gay studies (Saslow 1991). By the date of its founding, organized programs such as minors or certificates focusing on lesbian and gay issues and experiences existed at San Francisco State University, Yale, Duke, MIT, Princeton, and UC Santa Cruz, among others (Ocamb 1990). Queer studies has not been limited to the United

States, either: though it is represented in a variety of European countries, it has achieved perhaps the greatest penetration as "homostudies" in Holland (Hekma and van der Meer 1992). In Canada, there has been a unique focus on building lesbian studies as a separate field from gay studies, informed more particularly by lesbians' experiences as women (Gammon 1992).

While for the sake of simplicity, this book refers to queer studies and gay and lesbian studies as a unified discipline, there are in fact some significant differences between the ideologies and values underlying these terms—even as both continue to face marginalization (O'Connell 2004). In fact, there are differences even in the activist roots of the disciplines. Gay and lesbian studies is linked more to the older gay rights movement, with its emphasis on assimilation and equal rights, while queer studies is linked to the more radical queer movement's postmodern critique of sexual and political convention (Yoshino 2006). As a consequence, gay and lesbian studies focuses on the possibility of assimilation; the claiming of specific sexual identities; and the inclusion of gay and lesbian people in the master-narratives of history, literature, and culture, such as by reclaiming significant historical figures as gay or lesbian (Gross 2005; O'Connell 2004). Or as Mohr (1989:130) says, "gay studies is the study of gays as a minority." In contrast, the more theoretically informed queer studies focuses on gender inclusivity, the fluidity of sexuality, and the celebration of difference (O'Connell 2004). Its aims include bringing sexual power to light and understanding the social power of binary boundaries; analyzing how sex and gender categories are always problematic; utilizing the theoretical tool of deconstructionism; and showing how sexuality affects everything (Gamson and Moon 2004). Queer studies seeks to challenge restrictions on sex roles and behavior as well as heteronormativity, and to emphasize the fluidity of identities (Gross 2005). And while gay and lesbian studies limits its focus to issues of sexuality, queer studies "makes sexuality a central category of analysis" (Halberstam 2003:361), even as the focus of study moves on to other global issues.

Queer Studies Today

According to John Younger of the University of Kansas, in 2006 there were about 50 schools offering some sort of formal program in queer studies (though program titles vary). Approximately 25 professional associations or caucuses focus on LGBT issues in professions or in disciplinary scholarship. A variety of journals offer outlets for scholarly publishing. Queer studies may not yet be institutionalized, but is on its way.

Like women's studies, Asian American studies, and other academic fields concerned primarily with oppressed groups, queer studies has faced significant opposition within and beyond the ivory tower. The opposition faced by queer studies, though, may be more detrimental to the field. While opponents of women's studies and Asian American studies often object to the content of the courses, the pedagogical methods they employ, the mission statements of programs, the radicalism of the faculty, or the time these subjects divert from the "traditional canon," they are less likely to object entirely to the study of women or Asian Americans as people. In contrast, many opponents of queer studies believe that homosexuality is morally objectionable and that academic study concerning it has no place in the curriculum. Those who wish to study issues relating to the diversity of human sexuality have faced particular obstacles at colleges and universities with religious identities opposed to gay and lesbian rights and communities as well as in public university systems under scrutiny by conservative politicians. For instance, in 2010, a candidate for an administrative position at Marquette University was initially offered the position and then rejected due to her scholarship in queer studies (June 2010).

At the same time, queer studies also faces competition for limited resources within the colleges and universities at which it has established itself. At some, such as Bard College, programs and courses on gay and lesbian experiences and issues have been incorporated into gender studies programs. These developments have angered advocates for both queer studies and women's studies, both of which see their resources, autonomy, and missions threatened by such combinations (Saslow 1991). In fact, conflicts over the relationship between women's studies and queer studies have been long-standing, particularly in relation to the place of lesbians in the curriculum. Lesbian activists and scholars were key participants in the process of building women's studies, but early programs often left issues of sexuality out of women's studies curricula because of political pressures or the fear that a course or a text on the lesbian experience would brand all women's studies scholars (and all feminists) as lesbians. Lesbian participants in the intellectual and activist projects of women's studies often experienced these fears and choices as a suggestion that perhaps lesbians, at least those who chose to emphasize their sexual identity on equal footing with their gender identity, were not really women (Joseph 2002). On the other hand, lesbians have experienced marginalization as women within the gay liberation movement as well as in the research and teaching of queer studies—so perhaps women did not really count as gay either. Both women's studies and queer studies still struggle with their history of marginalizing the lesbian experience, a marginalization which is still in the process of being remedied.

Despite these ongoing difficulties, students, faculty, and activists at colleges and universities which do not yet offer queer studies programs continue to push for their inclusion in the curriculum, and new programs and courses continue to be added. Struggles around queer studies continue to have important links to the activist movements that first inspired the discipline: "GLBT studies ... emerged out of a political movement and has always had a necessary, if often fraught or distant, relation to the political conditions facing gay people and the movements and organizations engaged in the struggles for equality" (Gross 2005:524).

Comparisons and Contrasts

The three disciplines upon which this study is focused all emerged out of the same historical period. All three emerged at a time when groups previously excluded from full participation in the academy were gaining access to and acceptability within the higher education sphere. As women and Asian Americans entered higher education in increasing numbers, and as gay and lesbian students and faculty began to be open about their identities within their colleges and universities, these students and faculty, along with their administrative mentors and community allies, began to emphasize the fact that the traditional curriculum excluded their experiences. Each group, in turn, joined with students from other backgrounds to push for a curriculum that was "relevant" to their lives and needs. For women, Asian Americans, and gay and lesbian people, those curricula were women's studies, Asian American studies, and queer studies.

These curricular innovations all had close ties to activist movements concerned with increasing social and legal rights for the same identity groups. As noted above, women's studies has been seen as the institutionalized arm of the feminist movement, as the place where feminist ideals were put into practice within an organizational framework. Similarly, Asian American activists have relied on Asian American studies to increase the visibility of their cause and to create openings within the academic and political fields for activist intervention (Chiang 2009). And various LGBTQ movements have utilized the academic status of queer studies to buttress their case for equality and sexual freedom.

But it is not only the disciplines that help the movements. In fact, as we have seen in this chapter, the movements have played an important role in helping to initiate the intellectual projects and classroom experiences that eventually became the disciplines. In part, this is because in order to achieve their goals, each movement has had to change and expand the knowledge that existed about the identity group with which it was concerned. These linkages suggest that all three disciplines can in fact be seen as new knowledge movements (NKMs). The NKM model (Arthur 2009) suggests that academic disciplines can emerge through a social movement process where outsiders (those who are not able to claim a legitimate role as knowledge-makers in the academic or intellectual world) engage in contentious intellectual politics that have as their goal the creation of new knowledge. In other words, women's studies, Asian American studies, and queer studies all emerged through a social movement push to change what was known about their identity group and what it mattered to know in order to count as an educated member of society. As Taylor (1998) notes, "identity-based study areas" such as Black studies, Native American studies, and Jewish studies, along with the cases explored here, are called "progressive" because they aim to use the liberal arts to work for social change, sometimes revolutionary change. All of these disciplines are seeking change in the curriculum, the research environment, and pedagogical practice; all are seeking affirmation of the lived experience of students with these identities; all are seeking to open up the curricular system to the realities of diversity; and all are seeking to transform the social order so as to ensure a better life and better future for their students.

The progressive and sometimes revolutionary intellectual self-definitions of these fields have meant that they have all faced significant opposition throughout their existences. This opposition has come in many forms. Other constituencies within and outside the higher education field have objected to women's studies, Asian American studies, and queer studies as reducing the intellectual rigor of the college curriculum, as competing unfairly for classroom time and financial resources, and as distracting attention from the core competencies necessary for a college graduate. These sorts of arguments can have many roots. Sometimes it is merely competition for limited time and resources that leads entrenched fields to try to protect their own interests. But in other instances, the opposition has claimed that women's studies, Asian American studies, and queer studies are inappropriate participants in the curriculum. These critics suggest that education is best served when a traditional focus on the Western European canon and American history is maintained (see, for instance, Bernstein 1994). Even harsher are the critics who believe not only that identity-based fields are intellectual fluff, but that they are indeed harmful to students or to society. These types of arguments tend to suggest that women's studies curricula will cause female students to abandon marriage and motherhood, that ethnic studies curricula will create racial strife on campus, and that queer studies programs are merely recruitment fronts where lecherous professors try to seduce unsuspecting students. Unlike the prior arguments, which are often grounded in a rational debate about the purpose of higher education, these last critiques are instead rooted in beliefs about who and what should legitimately have access to education itself.

There are differences between these fields as well. These differences can be seen most clearly by looking at the outcomes of attempts to institutionalize and legitimate the fields. Despite having emerged at the same general point in time, despite similar backgrounds in social movement activism, and despite facing similar types of opposition (if perhaps somewhat stronger opposition in the case of queer studies), the three disciplines have ended up in very different places. Women's studies is now a mature and institutionalized field. Many colleges and universities would feel incomplete without offering at least some women's studies coursework today, and graduate training in women's studies is not uncommon. In fact, women's studies has reached such a point of institutionalization that some critics charge that is has abandoned its feminist roots as it seeks to preserve departmental interests by conforming to organizational bureaucracies (Martin 2001; Wiegman 2002). Queer studies is in a quite different position. Though courses in queer studies are now common, programs remain rare, and only one full major exists. Graduate students cannot complete their training in a queer studies Ph.D. program and can only rarely be hired as faculty members in full-time tenure-track positions focusing entirely on queer studies. Those programs which do exist are often precariously positioned with respect to resources and funding, and face the threat of being combined with other units to save money or disbanded to save political face. Asian American studies is in something of an intermediate position. It is a mature field today. Programs many not be common, but they are available, as are faculty positions and graduate training. Professional associations, conferences, and journals provide a disciplinary space for Asian American studies. Though it does face constant threats of absorption or dissolution on specific campuses, the discipline also continues to expand into new frontiers.

These differences in institutionalization make these three disciplines useful for examining the answer to the question that drives this study: how, why, and when is it that new curricular programs emerge on college campuses? By comparing three fields with very different overall outcomes but with similar pasts and similarly radical political positions, this study is better able to show the importance of political and organizational context on individual college and university campuses. In other words, there is a differential likelihood of disciplinary adoption both across campuses and across disciplines. This variation helps to illuminate the dynamics of change within individual colleges and universities. Additionally, the use of these three fields will help to make the findings of this study generalizable to other curricular and campus changes which may look somewhat different from the three explored here. This chapter has shown how each of these three fields developed in the larger national and international contexts and has documented when, where, and in what form women's studies, Asian American studies, and queer studies have entered the academy; it has also considered the ways in which institutionalization and broader acceptance have reshaped these fields, as well as the types of internal conflicts that have divided activists and intellectuals working within and around these fields. The remaining chapters of this book will consider the ways in which programs in women's studies, Asian American studies, and queer studies have emerged within the organizational structures of individual college and university campuses. But these programs have not emerged in a vacuum. Instead, their emergence, the shapes they took, the ways in which their opponents responded to them, and their current state of institutionalization have all been shaped by the larger picture as the fields these individual programs are part of have fought for a place in the intellectual world.

PART II
Six Cases

Introduction

The stories of how women's studies, Asian American studies, and queer studies emerged as disciplines in the United States in the latter half of the 20th century go far in propelling an understanding of how disciplines work, how knowledge expands and changes, and how previously excluded groups find a seat at the academic table. But these broader tales tell us little about how individual colleges and universities change. After all, a disciplinary subject may arise and spread without becoming an integral part of the education of undergraduate students (see, for instance, the discussion of the rise of genetic toxicology in Frickel 2004). As highlighted in the previous chapter, women's studies, Asian American studies, and queer studies have—to different degrees—become part of the undergraduate curricula at colleges and universities; in some cases, these programs have even emerged at two-year colleges. However, even women's studies, the most institutionalized of the three disciplines, is not available everywhere. Some well-known, highly selective, and even progressive colleges and universities such as Reed College and New School University do not offer programs in it as of this writing.

This fact means that we cannot look to the stories of the emergence of women's studies, Asian American studies, and queer studies in disciplinary terms as if they offer all of the answers about how such programs ended up where they did in organizational terms. Instead, we must look to the stories of individual colleges and universities. In examining individual colleges and universities, we can ask more particular questions. What is the mission of the college or university, and how might that relate—or not—to its willingness to adopt new curricular programs? Did anyone ever seek to create a program in women's studies, Asian American studies, and/or queer studies? If so, who were they and what strategies and tactics did they employ in their campaign? Did they ultimately manage to create a program? If so, what does that program look like today? In any case, what kind of obstacles did they encounter, and how did they respond to such obstacles?

This section of the book lays out the answers to such questions in terms of six very different colleges and universities, all of which offer four-year liberal arts undergraduate degrees. Three are public universities, while three are private. They include several colleges and universities that have the most selective undergraduate admissions policies in the nation as well as those that accept well over half of their applicants. Their campuses are located in cities, small towns, and sprawling suburbs ranging from the Northeast to the West coast. One is a college that enrolls only female students, while one is governed by a conservative Catholic tradition. More details about the differences between these six colleges and universities can be found in Table II.1, as well as in the narratives about each particular case.

Among these six colleges and universities and the three disciplines under consideration here, there were fourteen attempts at creating curricular change. Four of these attempts did not result in changes to the curriculum at their college or university, while ten did. However, these ten campaigns varied widely in terms of their degree of institutionalization. Some resulted in the development of a concentration of a few courses within a major; others became programs that offer graduate degrees. The differences between these six colleges and universities and the fourteen curricular campaigns between them will enable a better understanding of the dynamics of curricular change: what works, what doesn't, and why. Later in the text we will develop a comparative analysis that permits the drawing of conclusions from the cumulative picture that all six campuses provide.

Table II.1 Overview of Cases

	Abigail Adams College	College of Assisi	Promenade University	Technopark University	Sagebrush University	Jeffrey University
Control	Private Secular	Private Catholic	Private Secular	Public	Public	Public
Founded	Late 1800s	Early 1900s	Early 1900s	Mid 1900s	Mid 1900s	Mid 1800s
Total Students	Under 4,000	Under 6,000	Under 10,000	Under 15,000	Under 25,000	Under 25,000
Total Undergraduates	Under 3,000	Under 6,000	Under 6,000	Under 10,000	Under 20,000	Under 20,000
% Students of Color	Over 20%	Under 10%	Over 40%	Over 30%	Over 50%	Over 10%
% Students Female	100%	Over 50%	Over 60%	Under 50%	Under 50%	Under 50%
Region	Northeast	Northeast	Mid-Atlantic	Southeast	West	Northeast
Campus	Traditional	Traditional	Urban	Modern	Modern	Modern
Setting	Rural/Town	Small City	Large City	Suburban	Suburban	Rural/Town
Student/Faculty Ratio	Under 10/1	Under 15/1	Under 20/1	Under 20/1	Under 20/1	Under 20/1
Graduation Rate	Over 80%	Over 80%	Over 20%	Over 50%	Over 80%	Over 60%
In-state Tuition/Fees	Over $30,000	Over $20,000	Over $20,000	Over $5,000	Over $5,000	Over $5,000
Out-of-state Tuition/Fees	Over $30,000	Over $20,000	Over $20,000	Over $15,000	Over $20,000	Over $15,000

continued

	Abigail Adams College	College of Assisi	Promenade University	Technopark State University	Sagebrush University	Jeffrey University
% Receiving Need-based Aid	Over 75%	Over 50%	Over 50%	Over 40%	Over 40%	Over 40%
Selectivity	More Selective	More Selective	Less Selective	More Selective	Most Selective	Selective
Acceptance Rate	Over 40%	Over 40%	Over 60%	Over 60%	Over 40%	Over 80%
Ranking	Top 50	2nd Tier	4th Tier	2nd Tier	Top 50	Top 100
% Students Living off Campus	Under 20%	Over 20%	Over 80%	Over 60%	Over 60%	Over 20%
% of Students In-state	24%	10%	93%	89%	95% (23% local)	82%
Women's Studies	Major	Minor	Minor	Minor	Major	Major
Asian American Studies	Certificate	None	None	None	Studies in Major	Certificate
LGBT Studies	Minor	None	None	None	Studies in Major	None

Chapter 3
A Place to Become Women: Abigail Adams College

After getting off the crowded interstate and driving through a quaint New England town complete with stately inns, cute chocolate shops, and eclectic restaurants, visitors to Abigail Adams College drive up a steep hill and enter the crowded campus. Dignified brick buildings and elegant Victorian mansions huddle around neatly manicured green quads as groups of young women hurry past on grey pathways. Abigail Adams was founded over a century ago by a wealthy woman who wanted to give female students the same opportunities that men had, and it has remained a single-sex college while many others have closed their doors or chosen coeducation. When it opened its doors, Abigail Adams was deeply rooted in the Protestant traditions of the New England countryside, but today it is a private secular college which is seen by many as a bastion of liberal education and radical students.

Several thousand undergraduate students live in the dorms here, many of which are small and retain a familial feel. Few students are permitted to live off campus and even many of the small number of non-traditional students who are over the age of 25 choose to live in College housing. Abigail Adams does enroll graduate students in a small number of programs, but its main focus remains on undergraduate education and classroom instruction is primarily conducted by a distinguished faculty with credentials equal to those at many Ivy League universities. The faculty are matched by an equally distinguished student body— Abigail Adams is a highly selective college enrolling some of the most academically talented students in the United States. There are fewer than ten students enrolled for every one faculty member.

This sort of education does not come cheap, and Abigail Adams students pay some of the highest tuition and fees of any college students in America. The price tag on a year's worth of classes, room, and board in 2010 is over $50,000, though the vast majority of students receive some financial aid. In fact, Abigail Adams scores high on measures that track its enrollment of those from lower socioeconomic backgrounds as well as students of color and international students, making an education at Abigail Adams much more diverse than one at many of its peers. Students participate in a busy extracurricular life of student government, community service, social organizations, and intercollegiate athletics, many so overcommitted that faculty wonder how students have time to complete the excellent academic work they turn in. After graduation, students are sought after for graduate school and corporate employment, but many choose public service careers instead.

Students at Abigail Adams can choose from hundreds of courses and dozens of majors across the liberal arts, with a few more professionally oriented fields available as well. The College's setting in an area close to other colleges and universities also permits students to cross-register for courses on other campuses and has allowed for several cooperative academic programs to develop. Included among these rich academic options are a major in the study of women and gender, a multi-campus certificate program in Asian American studies, and a concentration in queer studies. Yet as recently as 1980, none of these programs existed.

"An Education Comparable to that of Men"

As a private women's college, Abigail Adams always placed the education of women at the core of its academic mission. Unlike many other women's colleges, however, Abigail Adams defined women's education not in terms of the unique educational needs, talents, or social roles of women but instead aimed to provide women with an education comparable to that provided to men. This distinct quality of the Abigail Adams culture makes it less surprising that Abigail Adams avoided instituting a women's studies program in the 1970s when some other women's colleges established their programs in the field—before women's studies became gender studies, the study of women was not comparable to anything that men did. Yet a few courses that might be categorized as women's studies were offered in the early 1970s, adopted in response to student strikes that occurred in the wave of protests that swept the nation in 1970.

A few years later, in 1974, the College's educational policy committee mandated that academic departments find ways to integrate the study of women into their disciplines, ensuring for the first time that an education comparable to that of men did not mean an education that ignored women completely. The new courses developed in response to this mandate were all housed in traditional academic disciplines and included courses on topics such as women in literature and the psychology of women. When faculty first began to offer these courses, others in their departments were sometimes skeptical of whether there would be enough material to fill an entire term, and the decision to encourage courses on women's issues was made in the aftermath of a faculty-wide vote not to establish a women's studies program on campus. Many faculty members believed that the development of a women's studies program would ghettoize the study of women's issues and that a separate program might make "all teaching and learning in terms of gender differentiation" and "might break the natural link between women's studies and the departments where these considerations logically deserve study"—fears that at least some contemporary scholars of gender believe have come true. In contrast, the voting faculty believed that women's issues would be better served by being treated as "integral parts of larger subject matters."

The initiative to integrate the study of women's issues throughout the curriculum was an unusual move among higher education institutions in the 1970s, and it attracted the attention of a major national foundation that solicited the College to submit a proposal for a grant that would fund a center for research on women. A committee of faculty formed to craft such a proposal. The document that resulted highlighted the ways such a center would fit the mission of the College, focusing as it would on women's education, faculty research opportunities, and the involvement of undergraduate students in research. The proposal also noted some of the unique features of the College that would make it an ideal location for such a center, including significant archival resources focusing on women's history. But even this proposal proved too controversial on campus.

Faculty raised a number of objections to the proposal, which were formalized in a letter signed by twenty male and female faculty members. They argued that the presence of a center focusing on research on women would provide an improper incentive for faculty members and students to divert their attention away from their true research strengths and instead focus on projects that might prove insubstantial. They worried that such a center would conflict with the College's mission to provide an education comparable to that of men, and that the center might attract "the wrong kind of student" in part by defining the purposes of the College too narrowly. Some faculty members even worried that despite the grant funding, sufficient resources would not be available for faculty members to conduct the kind of ambitious research the College expected of them. Ultimately, these objections won out and the proposal was not submitted. Instead, faculty interested in research on women turned their attention to winning funding for more specific individual projects.

Though these faculty members did get some institutional support for their research on women, the climate for feminist faculty at Abigail Adams in the 1970s was less than supportive. Abigail Adams, like other women's colleges, faced a constant barrage of comments and complaints that equated all feminism with lesbianism, and many feminist faculty felt that the conflation of misogyny and homophobia that this entailed left Abigail Adams in a defensive posture that brought about hostility to not only feminism but also to women's studies. A number of faculty members who worked to initiate courses on women in their departments or whose research focused on women were not reappointed or were denied tenure. An article published in a national newsmagazine during this period claimed that a primary determinant of tenure at Abigail Adams was the "degree of allegiance a scholar has to traditionalists who see women's studies as trendy, peripheral, subjective, [and] parochial," though the reporter could find no one willing to go on the record with this claim.

In contrast to the environment for faculty, students found a climate more supportive of feminism and work in women's studies. Throughout the late 1970s and the 1980s, students used their ample extracurricular funding to bring notable feminist speakers to campus. A student organization formed to do work around women's issues, including women's studies. Though the group remained small and was often regarded with some skepticism by others, students working on women's studies did not report any hostility to their work—only to their perceived lesbianism. As noted above, the conflation of feminism with lesbianism led some students to believe that the student group which ran the campus women's center was so lesbian in nature that simply being part of the group would taint one. This fear discouraged many campus feminists from becoming actively involved in organizational life.

The contradictions of the campus response to women's studies at Abigail Adams continued to multiply. The College president for a decade spanning the period under consideration here was a vocal female educator with a passionate dedication to women's education and who herself had done research on women. Yet an article in a national women's publication quoted her discussing her opposition to women's studies:

> I just think that, intellectually, women's studies as a major would be solipsistic. Women have been handicapped by being directed toward 'women's things' in a non-rigorous way for so long, and the culture is so profoundly sexist that if someone has a major in women's studies she is handicapped ... women should be directed to abstract from their own experience, but by using all the intellectual tools that have always been important for anyone.

Though the internal politics of the College continued to be hostile to women's studies, external foundations and other funding sources proved to be a source of support, as they had from the beginning. In the early 1980s, an alumna donated stocks in her family's company to the College with the stated purpose of increasing course offerings dealing with women's experiences. These funds were used to create an interdisciplinary course in women's studies and ultimately became the foundation of a departmental endowment that now allows the program on women and gender substantial programmatic flexibility. Earlier, in the late 1970s, a major national foundation spent over $300,000 to fund an interdisciplinary program on women and social change that still remains on campus in a modified form to this day. Though the project was based on the proposal that faculty had found so objectionable earlier in the decade, this time it won campus support. Key elements of the program included faculty seminars open to faculty members from nearby colleges, annual conferences, summer workshops on particular topics that provided employment opportunities for undergraduate research assistants, the publication of several volumes, workshops for planning curricular changes, networking opportunities for faculty and students interested in women's studies, and a new curricular initiative called the "course cluster." The course cluster project connected a public lecture series on a particular topic each semester with four different courses, each in a different discipline. It was instrumental in leading to the development of new courses, particularly those in politics, history, and psychology. The project on women and social change proved popular on campus. By 1982, after only four years, 200 students and 25 faculty members from 14 different disciplines had been involved.

Like many liberal arts colleges, Abigail Adams offered students the option of designing their own majors. Students with an interest in women's studies often sought to use this option to develop a program of study, but most found the process quite challenging. Students had no way of identifying which courses might fit into their programs or which faculty members might be willing and able to serve as advisors. At least one student who sought to create a women's studies program for herself was prohibited from doing so. She chose instead to major in a single discipline and then take as many women's studies courses as she could, a course load that largely amounted to a double major. Yet her primary department still criticized her for taking too many women's studies courses. By 1979, the situation had reached such a point that faculty and students began urging the creation of a guide that would help students who wanted to pursue a self-designed major in women's studies, but students largely continued to help themselves. By 1983 at least four students had created women's studies majors and many more had unsuccessfully sought to do so. A number of students also created their own independent study courses in a process one alumna described as "making it up as we go along."

"If Our Goal is to Change the World, First We Must Understand It"

Frustrated with the lack of progress in creating women's studies opportunities on campus, the feminist student organization that ran the campus women's center created a women's studies task force in 1979 to coordinate efforts towards a women's studies program. Once it was created, this task force began meeting with the faculty members who did teach women's studies courses as well as with the students on the educational policy committee of the campus government. The members of the task force and their faculty allies thought carefully about strategy. They thought big. They knew that winning a major in 1979 would be unlikely, yet they continued to campaign for one because they thought that this would make the adoption of a minor as a compromise more likely. Working together, students and faculty developed a pressure campaign that included the creation of a curricular proposal, a curriculum study aimed at measuring compliance with the earlier College commitment to offer more courses on women's experiences, requests to hire more faculty working in women's studies, and coordination with student departmental liaisons to request more departmental courses on women's issues. Even though all of the nearby colleges had women's studies programs, the educational policy committee continued to see women's studies as a minor issue.

However, the students on the task force began to think that women's studies faculty were becoming less supportive of their efforts, even as these faculty members made the commitment to advise students and to work for a page in the course catalogue that would discuss women's studies. The faculty told students that the students could accomplish just as much as the faculty could, and that therefore the students should be the ones doing the work. This points to another of the contradictions of curricular change at Abigail Adams—the debate over who actually had the power on campus. Prior to the mid-1970s, even experimental courses to be offered once or twice had to be approved by the entire faculty senate, an unusual arrangement that surely kept the curriculum more stable and traditional than elsewhere. Later on, experimental courses could be approved only by the committee on educational policy, but courses to be offered on a more permanent basis required both committee and faculty senate approval. New programs or departments required a further level of administrative review and approval. While students had their own curriculum committee, it served only in an advisory capacity and had little formal influence. Yet the faculty generally perceived the students as being a powerful force, if one that did not always know what to do with their power. One faculty member was even quoted in a national publication saying that he sometimes thought the students at Abigail Adams were more powerful than the faculty.

These contradictions led some students involved with the campaign for women's studies to believe that they had been "recruited" to do the work by faculty members who "capitalized on their enthusiasm" at the same time as faculty members supportive of women's studies believed students were the only ones who could make a change. Yet other faculty members pulled back from involvement because they were concerned it was not the right time to go forward, either because pushing too hard would derail subtle behind-the-scenes activities by faculty, because women's studies did not yet have sufficient intellectual rigor, or because women's studies did not deserve departmental status. At the same time, students and faculty who were interested in women's studies began to receive substantial support from a large and vocal local feminist community that was able to support a number of feminist businesses, social service agencies, and activist groups. This community provided support not only to women's studies but also to feminist campus activism on a variety of issues, such as a march protesting violence against women. A local feminist activist showed her support by being quoted in a national magazine arguing that it was important that women's studies programs and curricula be kept in the hands of women.

Yet the faculty did form a women's studies committee in 1978. Though this committee was not as activist as the student task force, it did aim to coordinate the efforts of faculty teaching women's studies and to make it easier for students with an interest in the field to find courses and advisors. The committee provided information about women's studies to both the faculty and the students, it helped students draft independent study proposals and design their own majors and minors, it developed an archive of course syllabi and independent study documents, and it made good on the commitment to advise students and to add a page to the catalogue listing women's studies courses. By 1979 at least two dozen women's studies courses were being offered at Abigail Adams. All of this work was justified by women's studies faculty with the explicit statement that there was no need for a women's studies department, and a story about the College in a national feminist magazine stated that "there is not, and by universal accord, will not be a women's studies major."

Though faculty were urging students to go slowly, the student women's studies task force submitted a statement to the educational policy committee in early 1979 proposing that a feasibility study be conducted for the creation of an interdisciplinary women's studies major. The study did take place. Students gathered data on the percentage of students taking women's studies courses, surveyed student interest in and faculty commitment to women's studies, and compared the Abigail Adams curriculum with that at similar colleges. The feasibility study found strong support for women's studies among students on campus. Over 200 students a year were enrolling in women's studies, or about 10 percent of the total student body. Additionally, a student activist who surveyed students for a class project found that most students had an interested in women's studies coursework. Student activists embarked on a number of additional initiatives as well. They began collecting past course papers on women's studies topics to create an archive in the campus women's center, held a student research conference, and compiled booklets on women's studies courses available on campus as well as through cross-registration. Frustrated with courses that claimed to address women's issues but barely touched on them, students began collectively evaluating courses so that students could more easily choose those with significant women's studies content. They also coordinated an electoral campaign to ensure that a sympathetic student would be elected chair of the undergraduate student curriculum committee. And though debates continued to rage both within and beyond the student body about whether it would be better to integrate the study of women into the curriculum or to develop a women's studies program, students and alumnae began writing letters to the College president urging her support of women's studies and explaining the importance of women's studies to women's education.

Perhaps the most unique activity that women's studies student activists engaged in at Abigail Adams College was the Interterm Project in January 1980. Like many other selective liberal arts colleges, Abigail Adams maintained a long break between the end of the fall semester in December and the beginning of the spring semester in late January. Students could and still can choose to use this time as an extended vacation, an opportunity to make extra money, a chance to take a short internship or travel abroad, or a time to take a for-credit or non-credit course in a topic they did not have time to explore during the regular semester. In January 1980, women's studies student activists chose to create a workshop on women's studies. The initiative for this project sprang from one of the many articles that appeared in the national press that discussed the College president's views on women's studies. Students decided that it was time to demonstrate not only their interest in women's studies but also the fact that women's studies could be a serious intellectual pursuit.

The group that planned the Interterm Project lived primarily in the same residence hall, one that was known for housing feminist students. The syllabus they created for this project, a detailed and extended intellectual work that shows just how gifted Abigail Adams students are, was an attempt to educate workshop participants in the key issues of women's studies. The students who planned the project believed that if they could demonstrate to the faculty that students really wanted women's studies and that they would spend their Januaries engaged in it, and if they could provide the faculty with an intellectually rigorous skeleton of a program, the faculty could and would take it forward. At the heart of the project was the question of how women's studies was related to the liberal arts.

In the weeks before the workshop, students laid out a set of goals for the program. These goals included raising campus consciousness about women's studies, training women to ask questions, building discussions around the notions of the liberal arts and the goal of anti-specialization, finding a way to address the notion that women's studies majors are a handicap for graduates, and publicizing other efforts and problems around women's studies on campus. In thinking about curricular initiatives, the students highlighted the importance of mechanisms to help students enroll in upper-level women's studies courses even when they had not completed prerequisites within the relevant departments, the need to develop sequencing and an introductory course so that material is not duplicated across different women's studies courses, and the difficulties students had faced in creating self-designed majors. The students also collected data on how other colleges and universities had gone about establishing women's studies programs.

The syllabus that was provided to program participants included a recommended reading list as well as a schedule of topics for discussion. The schedule included discussions on what women's studies was, what sorts of programs existed elsewhere, the status of women's studies at Abigail Adams, the reasons for developing a women's studies program, what the program and its courses should look like, and how to get support for the program. Participants were asked to read some of the classic texts on women's studies as well as many of the recent articles published in the national press about women and women's studies at Abigail Adams. Project planners hoped that the workshop would serve as the starting point of a process that would lead to the development of a formal proposal for a women's studies program, complete with an intellectual and academic justification and a plan for implementation, by May. They expected that this proposal would include a formalized opportunity for students to create self-designed majors in women's studies, calls for the creation of more women-focused courses in the disciplines, and the development of several interdisciplinary women's studies courses, particularly a feminist methodology course and introductory and advanced feminist theory courses.

The students working on the Interterm Project were quite aware of the integration between their academic work and broader goals around social change in a way true to the initial promise of women's studies itself. These students believed that women's studies would give women the intellectual tools to understand oppression, raise their consciousness, and address individual attitudes towards academia and power. Their slogan of sorts was the claim that "if we want to change the world, we must first understand it." The project itself shows their eagerness to develop understanding, but they were eager to change the world as well. At graduation in 1980, as a group of women's studies advocates graduated without seeing their dreams for a program come alive, students wore red armbands with black women symbols on them to show their support for women's studies.

"The Forefront"

In the early 1980s, developments in women's studies at Abigail Adams sped up. By 1981, women's studies faculty had argued for and successfully implemented a page in the course catalogue that listed faculty members willing to serve as advisors to students with an interest in women's studies, though no courses were listed there. In 1982, courses formally called women's studies began to be offered. In 1983, faculty members proposed the creation of an advisory committee to coordinate curricula relating to women. The committee was created and served to advise students working on independent majors or research projects, to coordinate the still-strong course cluster project, and to sponsor faculty development programs.

But not all news was good news. In 1983, an outspoken lesbian feminist professor was not reappointed to her teaching position. Though the non-reappointment decision cited issues with her scholarship as justification, many on campus believed that the real motivation was this professor's lesbianism and feminism. In addition, this denial of reappointment was quite controversial due to the unorthodox procedure that was followed, which involved a revote in the department, the intervention of the president, and the solicitation of a larger-than-usual number of outside reviews. Many students were particularly outraged by this decision, as she had been extremely popular as well as quite involved in teaching women's studies courses and advising women's studies students. These students, as well as a few faculty members, organized in response. Students held a picket and distributed leaflets, the lesbian alumnae group coordinated a letter-writing campaign in her support, and the student body selected her to give a speech during their commencement weekend.

The official topic of her speech was the development of feminist consciousness among students at Abigail Adams, as seen through the lens of psychological theory. However, she devoted significant attention to the climate for women and lesbians on campus as well as the issue of women's studies and why the College was not retaining feminist faculty. In discussing women's studies, she said

> ... you can see that the College has not been at the forefront in getting the study of women into the curriculum; in recruiting and retaining feminist scholars and those dedicated to the teaching of women; or in respecting the opinion of students (who happen to be women) ... Have you questioned why there is no Women's Studies Program at Abigail Adams College, a woman's college? It is because women's studies is not considered a legitimate subject of scholarly

inquiry? Is it because women are already so visible in the curriculum at Abigail
Adams that we don't need a Women's Studies Program and more courses?

Though this professor landed on her feet elsewhere, the students outraged by her
departure continued to press for more women's studies courses. In the 1983–84
academic year, they were rewarded with 20 women's studies course offerings,
and by the end of 1984 students could earn a minor in women's studies. The
committee charged with administering the minor sent out a document soliciting
courses for inclusion. To be included, courses were required to be rooted in some
discipline; focus on women's experiences, expression, or production, as well as on
debates about issues involving women; and involve serious consideration of how
the inclusion of women reshapes assumptions and the organization of knowledge
within the discipline. Shortly after the minor was initiated, a new president
came to campus. Like the prior president, this president was deeply committed
to women's education and did research and teaching about women; unlike the
prior president, she was supportive of women's studies as a discipline. She used
her own personal funds to support a collaborative center for women's studies
research nearby Abigail Adams College, though the center was not itself part of
the College. Three years into her term, a women's studies major was adopted.
The heavy enrollments in women's studies courses and in the minor prompted
the adoption of the major as faculty sought ways to avoid having their women's
studies courses count as overload; in addition, the faculty realized that curricular
integration was not coming as quickly as they had hoped and became more willing
to consider a separate program.

Within the first week of the availability of the women's studies major, three
students signed up. A report by outside evaluators later in 1987 noted that more
than 30 students each year chose to major in women's studies and more than 60
different courses were offered over a two-year period by faculty from 18 different
academic departments. The evaluators did have some concerns, however. The
program was not housed in a department. This meant that it was hard for the
faculty running the program to develop a coherent program or to address gaps
in the curriculum and that the program had little to no influence over hiring and
tenure decisions. In addition, the program had limited control over its small budget,
which came primarily from an anonymous donor.

While the course cluster remained a central part of the women's studies
experience in the early days of the major, it was abolished in 1993. In its place,
the women's studies program began to offer upper-level interdisciplinary courses
open only to majors and minors. From the earliest days of the program, faculty
had been contemplating the development of a "study away" program that would
allow students at other colleges and universities to come to Abigail Adams to do
research on women's issues, and this initiative was made part of the offerings of
the women's studies program in 1994. By that year, there were 1,100 students
enrolled in 42 courses offered by the program, and the 76 enrolled majors made it
one of the top ten majors at the College.

The program has remained a strong and central element of the Abigail Adams curriculum in the years since its founding, but has not been without controversy. In the late 1990s, the curricular program expanded to include more coverage of sexuality and of masculinities. At the same time, there was some pressure from students to incorporate a significant focus on gender as apart from women, particularly from a vocal group of students who identified as transgender. Other students and faculty were committed to retaining the historical focus on women's issues. The conflict came to a head in the early 2000s as the faculty considered changing the name of the program to gender studies. Some faculty involved in the women's studies program were reluctant to change the name because they felt it would be a conservative move away from the program's feminist roots, while others believed that "gender" was a more accurate description of the program's current curricular focus. Ultimately, faculty settled on a compromise position that retained both women and gender in the program's name. Though some students applauded the change, many were not as happy as the faculty expected and some wished they could graduate with "women's studies" on their transcript. As the name change was only finalized in 2006, perhaps students who enter Abigail Adams in the future will see the new name as the way things have always been. The constant turnover of student bodies leads to short memories.

"Go Back to Where You Came From"

Though Abigail Adams has never been a locus of Asian American student activism, its location in a community near other colleges and universities has given its students the opportunity to become involved with social and academic initiatives they would not otherwise have had access to. These opportunities began as early as the 1980s, when Asian Americans were just starting to make a demographic impact in higher education in the United States (Asian American students constituted just 2.4 percent of college students in 1980, while in 2008 7 percent of college students were Asian American, according to the National Center for Education Statistics). In the mid-1980s, for instance, the Abigail Adams campus served as the site of a conference for Asian American students across the entire East Coast.

Abigail Adams came to be a frequent location for Asian American student conferences. Throughout the 1990s, students held conferences every year, most drawing students from the local area. At one of these conferences, held in 1995, a faculty member in Asian American studies from another university came to campus to lead a workshop intended to instruct students on how to start an Asian American studies program on their own campuses. As might be expected, students had already begun asking for Asian American studies courses. However, unlike many other campuses, Abigail Adams still offered few courses in East Asian area studies or in Asian languages. For many students on campus, including the large number of international students from Asia as well as the undoubtedly large group of students who were still themselves part of the post-1965 Asian immigration boom, these courses seemed more of a priority. Conflicts thus developed between students interested in Asian area studies and students interested in Asian American studies. Nonetheless, by 1993 a course in Asian American studies was being offered on campus. Students also formed a student group focusing on Asian American studies and began to sponsor lectures on Asian American studies topics.

In the mid-1990s, students enrolled in the pioneering Asian American studies course, the Asian American Experience, wrote a letter to the student newspaper alerting the campus to the fact that "go back to where you came from" was written on the "diversity board" posted in one of the residence halls. This was not an isolated act—other acts of minor racism occurred over the next few years. Coupled with the sense of isolation many students of color felt at an elite college in a small New England town, these events prompted many students to ask for a multicultural housing option. But the primary activism around Asian American issues at Abigail Adams was directed outward.

In the late 1990s, students at a nearby university engaged in a building takeover related to racial issues, among them demands for Asian American studies. Students at Abigail Adams wrote a statement of support, participated in a solidarity walkout, and delivered supplies to those students occupying the building. A few months after this building takeover, students at another nearby college held a building occupation to demand the implementation of a collaborative cross-campus Asian American studies program that would involve Abigail Adams College. This wave of activism was the culmination of two decades of pressure for Asian American studies in the area, as students had been demanding Asian American studies since the 1980s. This activism was never as strong at Abigail Adams as it was elsewhere, but these efforts laid the groundwork for what came next.

In 1999, a conference was held by a group of area colleges to explore directions in collaboration around Asian American studies. A faculty member at Abigail Adams gave a speech at this conference promoting the collaborative program. This year proved to be a landmark one for efforts to establish a program. Before 1999, despite student and faculty interest in a program, there had not been sufficient faculty resources to allow one to proceed. A number of new hires in and just before 1999 finally provided these resources, and campus collaboration and the support of allies allowed the program to go forward. It was also in 1999 that a group bringing together faculty and students interested in Asian American studies in the local area was first organized.

This progress occurred despite considerable skepticism about new programs from many faculty members uninvolved in the initiative. In particular, the majority of the faculty members involved with the program were junior faculty, many of whom were discouraged by deans from participation and told it might hurt their chances of tenure. The program suffered from significant financial constraints as well as from a general lack of knowledge about what Asian American studies is. In addition, there were debates as to whether Asian American studies merited its own separate program or whether it should be subsumed into American studies.

Unlike in the case of women's studies at Abigail Adams, students played a more minor role in the campaign for Asian American studies. While students had a strong interest in taking more courses, they were not necessarily the ones playing a major advocacy role. They were involved throughout the process of program development; though students did not draft the proposal for the cooperative certificate program, they did provide input on it and attended a series of committee meetings. In its final version, the proposal emphasized the benefits of cultural diversity on campus, the program's role in making new scholarship available, and the community's responsibility to include marginalized groups in scholarship. In addition, external funding was made available to support Asian American studies programming and efforts to recruit and retain a diverse group of students and faculty, and this money supported a visiting faculty position in Asian American studies.

In order for cooperative certificate programs such as the Asian American studies program to be adopted among this group of area colleges, they must first be approved by a committee of deans from each of the colleges and then approved by the normal curriculum committee process on at least three campuses. At Abigail Adams, the certificate program was approved in 2000. The certificate program requires fewer courses than a major would, but more than a minor, and in addition requires the completion of a special project consisting of research, community action, artistic production, or some other sustained independent engagement with Asian American studies. By the mid-2000s, about two Abigail Adams students per year earned a certificate, with between 20 and 50 enrolling in Asian American studies courses on campus each semester. Low enrollment is not the only obstacle the program faces. The lack of sufficient teaching faculty is the most significant obstacle to program expansion. A 2003 report suggested that counting up all of the Asian American studies courses offered by faculty at all of the participating campuses would employ less than one full-time-equivalent position per year, though a few additional courses are taught by adjuncts or graduate students and course offerings may have expanded slightly in the years since 2003. Current initiatives designed to respond to this limitation are focused on encouraging faculty with relevant expertise to teach more Asian American studies courses as well as hiring more faculty in Asian American studies, including through joint appointments at multiple campuses. A faculty search of this nature was conducted in 2007. In addition, there is an initiative to return to offering student conferences on a regular basis, in part to allow for better coordination of student activism in the area. While the program remains small, it is not surprising that it does. Student and faculty pressure can go far in getting a program started. A critical mass of interest is required to sustain it, and it is hard to find that in a small New England town far from centers of Asian American studies scholarship.

"Militantly Recruiting Others"

As was mentioned above in the discussion of women's studies at Abigail Adams, the campus had long struggled with popular culture images that equate feminism and women's community with lesbianism. The College's attempt to fight these images has often resulted in hostility towards the queer community on campus, and yet a sizable community of lesbian and bisexual women has been a part of campus life for years, with a transgender community growing more recently. Many of these students were attracted to Abigail Adams because it is a women's college and because it is located in a feminist community, but the College has not always been happy to see them arrive.

Queer issues first became topics of public conversation at Abigail Adams in the 1970s at the same time as they were hitting the scene nationally. In 1973, an event called "Women's Weekend" hosted a workshop on bisexuality at which about 50 people came out as lesbian or bisexual. After this, an underground support group for lesbian and bisexual women formed. When it failed to win formal recognition and funding, it disbanded. Students tried again to form a student organization in 1976. This lesbian organization was denied funding by the student government in the late 1970s. The official explanation for the funding denial had to do with budget irregularities, but many students believed this was a pretext. Lesbian students also struggled in their private lives and many experienced significant fears about their place at the College. Documents in the College archives show that there were rumors in the mid-1970s that students found to be lesbian would be expelled and that the dean of students kept secret files on lesbian students.

The divisiveness of issues of sexual orientation on campus was intensified by the fact that the national media made a sport in the late 1970s of writing articles about lesbianism at women's colleges, articles that often featured Abigail Adams. Every time one of these many articles was published, the College administration and the public relations department went into overdrive doing what they saw as damage control. For instance, one College-issued "Statement on Lesbianism" noted that claims of lesbianism were often used to fragment women's communities and that general perceptions of an increase in lesbian students were actually due to increased openness among students, with the real lesbian student population remaining quite small. By the early 1980s, things had reached such a state that alumnae were writing to tell the College that they would stop donating money because they perceived the College as too supportive of lesbianism while faculty claimed students were transferring because they were uncomfortable with lesbian classmates.

The College president had written a memo in 1979 that urged a policy of non-discrimination based on sexual orientation. In the same memo, she wrote that "in any instance where lesbians are militantly recruiting others to join their way of life they must be required to live off campus." While there is no evidence that lesbian students at Abigail Adams were trying to "convert" their classmates, the fear that this might occur was rampant on campus. A dean in fact confronted students in one residence hall to ask if they were recruiting younger students into lesbianism. Things reached such a state that the administration decided that lesbian and feminist students should no longer be allowed to concentrate in the residence hall of their choice and instead dispersed them into different dorms. In the words of one alumna, the result of this decision was to "seed the rest of the campus with radicalism" instead of keeping it contained in one location.

Lesbian alumnae, not subject to the same fears as current students, played an important role in organizing. In the mid-1980s, alumnae who were developing a lesbian feminist alumnae group wrote to 400 supportive alumnae to provide a sort of climate statement about what was occurring on campus. This statement documented the dismantling of the lesbian feminist residential option described above and noted that the alumnae magazine would not publish letters supporting lesbian feminist issues or news of lesbian-related accomplishments as well as that the campus non-discrimination statement still excluded issues of sexual orientation. The alumnae group was also involved in developing workshops on lesbian issues to be presented at the College or to alumnae groups. Besides alumnae, students on campus could count on feminist and queer women from the community to be strong supporters of their activities on campus.

Once they obtained official approval, one of the first activities the lesbian student group engaged in was presenting workshops to the administration and to other students. Student-run workshops soon were prohibited by an administrative moratorium. Coupled with their increasing frustration over the climate for lesbians on campus, this moratorium spurred students to action. In 1983, the lesbian student group issued a list of demands. These demands included permission to resume offering campus workshops, the addition of sexual orientation to the non-discrimination statement, and the opportunity to pre-approve College statements on lesbianism. The group also requested a lesbian counselor in the health services department, the creation of a lesbian issues task force, and curricular development focusing on lesbian issues. Administrators held a meeting with students to discuss these issues, and though it seems that some workshops became permissible after this meeting, the general response from the administration was that they were unwilling to discuss "non-negotiable demands."

Throughout the 1980s, lesbian students continued to work towards a more open and inclusive community as well as towards developing lesbian curricula. At first, students worked with faculty to improve issues of classroom climate. They also developed an archive of course papers dealing with lesbian topics or issues, much as students had earlier done for women's studies. By 1988, at least one course explicitly focused on gay and lesbian issues was available, though it was offered under an alternative title so that words related to sexuality would not appear on students' transcripts—a common practice in the early days of queer studies and one that some students still wish for today. In 1989, about 80 people held a campus rally to demand that sexual orientation be added to the non-discrimination statement, that an administrator dealing with LGBT issues be hired, and that a committee to "examine the need and possibilities for a Program for

Lesbian Bisexual and Gay Concerns" be created. Though many lesbian students in this period experienced the climate at Abigail Adams as one of substantial freedom and support for experimentation and self-discovery, particularly in comparison to the way lesbians were treated in the outside world in these years before the highly-publicized coming out of stars like Ellen DeGeneres and k.d. lang, there were also moments when the administration intervened directly in the lives of lesbian students on the request of their parents.

"Making More Visible"

The new president who arrived on campus in 1985 and who supported women's studies also had quite a different relationship to queer studies than did her predecessor. Though she did not use Abigail Adams' name in doing so, she added her personal endorsement to an ACLU resolution against sexual orientation discrimination in the military. In 1991, she issued a statement proclaiming tolerance towards lesbian students, a move that received attention in the national news media. Some anti-lesbian incidents continued to occur on campus, but students responded by creating an activist climate that celebrated openness around sexuality. The faculty, on the other hand, still experienced an unsupportive climate and were warned to be careful.

In 1992, the college president met with the lesbian (and now bisexual) student group. At this meeting, students asked for more inclusion of lesbian and gay issues in the curriculum. The president's response was that students should not have the responsibility of suggesting course content, but students argued that they had been asking for attention to these issues for years without receiving a response. The president committed to discussing gay topics at a meeting she held with faculty but no additional action was taken on curricular issues. In fact, this period involved a move to intensify the curricular focus on core academic areas. Late in 1993, gay and lesbian faculty members were first offered domestic partner benefits, but the only openly gay (male) faculty member was denied reappointment.

No faculty on campus listed queer studies among their interests in the 1996–97 academic year, but a number of faculty were indeed doing research and teaching related to queer issues. Due to the coordinated efforts of a group of area colleges, a brochure listing courses in gay, lesbian, and bisexual issues available for cross-registration at each of the colleges was created yearly starting in the early 1990s. Five Abigail Adams courses were included in the brochure from the politics, theatre, sociology, and psychology departments. Despite the presence of these courses, Abigail Adams faculty were involved in these collaborative efforts to only a very limited extent. There was strong student demand for more courses on the queer experience, and faculty focused on raising the visibility of the few courses already offered. Students also began to demand a faculty hire in queer studies, a move that existing faculty with interests in queer studies found troubling.

Visiting faculty in queer studies did become available, supported by money from an external foundation.

In the fall of 1998, a symposium on queer activism and queer studies was held on campus. More than 750 people, including students, faculty, staff, and community members, attended. The then-president of the college addressed the symposium, saying

> Abigail Adams has a long-standing commitment to diversity, and sexual orientation is explicit in that commitment ... we need to create a climate in which gay faculty, staff, and students can live productively ... [queer studies] is an exciting example of the role colleges and universities should play in raising awareness of issues of the day.

This symposium marked the beginning of a period of rapid change in queer studies on campus.

A course on queer studies was first offered within the women's studies department in 1998. The next year, an introductory course was developed. This course was organized as two-credit lecture series, one of the first two-credit courses on a campus where courses are ordinarily worth four credits, and drew 250 students. The course was expensive to offer, but faculty drew on their own resources and the women's studies endowment to make it possible, as the administration was wary of supporting an expensive experimental initiative. The same year, a three-course concentration in queer studies was approved within the women's studies program.

To the faculty involved in creating the concentration, it was really a matter of "making more visible" what already existed on campus. A group of faculty worked to create the concentration at the same time as the women's studies department was undergoing a curricular review, and in fact the department also added a requirement that all students majoring in women's studies take at least one queer studies course. There was no significant opposition to these changes, and in fact some of the advances made by the program, such as the interdisciplinary two-credit course, are now seen as assets by the administration.

The program has not been without difficulties. Faculty have trouble offering a sufficient number of queer studies courses in a situation in which most faculty have primary appointments in traditional academic disciplines and thus primary responsibilities to teach courses there. Some queer and trans-identified students were also historically somewhat wary of enrolling in courses in women's studies because they saw the program as promoting gender essentialism—concerns that were largely addressed by the name change to women's and gender studies, after which these students felt "more accommodated." In 2006, the College opened a resource center dealing with issues of gender and sexuality that offers programming and other resources to students, faculty, and staff. Today, the College has a reputation as unusually friendly to queer students and often shows up in lists of the most queer-friendly colleges.

"From Pearls to Pickets"

The Abigail Adams College of the 1960s was a largely traditional place. While not immune to the waves of campus protest sweeping the nation by the end of the decade, the College was more a place to find elite women preparing for motherhood or careers than it was a place to find crowds of students carrying picket signs. Yet by the year 2000, Abigail Adams offered programs in women's studies, Asian American studies, and queer studies. The paths to all three of these programs were scattered with periods of confrontation and controversy even as the ultimate approval of each program went smoothly.

The story of curricular change at Abigail Adams provides several important insights that we will return to in later chapters. First, curricular change was not possible without students and faculty working together. The relative involvement and importance of these two groups can change. In the campaign for women's studies, students were clearly in the driver's seat, with faculty providing background support and stepping in at the end to shepherd the new program through the approval process. In the cases of Asian American studies and queer studies, intermittent demands and protests gave way to an entirely faculty-driven process with minimal student input. But the formation of all three programs involved both faculty and students. Second, processes of curricular change take time. In all three cases, students first began asking for a curricular initiative years before the program was implemented. In an environment in which the student body turns over completely every four years and in which even the faculty is not known for its longevity (Abigail Adams employs large numbers of temporary faculty and does not always have the highest tenure rates), institutional memory can be short. The activists involved in the ultimate push for approval for each of these disciplines may have seen themselves as the people who got it done. But they were building on legacies of students and faculty who went before them and set the stage for what they would ultimately accomplish. Finally, the political environment within the college or university matters. A president and a faculty hostile to women's studies or queer studies can certainly prevent their establishment, and a community more accepting of these innovations can make them possible. This does not mean that a simple change in administration solves everything. When the new president arrived on campus in the mid-1980s, complete with a commitment to women's studies and queer studies, it still took several years for the women's studies major and the queer studies concentration to come to fruition. This president was willing to support the initiatives that were developing, but she did not implement them single-handedly.

Though these insights will be important for the cases presented in the chapters to come, not all colleges and universities work like Abigail Adams. As a private college, Abigail Adams does not need to worry about the vagaries of state politics in seeking approval for new programs. As an expensive and elite college with a sizable endowment, Abigail Adams has the funding available for pursuing experimental programs. As a college that despite a more conservative history has always had a mission of educating women and which had a more contemporary mission of diversity, Abigail Adams found it difficult to claim that women's studies, Asian American studies, or queer studies did not fit with its curricular identity. And as a college with a large and diverse faculty, a motivated student body with time for leadership and access to activist resources, and a location in a diverse and activist community, Abigail Adams was an ideal location for the incubation of new ideas and campaigns. Yet even without these advantages, new programs emerge at other types of colleges and universities.

Chapter 4

Our Work is Never Done: Promenade University

Visitors to Promenade University usually arrive on crowded public transportation, as parking in the neighborhood where it is located is rather limited. On one side of campus is a busy commercial shopping district, on the other a public park in a gentrifying residential area. Though the crime rate is comparable to other areas in the large mid-Atlantic city in which the University is located, the campus is fortified with high fences and guard towers, and visitors are not allowed to set foot on campus without some sort of official permission to be there. Once inside the gates, they find a small courtyard surrounded by tall concrete buildings connected by a warren of corridors, elevators, and skyways.

The University was established in the early 1900s. From its founding, it has enrolled a student body far more diverse than most colleges and universities, including large numbers of low-income and non-traditional students. Today, about half of enrolled students are students of color, with about a tenth of the students identifying as Asian Americans, and like many colleges and universities today, two-thirds or more of the students are female. Many students are immigrants or the children of immigrants for whom the University offers a chance to claw their way up the economic ladder within an easy commute from home. Though it is a private university with tuition rates topping $10,000 a semester, many students cannot afford those rates and struggle through school part-time with heavy loan burdens. Few students live on campus; many live at home with families and children of their own. Almost all students come from the local area.

Though Promenade University is not selective in its admissions policies and ranks low in prestige in comparison to other private universities, it has several respectable graduate programs, particularly in the health sciences. Promenade University is one branch of a multi-campus system spanning the metropolitan area in which it is located. Other campuses enroll less diverse student bodies, including more traditionally-aged residential students, but each campus has a distinct curriculum and control is largely local.

The University enrolls over 10,000 students, about half of whom are undergraduates. The student-faculty ratio has not kept pace with the enrollment growth, and today there are almost 20 students for every one faculty member. Many courses are taught by low-paid adjuncts who are earning their Ph.D.s at other universities in the area. The University also has a retention problem, as students who initially sought it out for its convenient location and status as a private university often realize that transferring to a low-cost public alternative might suit them better, while others simply run out of funds. The low graduation rate is also due to the fact that the many part-time students mean that few students are able to finish their degrees within the six-year window measured by the Department of Education.

Though today Promenade is viewed as a low-status option for those who face difficulties in achieving a college degree, it used to be a locus of political activism. On campus, students have organized to demand more reasonable fees, changes to the professional school curricula, and more fair grading policies. They have also participated in city-wide and national protests about a variety of issues affecting the student body. Yet most students are so busy balancing school, work, and family that they simply do not have time for politics.

Students at Promenade have to fulfill a long list of general education requirements alongside their major programs and so often have little time to take electives. Undergraduate programs are primarily pre-professional or vocational in nature, with an emphasis on health care, education, and other service work, though liberal arts majors are available. Though students have organized campus groups for Asian American and queer students, no courses are offered in Asian American studies and only occasionally are there courses relating to issues of sexual orientation. In fact, in 2008 the campus was just considering organizing an Asian area studies minor program. Promenade University does offer a minor program in gender studies.

"Something for Women"

Despite the history of campus activism at Promenade University, significant attention did not become focused on women's issues until the early 1990s. This first wave of attention was primarily focused on non-academic issues. First, in the aftermath of the Anita Hill controversy and a rape scandal at a nearby college, students pushed for campus education about sexual harassment and sexual assault. Second, students concerned with the plight of working mothers on campus pushed for decreased tuition rates as well as the opening of campus day care facilities. A conference on women's history in 1990 marked the first time significant attention was paid to women's studies issues, and at that conference students called for courses on Black women's studies. Throughout the early 1990s, students frequently complained about the lack of diversity in the curriculum on a rapidly diversifying campus, with the general education curriculum that provides the only exposure to the liberal arts for health professions students bearing the brunt of these complaints.

By the mid-1990s, over two thirds of Promenade students were female. Yet the campus organization and culture remained male-dominated, and little was done to address this disjuncture. Many faculty members believed that the large population of women of color in the student body particularly needed attention paid to their experiences. These faculty members saw women's studies as a way to help these students find their voices. Students, in turn, did have an interest in women's studies, but as first generation students at a commuter campus who had busy lives outside of school, they lacked the means and the knowledge to act on their desire.

Female faculty members were particularly concerned about the inequities they faced. Women earned lower salaries than men did, experienced a pervasive lack of respect, and were unable to obtain access to administrative positions. According to a female faculty member who now works in the Promenade administration, conditions in some departments were so bad that most female faculty members left shortly after they were hired. Female faculty members were equally frustrated with national politics and with the fact that Promenade was not playing a leading role in curricular innovation. As one faculty member put it, a large university in an urban area "should have" women's studies. By the early 1990s, female faculty members began to believe that they needed to start "something" for women on campus.

A small group of faculty began meeting to work together on women's issues. Faculty with an interest in women's studies began to incorporate more material on women into their courses, developing what one faculty member called "a modern orientation towards women's issues." They also urged other faculty to review their courses to ensure that women and gender were integrated into the material, and while some participated, others simply laughed. This was an important strategic move, however. The goal was to build a track record of student interest in women's studies and to ensure that there would be sufficient coursework in women's studies available to ultimately build a program. However, faculty interested in women's issues were more focused on co-curricular initiatives than on the curriculum. Their first prolonged project was to develop a campus women's center. For many people, this project was much more important than women's studies was. A center would provide a safe space and offer student services. The faculty group was able to obtain a small amount of funding, eventually enough to hire a coordinator, as well as a moderately-sized office for holding meetings, open hours, and counseling sessions. Staffing was provided primarily by volunteers from the nursing and psychology programs. While these volunteers did allow the center to remain open, their lack of professional training and experience often left the center in chaos.

In the early 1990s, a wave of faculty hiring resulted in the employment of a new group of young female faculty who were better educated in women's studies and who energetically pursued the prospect of a major program in the field. Some even began to work on women's studies before they came to campus to begin their jobs. They were quickly told by the administration that a major would be impossible, so they turned their attention to developing a minor or concentration program. The administration was particularly skeptical of the potential for a women's studies program given the dearth of courses already offered. The other major obstacle that the planning committee faced was their inability to find any department that was willing to house them.

At Promenade University, the process of offering an experimental course was easy—these did not even have to go through the curriculum committee. But winning approval for a new program is hard. All programs must be offered within departments, making the interdisciplinary non-departmental organization of programs like those at Abigail Adams College highly difficult. The only alternative is to create a program that is housed within an academic division such as social sciences and is under the auspices of the divisional dean. When a department is interested in offering a new program, faculty must first vote within the department and then within the division, and if approval occurs at both levels, the proposal then passes to the curriculum committee. The administration has the final say, but generally abides by the recommendation of the department. Requirements for program proposals are extensive and include syllabi for the courses to be part of the program as well as a detailed rationale and a list of necessary library resources.

Despite the fact that the early 1990s brought a wave of interest in expanding interdisciplinary coursework opportunities from the campus curriculum committee, traditional departments were reluctant to house an interdisciplinary program. The dean of arts and sciences, the next logical place to turn, was particularly unsupportive of women's studies and refused to provide any funding for the nascent program. Furthermore, the University had little experience in supporting new curricular initiatives. The university did not approve hiring lines for faculty to teach in women's studies and the program director only occasionally got release time from her heavy teaching load to administer the program. Eventually a provost who was more supportive of women's studies became involved and began to supply some funding to the program, but never as a regular budget item. This meant money came and went according to her whims.

The coordinating committee working on women's studies ultimately held a "summit meeting" at which the curriculum committee and various deans came together to find a place to house the program. The humanities division agreed to take the program in. Only then could a group of six faculty members begin to plan the curriculum and a series of special events. Students supported the creation of women's studies and signed petitions urging the establishment of a program, but undergraduates were otherwise uninvolved. Several graduate students, especially those from the English department, did become involved in the curriculum planning process. Committee members worked to find courses that could be cross-listed with women's studies from among existing course listings and developed new courses themselves as well as sponsored lectures to bring women's studies ideas to the broader campus. The women's studies minor was officially implemented in 1996 with a special event to mark its founding. Coverage of the event in the campus newspaper made explicit that feminism was a part of women's studies, and a course on feminist theory was one of the earliest course offerings.

At the end of the 1990s, the decision was made to change the program name from women's studies to gender studies. This change, as at Abigail Adams, was controversial. Some women's studies faculty members believed that the focus on women was essential to their original vision in founding the program. Others felt the change was necessary to reflect the growing attention to lesbian and gay issues in their courses, though queer studies coursework is not generally available on campus. In any case, the name change decision was less grounded in any academic or intellectual rationale as much as it was in the desire to appear inclusive of men's issues. After the decision was made to change the program name, several founding faculty who were particularly committed to women's studies became less involved in the program.

The gender studies program continues to face difficulties today. Funding and enrollment remain limited. Like courses in many programs at Promenade University, gender studies courses often face cancellation for lack of enrollments. About two students each year graduate with a minor, while about 30–40 enroll in gender studies courses. Many program supporters believe that the minor has not yet been fully developed, and the lack of sequencing and upper-level courses support this claim. Others would like to develop a major. A few years ago, faculty wrote a proposal for a B.A. in gender studies and got halfway through the formal approval process. They were ultimately discouraged by a dean from proceeding. Housing an interdisciplinary minor in a division was hard enough; all major programs at Promenade need to be housed in their own department. As departments are expensive and budgets remain tight, the administration was not supportive of the prospect of departmentalization. Once discouraged, the major initiative lost momentum, though at least one committee member believes that with a push it could have passed the curriculum committee. It seems unlikely that this will happen in the near future. Instead, Promenade faculty and students will continue to focus on the nitty-gritty of preparing working-class students for professional jobs.

"Working for Social Acceptance"

Despite their busy lives, at least some students at Promenade make time for student activities. These activities include student groups for both Asian American and queer students. The student groups that exist are, however, more concerned with social and cultural activities than with student activism. While the Asian American student group is active, it has little history of political involvement. No one on campus recollects any interest in Asian American studies from students or faculty despite the fact that the percentage of Asian American students at Promenade is at least as high as that at Abigail Adams, and no one remembers any activism around Asian American studies.

The queer student group is a different story. In the early 1990s, there was a campus scandal over lesbian content in some English classes. Students complained in letters to the campus newspaper that such content violated their religious sensibilities. These complaints spurred action. Students, faculty, and staff wrote in to the newspaper to voice their opposition to the complaints. The letters included one signed by 43 members of the campus community as well as another written by the students in a lower-division English course. Around the same time as this controversy, the first lesbian and gay student group at Promenade was founded. While the group became dormant at some point, it was resurrected in 2001.

Students and faculty had demonstrated interest in queer studies even before the women's studies program was founded. Yet no program exists and only a few courses have been taught, primarily in the English department. As noted above, part of the reason why the women's studies program changed its name to gender studies was to reflect the presence of lesbian and gay studies in program courses. However, most courses with a focus on queer content are disguised in some way. Though there is interest on campus in taking such courses, enrollment remains low and those students who do enroll are a tight-knit group who seem almost like a club. As one faculty member put it, Promenade has a conservative and church-going culture, and many students fear that they would be stigmatized if they took courses with queer content. Obviously societal acceptance for sexual orientation diversity and discussions of sexuality are growing, and perhaps one day even the students at Promenade will be interested in participating. For now, a few disguised courses will have to do.

"A Legacy of Struggle"

In some ways, the faculty who worked towards women's studies at Promenade had a very radical vision. They saw women's studies not just as a discipline that would give rigorous scholarship on women a place at the table, but also as a way to give voice to their socially marginalized and economically oppressed students. These women knew that curricula alone could not make a difference in their students' lives and so they supported the creation of a women's center, linking politics, praxis, and pedagogy much as the earliest women's studies activists had done in the 1970s. Their vision was explicitly feminist. But from looking at the program today, you would not see that legacy.

Instead, you would see a small and struggling minor program offering few faculty and fewer courses. The minor is stuck in much the same place it was over a decade ago when it was established, despite the name change to gender studies. Those interested in queer studies have not been able to make too many inroads either. The students and faculty interested in women's studies and queer studies had a hard task in front of them. They worked in a resource-poor environment full of students just trying to get through so they could earn enough money to support their families. The science and health professions focus of the University left little space for innovative interdisciplinary education. That they succeeded at all is an accomplishment, but more could have been done. In particular, the combined efforts of students and faculty on a campus with a history of student activism may have been harder for the administration to ignore. With a united front, perhaps Promenade University would be the site of an institutionalized women's studies program with healthy enrollments and a growing queer studies focus. It could have been, that is, more like Technopark University, a university that struggled with some similar limitations but that has been able to build a thriving women's studies program. We will visit Technopark in the next chapter.

Chapter 5

Reaching for Tomorrow:
Technopark University

Visitors reach Technopark University by traveling along a set of sweeping highways that surround the campus on three sides. Exit ramps give way to planned neighborhoods of nearly identical suburban homes and then to anonymous industrial parks with their dozens of flat black parking lots. Then, in the center, the young university rises up, an anchor and an engine of development in its Southeastern county. Though Technopark is not the flagship of its state university system, it has been steadily rising in selectivity and prestige over the past several decades as a program of intensive investment in research productivity begins to pay off. Its large campus holds just under 15,000 students, of whom about 10,000 are undergraduates. National commentators commend the university for its focus on undergraduate education, but the student-faculty ratio remains near 20 to one. More than half of students live at home and commute or find housing in the surrounding suburbs, as befits a campus originally built without dorms to serve suburban commuter students, but an increasing number have chosen to live on campus; over three quarters of freshman now live in the dorms.

About 90 percent of Technopark's students come from the state in which it is located, most from nearby the campus, though the university has made strides in attracting international students with its science and technology focus. In-state students pay less than $10,000 in tuition and fees, though living expenses can top the tuition costs, especially for students who choose to get an apartment off-campus and commute. Out-of-state students pay twice this tuition. About half of students receive some financial aid, but only a portion of financial aid is need-based at Technopark. Only slightly more than half of students graduate within six years of enrolling as freshman.

Despite its suburban location, almost 40 percent of Technopark students are people of color, with over half of students of color being Asian American. The heavy focus on science and technology degrees—the most popular majors include information systems, biological sciences, and psychology—has meant that the university is just under 50 percent female. Though students have organized many student organizations and have actively fought to protect their interests by demanding daycare and protesting tuition hikes, the campus and its students have been characterized by a lack of involvement in political or social issues.

Technopark University was founded in the mid-20th century as a response to the baby boom bulge in college student enrollment; it did not develop residence halls or a typical campus-based social life until after the 1960s era of student protest was already dying down. Its growth since that time has been extraordinary. Today, Technopark sees itself as a place for bright local undergraduates who want to combine a liberal arts experience, valuable professional credentials, and the resources of a research university. It offers approximately 50 undergraduate degree programs that span the liberal arts, sciences, and pre-professional programs; graduate students can choose from a variety of masters, doctoral, and professional degrees concentrated in the sciences, engineering, and education. The curricular options at Technopark include an undergraduate major and graduate certificate program in women's studies; though a few courses are offered that focus on sexuality issues, there is no queer studies program. Individual courses in Asian American studies have occasionally been offered by the American Studies department, but no program in Asian American studies is available at Technopark.

"My Consciousness Was Raised and I Want More"

A women's liberation group was formed at Technopark University in 1970, just as campus life began to develop. Both faculty and students were involved in this group, and it began discussing the potential of women's studies as soon as it was formed. It created the first experimental women's studies course in spring 1971. By fall 1971, a separate student women's group was founded, and it too began pushing for women's studies. Formal courses were soon offered, predominantly in the English department. In 1972, the Technopark Assembly formed a committee to consider women's studies. It found that the few women's studies courses which were offered at the time were all oversubscribed—even enrolling male students— and that many faculty were interested in teaching women's studies courses. In addition, those students who had taken women's studies courses or who developed mentoring relationships with female faculty tended to have their "consciousness raised" and want more. The committee developed a proposal to establish a women's studies program, but the proposal would have allowed women's studies only as a second major, requiring students to continue to complete a major in a traditional discipline alongside their women's studies coursework.

A lot of the support for the women's studies initiative came from the Technopark American studies department, which then was and to some extent has remained a center for educational innovation on campus. American studies hired a faculty member specifically to develop courses in women's studies. In addition, the open nature of the curriculum at Technopark in the 1970s—stemming both from the air of experimentation in higher education more broadly in the late 1960s and early 1970s as well as from Technopark's youth as a campus—meant that faculty who wanted to offer individual experimental courses could do so quite easily. Indeed, even graduate student instructors could offer experimental courses. Yet the proposal for a second major in women's studies did not get anywhere when it was first proposed.

The initial stages of the campaign for women's studies were taking place in an environment in which Black students and faculty were focused on the establishment of a Black studies program. Though there was little overt opposition to women's studies, the Technopark administration was unsupportive of both women's studies and Black studies. Though women were the majority of undergraduate students, only 20 percent of faculty members were female, and an even smaller percentage of those with tenure were women. In addition, the 1970s were difficult budgetary times for Technopark. Yet students, particularly a specific cohort of those involved in campus women's groups, remained involved in pushing for a women's studies program and were quite invested in the women's studies courses that they took. This core of support was enough for a group of faculty, staff, and students to build on as they developed a new proposal for a women's studies program that was based on courses already offered as well as new courses that faculty members were interested in teaching. This proposal went forward in 1978, but again the administration did not respond positively. Some conservative faculty members who saw women's studies as a passing fad also worked in opposition to the proposal.

One of the faculty members who played a major role in women's studies organizing in the 1970s was denied tenure in an ugly tenure battle in 1979, shortly after the proposal was again rejected. She received full support from the faculty and students at Technopark, but was turned down by the dean and the chancellor. The women's student organization then active on campus wrote a letter to the campus newspaper stating that she was the centerpiece of the not-yet-extant women's studies program, teaching two women's studies courses and providing advising to students interested in women's studies, and that not tenuring her would be a major disservice to the entire campus. At least one student transferred away from Technopark as a result of this tenure decision; and about one fifth of the entire student body signed a petition requesting reevaluation of the tenure case. The tenure denial was not specifically based on her involvement in women's studies; rather, the administration was unhappy with her writing and research activities, which they referred to as "activist journalism," and with her involvement in campus politics, including supporting student protests against tuition hikes, an effort to establish campus day care, and a sit-in of Black students as well as holding the chair of a committee working to deal with discrimination in hiring.

Though we don't think of the late 1970s and early 1980s as a time of campus radicalism across the United States, this tenure controversy was only one event among many political actions at Technopark in that period. In May of 1979, 15 students—some of them activists from the women's student organization—were arrested at a sit-in protesting the racially-disparate effects of financial aid policies. Around the same time, a university committee on the status of women was formed, along with a cabinet-level position on women's issues in the student government. The student who held this position had created her own double major in women's studies and business management. The next year, a women's center opened on campus; it was staffed on a volunteer basis by students involved with the campus women's organization. A research group within American studies created a project aimed at helping returning women students adjust to college life. Yet the administration remained insensitive to women's issues. For instance, in the late 1970s, there were a number of rapes on campus, and the official response from the campus security office was that female students should not go out at night.

In 1982, a minor in women's studies was approved. The planning committee went forward with its initiative based in part on strong interest from students in taking women's studies courses, but the process of establishing the minor was made easier by structural conditions on campus. Developing the minor did not require funding for more staff or faculty, and minors (unlike majors) did not require approval from the statewide university system. Though minors are common on campus now, in 1982 no other minors were offered on campus—so the women's studies program could be developed without seeming to threaten the established order of other disciplines or programs. Though the creation of the minor was a major step forward for those interested in women's studies, the faculty members on the planning committee continued to actively solicit faculty participation in planning a certificate program as well as in teaching and advising for women's studies.

By the late 1980s, things had changed. This time, when a high-profile rape occurred on campus, the committee on the status of women worked with the campus security office to increase awareness about crime on campus as well as to publicize the availability of safety services like emergency phones and an escort service. Seventy students, predominantly adult reentry students, traveled to the Rally for Women's Lives in Washington, DC. Students were developing their own women's studies majors through the interdisciplinary studies program, and the American studies program allowed majors to concentrate in women's studies—a program that remained available until the end of the 20th century; after a brief hiatus, it resumed as an option for American studies majors to develop a concentration in any academic department or program. Curricular options in women's studies were managed by a coordinating committee, and students were able to participate on this committee if they earned grades of C or better in their women's studies courses. In 1990, an introductory women's studies course was offered for the first time.

But further developments were contingent on the support of the statewide university system. By the mid-1990s, the system had begun to take women's issues more seriously. The flagship campus held a summer institute devoted to helping instructors incorporate gender issues into their teaching, while the system built a statewide network of faculty, staff, and administrators concerned with women's issues. This network sponsored scholarships and research awards, held an annual conference focused on the needs of female staff interested in career advancement, and defended (on the rare occasion that it was necessary to continue working on such a settled issue) campus women's centers. However, even in the 21st century, the network issued a newsletter featuring a recipe corner and an article about mother-daughter book clubs—so despite its support for women in the state, it was not an agent of political change.

Yet things did change. Between 2000 and 2002, women's studies at Technopark University gained its first full-time faculty line as well as a formal women's studies student organization and a post-baccalaureate certificate program. Later in that decade, the program changed its name to include gender. By 2005, the women's studies faculty developed a proposal to expand the program into a major, and it quickly passed several bureaucratic hurdles on its way to state approval. While this research was being conducted, faculty remained so concerned about their chances of success that they were extremely reluctant to discuss their program's history—they believed the retelling of their story might upset the campus administration and eliminate their chance at finally building a major. Yet in 2007, the major was approved, a quarter century after it was first proposed.

Today, the program employs one tenured faculty member and one full-time lecturer, along with a number of affiliated faculty who teach courses. It offers a wide variety of courses that enroll about 550 students per year and already graduated five majors in the first two years after the major program was approved (about three students a year earn certificates).

"A Fragmented Community"

Though about one fifth of Technopark's students identify their race as Asian American—the result of a rapid growth in the Asian American student population over the past decade—Technopark has not developed an Asian American studies program and there has been no mobilization towards such a program. A few courses on multicultural issues do specifically include material on Asian Americans, and an introduction to Asian American studies course has been offered sporadically by the American studies department since the late 1990s when instructors with the necessary expertise have been available. As noted above, the American studies department has traditionally been a site of curricular experimentation at Technopark, and the department's faculty observed the increasing percentage of Asian American students and thought there was a need for such courses.

Students, however, have not show as much interest in the field. Asian American student organizations at Technopark focus most of their energy on social and fundraising events rather than on education and political awareness. In addition, the Asian American students at Technopark are predominantly identified with specific ethnic groups rather than with a panethnic (Espiritu 1992) community. Indeed, one interviewee called the campus community for Asian American students "fragmented." Student organizations for Korean American, Vietnamese American, Filipino American, and Chinese American students all operate separately, coming together in an umbrella group only for special events. There is sometimes cultural conflict between Asian American students of different ethnic backgrounds.

Though the university does offer coursework through or beyond the intermediate level in Chinese, Japanese, and Korean, the only formal program focusing on any aspect of the Asian or Asian American experience is a minor in East Asian history, and efforts to expand Asian American studies as a discipline have not emerged. At the present time, there is little interest in Asian American studies among Technopark students, who are much more interested in fulfilling graduation requirements. According to an adjunct instructor who taught some of the first Asian American studies courses, it would require a sustained commitment to teaching the course to even generate the necessary interest to add additional coursework. Furthermore, a nearby branch of the state university system already offers a certificate program. Given the systemwide administration's interest in limiting curricular duplication, adding another program in the same area would require administrative commitment and a strong justification to the state governing board.

"Backwards and Forwards"

The queer community at Technopark has not always been the most active. The queer student group was first formed in the mid-1980s after a campus therapist who had been seeing many lesbian and gay students helped them form a support group. Gradually, this organization turned into a conventional campus organization, and a tight-knit group of students tried to bring awareness of queer issues to the campus through educational programs. The small queer community on campus also included some faculty, who often met with students as well. But it was not until the mid-1990s that the queer community became politically active on campus.

In 1993, demonstrations and public relations campaigns involving student groups culminated in an article critical of the gay rights movement in the student newspaper that was written by a gay campus journalist from a military family and then the subsequent outing of that student to his family by a gay campus activist. In 1995, queer students participated in a demonstration against the campus newspaper in coalition with students of color; the demonstration was held to protest the lack of coverage of gay issues and minority groups in the paper. An article later in the year did focus on the degree of anti-gay harassment on campus. Also in 1995, queer students celebrated National Coming Out Day by chalking the campus to raise awareness among their classmates, an activity used to celebrate this day on campuses across the United States. In response, other students staged a "counter-chalking," writing anti-gay slogans and "spewing AIDS ignorance" across campus. This sort of anti-gay chalking continued throughout the academic year. The queer student group, which was in the process of organizing for the first time, used this event to show that they needed more resources, particularly an office with space for a resource library. The same year, the state governing board voted against the extension of domestic partner benefits to the same-sex partners of University employees.

The first queer studies courses were organized in the mid-1990s in the midst of these conflicts by a lesbian, gay, and bisexual advisory council, which had been established by a provost with a strong interest in increasing the visibility of the lesbian and gay community on campus. The initiative had begun with informal meetings in the provost's office, but many faculty were hesitant to participate for fear of being outed and thus facing difficulties within their own departments. The council was thus formed as a sort of protective shield to ensure that semi-closeted faculty could stay that way. It drew heavily on Technopark's peers within the state university system for advice and resources.

The first queer studies courses were offered as experimental courses, offered like other experimental projects in the American studies department, and were so oversubscribed that they had a waiting list. These courses were taught by adjunct and temporary faculty members, but the faculty who taught them felt safe and welcomed in their roles. The advisory council thought that these early courses would be the first step towards building a formal program in queer studies. At first, the plan was to create a concentration within American studies and to hire a permanent faculty member to teach in this area, but budget constraints forestalled this plan. Students were excited about and highly involved in the courses that were offered, and the queer student organization was eager to show its support for the potential program. However, students were generally unaware of their power to push for more.

After the provost who had so supported the queer studies initiative left the University, the American studies department took on the initiative as its own project. However, there was not enough intellectual interest among the existing American studies faculty members to sustain further action, and additionally few tenured faculty members were available to support it. At the same time, the queer student organization had begun to experience internal divisions around the involvement of heterosexual students and thus turned its organizational energy inwards.

Queer life at Technopark continues to be difficult. Though fewer homophobic incidents occur, queer students and faculty perceive little support for their lives and issues from the administration. In the mid-2000s, a same-sex couple successfully won election to the homecoming court and kissed after the coronation ceremony. Several community members complained bitterly about this action, and while the victors were permitted to keep their crowns, the homecoming ceremony was disbanded after that year. Faculty members remain reluctant to come out for fear of damaging their careers, and a former social and support group for gay faculty has disbanded over the years.

Students have built a campaign to increase campus resources for queer students, asking for a resource center, gender-neutral housing, a queer-focused residence floor, a safe zone program, and a queer studies minor. While the safe zone program has become well-established, the student organization has an office with a library of books and resources, and a well-received gender-neutral housing program has been developed, the other programs have not gone forward. Students did develop a proposal for a minor in queer studies and brought it to the women's studies program, where faculty showed support for the idea. However, few courses are offered in queer studies, and the women's studies program's interest in preserving its own status has made it less likely to champion new initiatives.

"We Take What We Can Get"

Over the course of its short lifespan, Technopark University has gone from being a local commuter campus for the sons and daughters of the suburbs to a position as a rising star among research-intensive undergraduate-focused universities. It has built a reputation for technology transfer and for preparing undergraduates for competitive graduate programs. Yet it is not a flagship campus with the size and star power to be all things to all comers. It is not a private university with the resources to create all the programs its students may want. It remains a creature of its Southern and suburban neighborhood, with students and administrators a bit more reluctant to embrace progressive innovation.

Neoinstitutional models of curricular change would argue that the Technopark University of today—a university that is steadily working its way upward in the prestige hierarchy—ought to be imitating its peers as part of its scramble for acceptance and reputation. Within the state system that Technopark is a member of, women's studies first became available as a degree program in the mid-1970s and it is currently possible to earn transcript credentials in queer studies and in Asian American studies; many of Technopark's peer institutions offer such programs as well. So if neoinstitutional models would have predicted curricular change at Technopark, why didn't it happen the way these models would expect?

Technopark began as a commuter campus. Though various actors involved with the University saw its bright future as a goal to strive for, in the earliest years it was hard enough just to keep the classrooms staffed and work towards the approval of a residence hall. Political engagement can and does happen on commuter campuses—the Third World Liberation Strikes at San Francisco State College that marked the emergence of ethnic studies (Barlow and Shapiro 1971) occurred at just such a campus. But commuter students are less biographically available (McAdam 1986) and less engaged in the campus community. These factors reduce the likelihood that they will become involved in campaigns for curricular change.

Activism did occur at Technopark around women's studies. Here, we can see the important role that faculty play in catalyzing student demand and student activism. First of all, it took mentoring by faculty engaged in women's studies and exposure to women's studies courses for a critical mass of students to begin to demand access to women's studies curricula. These students learned what was missing from their education by having the alternatives laid out before them by faculty dedicated both to women's studies and to undergraduate education. Second, it took controversy involving a faculty tenure decision to get a broader group of students fully engaged with the women's studies campaign. The tenure denial in 1979 sparked a demand not just for more courses, but for a more fully institutionalized program, a program where the removal of one faculty member would not be enough to shut the entire program down.

The role of campus controversy can also be seen in queer issues at Technopark. It was conflicts between queer students and conservative students, as well as campaigns of homophobia, that spurred activism among queer students and some of the first tentative demands for queer studies. But these students fell short in their attempt to develop a program. On the one hand, they lacked confidence in their own power as students to make changes in their campus environment, and thus they held back when a more aggressive campaign might have paid dividends. On the other, they lacked meaningful mentoring and guidance from faculty, the mentoring and guidance that had encouraged and enabled activism among the students who supported women's studies.

The failure of the initiatives for Asian American studies and queer studies to get off the ground at Technopark also shows us that faculty pressure is not sufficient on its own. Faculty—and even a supportive administrator—wanted to develop a program in queer studies. The American studies department thought the campus needed Asian American studies and even found someone to teach a few classes. But these interests did not generate programs. At Technopark, as at many colleges and universities, it is relatively easy for a faculty member to offer a course on almost any topic he or she pleases. Even where formal approval is needed to add a course to the permanent catalogue, the course can typically be offered as a special topics course without such approval. Substantial and continuing enrollment in the course is then often used to justify the permanent approval of the course or the development of subsequent related courses. However, without such enrollment, experimental courses disappear.

The approval process for programs is much more complex. At Technopark, proposed majors and certificate programs must go through six layers of approval— by the dean of the appropriate academic unit, the provost, the undergraduate council, and the budget committee of the faculty senate on campus before moving on to be approved by the university system governing board and by the state higher education commission. Potential programs may be rejected at any stage in this process, meaning that only programs with substantial support and strong proposals are likely to succeed. This complex process highlights the importance of considering the implications of broader contextual factors on the ability to develop a new program.

It is worth noting, of course, that campaigns for curricular change are long-term processes. The women's studies major was approved a quarter-century after it was first proposed; it took a decade from the first formal proposal to the development of the minor. It may be that we have not yet seen the end of the story for Asian American studies and queer studies at Technopark. It may be that these programs just need more time. But right now is unlikely to be that time. While Technopark's state system has not suffered budget cuts in the recessionary period of 2008–10 that are nearly as severe as the worst-hit states in the country, they have closed several programs and laid off faculty members even in pre-professional programs. Even maintaining the status quo has become quite an accomplishment in an era when flagship campuses such the University of Maine (Carr 2010) are shuttering programs like women's studies. The story of budgets is one element of the story of curricular change at many colleges and universities, of course. Jeffrey University, where we will travel next, is one such campus, but it is also a campus where student activism has been maintained over decades—another example of the long time frame of curricular change, but one with a somewhat different ending.

Chapter 6

Fighting the Good Fight: Jeffrey University

After being stuck in a traffic jam that stretches from the interstate across seven miles of scenic landscapes and busy strip malls, visitors to Jeffrey University see the tall buildings that make up the heart of this campus rising above the flat farm fields on which it was built. Those farm fields were once an integral part of the education students received here. Jeffrey was one of the original land grant institutions founded in the 1860s after the Morrill Act funded an institution of higher education in each state for the purpose of developing and educating farmers about better agricultural methods. The campus today does not look like the campus of a university that is over 150 years old. Instead, modern buildings already showing the wear from the mid-century expansion that accompanied the GI bill and the baby boom are scattered in clusters across a vast landscape.

Jeffrey University is the flagship campus of the public higher education system in its New England state. This allows it to have selective admissions, though the concentration of public and private colleges in New England mean that there is less competition for slots here than one might find in the Western land grant universities. Still, it is able to draw about 20 percent of its students from across state lines, and these students pay almost $30,000 a year for the privilege. While the in-state costs run about $10,000 lower, Jeffrey is still among the most expensive public universities in the nation. Almost half of all students receive need-based financial aid to attend Jeffrey, but many students make do with a more affordable education elsewhere in the state system. Still, Jeffrey enrolls over 20,000 students, about three quarters of whom are undergraduates.

Though Jeffrey was founded as a small all-male college at a time when its state population was 99 percent white, it is experiencing a rapid increase in the diversity of the student body. Women were first admitted to Jeffrey towards the end of the 1800s, though they were only permitted to study certain subjects. Until the 1960s a Dean of Women worked to constrain female students to appropriate academic and social roles on campus. Today, the presence of agricultural and engineering programs keeps the percent of female students below the 50 percent mark. Students of color make up almost 20 percent of the student body and are overrepresented compared to their percentage of the state population. There are a significant number of international students as well, with international students making up over a fifth of the graduate student population.

Though students at Jeffrey can still earn degrees in agriculture and natural resources, liberal arts and pre-professional education are now the norm here, accompanied by a vast array of graduate degrees that place this university among the top 100 research universities in the United States. Among these offerings are a certificate program in Asian American studies as well as a women's studies program offering undergraduate majors and minors and a graduate certificate. While queer studies courses are often offered at Jeffrey, a program in queer studies is not available.

"Things Were Getting Interesting"

Jeffrey University came to gender integration, at least in employment, relatively late. By 1972, 42 percent of the student body was female—including a third of graduate students. Yet only 13 percent of the faculty and four high-ranking administrators were female. A committee on the status of women was formed to deal with the consequences of these disparities in part through the involvement of the Dean of Women, the highest-ranking female administrator on campus. Her role was a relic of a prior era when women experienced segregated and circumscribed roles even on coeducational campuses. Though her priority had been opening up access for women rather than transforming the content of education, her long-standing interest in women's issues made her a valuable ally for early advocates of women's studies. She was able to provide advice to these advocates on how to approach and to navigate the university administration. In particular, her decision to become involved in more direct efforts for change at the close of her career was due to the lack of response on the part of the administration to personnel problems. She also had long-standing commitments to equal rights issues beyond the University, including playing an active role in the American Association for University Women, and worked to help adult women returning to school. In the end, it seems that she wished she had done more—in her own notes, she wrote that she retired "just as things were getting interesting."

The committee on the status of women found not only that women were underrepresented among the faculty, but that they were also underpaid. The full-time pay for female faculty was as little as 76 percent of that which men received. The committee also called for the implementation of an affirmative action plan in faculty hiring in order to work towards parity. Female faculty members faced other difficulties in the early 1970s besides disparate numbers and disparate pay—many felt that the campus was inhospitable to women. Some female faculty, particularly those teaching in the English department, organized a support group to help themselves cope with the hostility they experienced. Yet those who participated in early women's studies efforts did not worry much about the risks of participation for their careers. Many at the University were opposed to women's studies, but a few senior male faculty members were strong allies. Besides, earning tenure in those years of massive expansion in the student body was quite easy.

Feminist activists were getting organized outside the University as well. A local women's center partnered with the University to develop adult education course offerings for local women. This organization had as one of its core missions the expansion of educational opportunities for women, particularly those for local adult women returning to school. Some of these courses were the first women's studies courses in the area—or, for that matter, the nation. At the same time, a campus women's center was founded with the explicit mission of turning the ideas of the women's movement into action.

These early women's studies courses offered through the continuing education program offered some students the chance to begin to put together individualized majors focusing on women's lives. The fluidity and flexibility that had developed at many universities as a response to student unrest in the late 1960s had left Jeffrey with an individualized bachelor's degree program that enabled any academically qualified student who found an advisor to create his or her own curriculum drawing on established courses at the University as well as on continuing education courses and courses at other area colleges. The first student to complete a major in women's studies at Jeffrey did so through this program, and by 1973 a number of students were graduating with women's studies degrees. The continuing education program itself also experienced little oversight and great flexibility. With the only requirement being that programs support themselves, the director of continuing education was generally willing to let people try anything. He granted those working on women's studies a desk and a phone from which to organize their program.

In 1970, the first women's studies course was offered as part of the regular curriculum rather than in continuing education. It was taught out of the English department, and by the second time it was offered, it enrolled over 100 students. Around 1973, the first faculty member was hired to teach in women's studies on a three-year temporary appointment. Her employment situation was unique—her position was split three ways, with a third of her time to be spent in the English department, a third in the campus women's center, and a third working on women's studies. Ultimately, she became the coordinator of the process of writing a proposal for women's studies. Many of the people who came to women's studies in these early years were refugees from their own departments, and students and faculty formed close and supportive relationships with one another.

A committee formed with the goal of writing a proposal for a major; the committee included graduate students, undergraduates, non-academic community members, and a small number of faculty. At first, committee members were radical in orientation. They planned to call their new program "feminist studies." This sort of name was then and still remains extremely unusual, but it highlights the degree to which the faculty saw academics and activism as intertwined. In fact, the original curriculum proposal would have required majors to participate in support groups and engage in community action projects. Early meetings focused on the role of men in feminist studies—even at a coeducational public university, many were opposed to their presence. The eventual decision was that men would be permitted to enroll in women's studies courses only if their numbers were significant enough to form all-male support groups, thereby preserving support groups as single-sex spaces that would permit women's empowerment. Of course, such a proposal was likely to lead to the complete absence of men from the women's studies classroom.

Even today men tend to make up less than 10 percent of women's studies students, judging from discussions of teaching on the women's studies email forum (WMST-L 2009), except at colleges and universities with a strong diversity requirement that encourages enrollment in women's studies.

The original curriculum proposal included a number of additional radical elements. The drafters included a focus on consciousness-raising, coming to know women's bodies, the roles of emotional and intuitive knowledge, the validation of women's experiences, and the study of "herstory." In addition, they wrote about their activist goals to establish revolutionary separatism and abolish the patriarchy. Such topics and methods depart from the traditional focus of the academy on rationality, enlightenment thought, and an intellectualism divorced from both the personal and the political. Both the students and the faculty involved in drafting the proposal were excited by their radical vision. However, not everyone agreed on how to achieve it. Deep conflicts existed between various groups of feminists and women's studies advocates on campus. Some feminists were committed to a Marxist perspective while others were more interested in race, gender, and intersectionality. Some women's studies advocates wanted to avoid hiring faculty or creating a department, while others believed that establishing a program that coordinated courses offered in traditional departments would be the most effective way to go forward. This last structure is the one that was ultimately adopted.

Because women's studies at Jeffrey University arose at a time of significant flexibility and innovation in both curricular and non-curricular matters, the program at first faced little difficulty in getting established. An undergraduate certificate program was proposed in the fall of 1973. A year later, a minor was in operation with tentative approval for a two-year pilot period. By then almost 1,300 students were enrolled in women's studies courses. The radicalism had been toned down. Committee members were reluctant to move away from the separatist model of women's studies they began with, particularly since they saw this model as able to develop the full potential of women's studies without worrying about traditional forms of academic legitimacy, but they began to realize that integrationist models would be more easily able to jump administrative hurdles. They began to recruit male instructors as a strategy to make the program appear less exclusionary and segregated. New courses proposed in 1973–74 were much more in line with those expected of a traditional discipline and were justified in terms of "need" as well as uniqueness. They included an introductory course asking the core question "what does it mean to be a woman?" as well as courses on theory and methods and a capstone course. Yet some of the program's prior radicalism continued to show through, particularly in the governance structure that was developed. Governance took place through consensus decision-making, participatory democracy, and deep discussions of ideology. Decisions were made by a policy board that held meetings which anyone involved in the program could attend.

The process of winning approval for the women's studies program was not as easy as it might at first have seemed. Proposals for curricular changes at Jeffrey University have to pass through a number of layers of approval. First, the committee dealing with academic issues must approve the proposal; this committee features student representatives. Second, proposals are put up for a vote by the full faculty senate. Then they are sent to the administration, where they must be approved by the provost, president, and chancellor, who also must allocate funding. Though the state system does not have an official role in individual curricular decisions the way it does at Technopark, there is a state board who has oversight over the University and its administration. Two members of this board are students and five are alumni from across the state system, but the remainder are laypeople without higher education experience who are appointed by the governor to staggered five-year terms, meaning that the governor has substantial control over the board.

When the program was first proposed by a subcommittee of faculty, the administration approved it without any allocation of funding. It is of course extremely difficult if not impossible to run a curricular program without any money, so this was the administration's way of saying "thanks, but no thanks." The committee chose to respond with force to the lack of funding. They organized teach-ins on campus and threatened to shut down the University. These threats had real currency, as the University had a history of student activism in the 1960s that had involved multi-day building occupations. In addition, strong ties between campus women's studies activists and local feminist women made it clear that the program could "call out the troops" if necessary. After experiencing the opening stages of this activist campaign, the provost provided a minimal level of funding, enough to hire four teaching assistants and a part-time program coordinator. Students were highly involved in this campaign. Not only did they provide the warm bodies at teach-ins and the numbers to back up threats of action, but they also mobilized to increase faculty support for women's studies by engaging in a concerted effort to ask women's studies questions in classes in traditional disciplines and to (on the part of graduate students) bring women's studies literature to the attention of their instructors.

The new program remained formally housed in the interdisciplinary studies program, but establishing a program gave faculty the ability to develop a standardized curriculum and to advise their own students. In the early years of the program, the planning committee was predominantly made up of very young faculty. Students were members of the planning committee as well, with some even earning academic credit for their participation, and they were dedicated to the idea of a major from the beginning. The planning committee spent a significant portion of its time developing strategies to make women's studies palatable to the rest of the campus community, with different messages for different constituencies. To those who believed that women's studies topics should be integrated fully into the curriculum rather than taught in a separate program, they explained that a women's studies program could "stimulate interest in current women's studies courses in the departments," "encourage the development of new departmental courses," and "create a framework in which successful experimental courses … [could] be strengthened as permanent course offerings." They emphasized that offering a women's studies program need not reduce the availability or primacy of departmental courses dealing with women. To those interested in administrative efficiency and fiscal responsibility, they highlighted the fact that increasing numbers of students were enrolling in women's studies through the interdisciplinary studies rubric and that a women's studies program could therefore "provide a service" to the individualized degree program by supervising women's studies students and helping them plan appropriate courses of study. To those with an interest in traditional measures of academic excellence, the committee promoted women's studies as a program that would "facilitate access to other students, faculty, appropriate courses, and independent projects" as well as "afford an opportunity for collaboration" for faculty doing research and teaching on women.

By the time the two-year pilot period was up, 3,400 students were enrolled in women's studies courses—well over 10 percent of the student body. The committee requested an extension and received two more years in pilot status. By 1978, the faculty senate unanimously approved a five-year extension for the program and the faculty union and graduate and undergraduate senates all issued resolutions in favor of the program, which was to finally be removed from the auspices of interdisciplinary studies. The university president ultimately returned the proposal to the administration asking for more budgetary information. The administration, of course, was not interested in spending more money and the move outside of interdisciplinary studies would cost money, and this decision to "stop the clock" on the funding process went outside the normal procedures for curricular change and was designed to frustrate women's studies advocates. But the women's studies faculty and students were committed to the move—administrative and curricular flexibility were constrained by the fact that officials in charge of interdisciplinary studies retained veto power over decisions made by the women's studies faculty. The most significant difficulty was the heavy paperwork burden required by interdisciplinary studies, but sometimes interdisciplinary studies officials went as far as to reject students' individual curricular plans when they had already been approved by the women's studies faculty. Faced with administrative intransigence, 100 faculty members and 1,000 students signed a petition in support of the program. The student signatures were gathered in just three days.

Women's studies finally did move out from the auspices of interdisciplinary studies and establish an undergraduate certificate in the late 1970s (and later a major), and it was placed in a division known as "special programs" that had been established to house various academic and non-academic programs that were new and experimental. Later, the program reported to the associate provost in charge of affirmative action. These arrangements left women's studies with significant resource constraints but expansive curricular flexibility (the program ultimately found a home as a regular academic department in the humanities division of the arts and sciences college).

"A Place to Do Something"

The campus climate for women's studies was never entirely hospitable. Continual budget problems, ranging from lack of administrative funding to state-wide budget cuts, made it hard for women's studies to keep up with basic needs like faculty hiring, never mind extra frills like guest lecturers. Conservative voices on campus continued to criticize women's studies. A campus publication in the late 1980s, for instance, invited the conservative political activist Phyllis Shlafley to write an editorial; in it, she called women's studies programs "dangerous to your male-female relationships." However, those involved in women's studies were able to take advantage of the environment surrounding Jeffrey to enrich women's studies. A local women's studies research center was a source of guest lecturers and sometimes visiting instructors, and a committee of faculty from area colleges built a network to support faculty curriculum development and research activities. By the 1980s, women's studies at Jeffrey was no longer the isolated and innovative program it once was. It was being joined by many other women's studies programs in the area.

As Jeffrey University is a major research university with extensive graduate offerings, women's studies faculty had long discussed incorporating a graduate component into the program, with the first significant discussions taking place in 1982. Budget and other difficulties, however, led to lengthy delays. While the graduate certificate was proposed in 1984, the program was not approved until 1990 and students were not able to enroll until the 1996–97 academic year. These graduate students were then able to serve as teaching assistants for the undergraduate courses, providing for the first time instructional support from individuals well-educated in women's studies. In establishing the certificate, the faculty returned to the radical roots of the program by including "feminist" in the certificate name. There had been some talk of making the certificate a collaborative program with other area colleges, but that initiative fell through. The certificate program was the result of years of faculty effort. While graduate students enthusiastically signed on once it was established, they were less involved in getting it started than they had been in earlier phases of program development. However, students often did ask for the availability of graduate options.

This enthusiasm on the part of current and potential graduate students, coupled with faculty interest in working with more advanced students, convinced the women's studies faculty to begin working on a proposal for a master's degree in women's studies in 2001. A number of students had let the faculty know that they would have enrolled in such a program if they could; instead, many chose to do graduate work at other universities in the state that did offer women's studies graduate degrees. However, the master's degree initiative has not gone forward. Budgetary problems have been a major concern, as has the fact that with only a handful full-time faculty members, at least one of whom tends to be on sabbatical each semester, there would not be sufficient faculty resources to support advanced graduate work, though there are other affiliated faculty. When the terrorist attacks of 9/11/01 led to major state budget crises, there were decreases in the number of tenure-track faculty lines to the point that some feared the program was being destroyed. In more recent years, new hires have invigorated the department, but state public higher education funding became tight again during the economic crises of 2008.

Women's studies at Jeffrey University has changed in other ways as well. As the program became an institutionalized academic department, its culture changed. No longer could decisions be made through participatory democracy. Undergraduates who wanted a voice in departmental matters had only the student organizations they themselves formed and a seat or two on the program committee. Fluid personnel policies that had allowed graduate students and academic advisement staff to seamlessly transition into faculty roles were abolished in favor of traditional models of faculty hiring and tenure. A student involved in the early stages of the women's studies program said that once it became a department, women's studies lost its energy and excitement. In exchange, and despite the budget woes, it gained strength and permanence. Today, approximately 20 to 25 students major in women's studies each year with about the same number earning minors. About five students earn graduate certificates. The department estimates that over 1,000 students enroll in women's studies courses each year, not counting those who enroll in interdisciplinary and cross-listed women's studies courses through other departments.

It is worth mentioning that Jeffrey was unique in several ways. Women's studies started early there. Faculty and students interested in women's studies had few places to turn for models, mentoring, or support. They could not draw on established patterns or time-tested curricula. Instead, they were the ones doing something new. When they got started, feminism was not yet associated as strongly with lesbianism and with separatism, and thus women at Jeffrey did not have to worry about the kinds of questions that their peers at Abigail Adams College faced. Some of those who were involved in the early days of women's studies at Jeffrey explain their successes by saying that they were just "in the right place at the right time," that the University was "a place to do something" in the 1970s. There were also some aspects of the organizational context that made change easier. Jeffrey was a campus that was hospitable to curricular change and innovative programs and which had a history of responding to protest without major repression and it was located in a highly political area. The women's studies program developed strong ties to the Black studies program, including holding a joint conference on Black women. These ties prevented the two programs from becoming competitors for funding and campus support, as they did at Technopark. Jeffrey was also undergoing a major expansion in the student body at the time women's studies emerged, and this expansion made room for new faculty, new areas of study, and new ways of doing things. When those involved in women's studies at Jeffrey say they were in the right place at the right time, however, they do not give themselves enough credit. They worked hard to develop proposals that would remain close to their ideals while still being palatable to the campus as a whole. They built

alliances and cultivated supporters across campus and beyond its borders. And they engaged in careful strategic planning that increased their strength and helped them slowly win concessions that resulted in a strong, institutionalized program. It may not look like what the early advocates of "feminist studies" had in mind, but women's studies has made Jeffrey a different place than it was in 1971.

"Where Interest and Demand are Sufficient"

Though Jeffrey University now has a student body in which almost one fifth of students are students of color, things were not always this way. Students of color did not surpass 10 percent of the student body until 1992. This increase took time. The University initiated strong efforts to increase the recruitment of students of color as early as the 1960s. Asian Americans have been the largest minority group on campus since 1990 and now make up almost half of all students of color. The campus is more diverse than its surroundings—the county in which Jeffrey is located remains 90 percent white, with most people of color being Asian American or Latino immigrants who arrived within the last decade, some of whom are refugees. Since Jeffrey and its surrounding community were historically so White and located in such a White environment, they had not been a center of Civil Rights protests or race riots during the 1950s and 1960s.

Nonetheless, racial politics at Jeffrey did eventually become contentious. As far back as the early 1980s and through the 1990s, small groups of students advocated for the establishment of ethnic studies programs, including Asian American studies. They advocated for other services for students of color at the same time. To these activists, curricular and non-curricular changes went hand-in-hand. Individuals with relevant subject-area knowledge or skills began doing what they could to satisfy student demands. In the mid-1990s, for instance, a graduate student taught a one-credit colloquium in Asian American studies (most courses at Jeffrey are worth three credits). This course marked the beginning point of sustained efforts to establish Asian American studies. By 1999, a task force made up of faculty, graduate students, and undergraduates had been working on the issue of Asian American studies for five years. Though many involved wanted to see some sort of program, the task force primarily focused on expanding individual course offerings. But the student body was frustrated with the lack of progress. The University did little to respond to student demands for ethnic studies programs of any kind and even less in regards to Asian American studies. This lack of action caused students to become increasingly frustrated. Curricular issues were not the only factor leading to their increasing anger. Students claimed that there was a lack of effort towards recruiting students of color and that there was a lack of communication about racial issues on campus. In addition, Jeffrey University had maintained a tradition of hosting Columbus Day celebrations that did not refer to the experiences of indigenous people in the United States and their role in American history, a tradition that angered many students of color.

Students eventually became frustrated and angry enough to plan a disruptive campus action. 150 students occupied one of the main administrative buildings on campus for six days in the spring of 1997 while 300 more students demonstrated outside. The goal of this building occupation was to persuade the administration to take the demands and needs of students of color more seriously. As noted in the discussion of women's studies above, Jeffrey had a history of building occupations and other disruptive protests. One student who was enrolled at the University in the late 1960s said that during a building occupation while she was a student, administrators simply stepped over the students sitting on the floor, went into their offices, and continued to work. This prior experience with building occupations may have lead to a less confrontational reaction to the student demonstrators, who eventually did agree to leave peacefully. The building occupation was dramatic enough to make national news. Even the federal government took notice, with the United States Commission on Civil Rights stepping in to investigate whether any violations of students' civil rights occurred during the occupation. No indication of human rights violations was found.

Administrators agreed to meet with a negotiating committee representing the student demonstrators. Together, the administration and the students worked out a series of agreements that included recruiting and retaining more students of color, the expansion of academic support services, the creation of a non-academic department of minority affairs, funding for child care subsidies, and more student involvement in faculty and staff hiring decisions. In addition, the agreements included a commitment to build programs that would eventually be upgraded to majors in Irish studies, Native American studies, Latin American studies, and Asian American studies (Black studies was already available at the University) and to hire tenure-track faculty in each of these areas. In the short term, the administration committed to building certificate programs "where interest and demand are sufficient," leaving students the task of demonstrating such interest and demand.

In 1998, 500 students signed a petition asking that the Asian American studies task force be given official status and sent it to the Chancellor. The petition claimed that there was "proven student interest in Asian American Studies," that "Asian American Studies is related to, but DISTINCT [*sic*] from, Asian Studies," that it is "but one branch in the broader discipline of Ethnic Studies," that it is "legitimate," and that the long term goal of the task force would be "to establish a department in Asian American Studies." The claim that Asian American studies is distinct from Asian studies was a particularly important one. Many people, including academics, have trouble distinguishing between the two and conflate the Asian experience with the Asian American experience. Asian Americans see this mistake as perpetuating the "forever foreigner" myth (Park 1950) that leads many whites to see all Asian Americans as recent immigrants, even those whose ancestors arrived in the 1700s. Additionally, those unsupportive of Asian American studies at Jeffrey frequently stated that students ought to be satisfied with Asian studies. This claim would be like telling students interested in studying hip hop culture in North American cities that they ought to be satisfied with a class on African civilizations before colonialism.

This petition was not the only tool that students used to demonstrate sufficient interest in and demand for Asian American studies. They also developed a concerted publicity campaign. A key element of this campaign was the creation of brochures that explained the need for Asian American studies with a particular focus on the importance of learning one's own history in order to understand one's own experience—a framing strategy reminiscent of the one used by students working for women's studies at Abigail Adams College. During this time, Asian American studies advocacy became one of the central activities of Asian American student organizations on campus. While students played a central role in advocacy and continued to staff the task force, their efforts were supported by a diverse group of faculty members as well as two deans. Some of these faculty members wanted to teach Asian American studies, while others had no academic interest in the discipline, such as one who taught courses in geosciences.

Full-credit Asian American studies courses were first offered around the time of the building takeover. Courses do not appear in the course catalogue at Jeffrey until after they have been offered once or twice, but Asian American studies first appears in the course catalogue for the 1998–99 academic year with course listings in the English department. The task force also drafted a proposal for a certificate program after the building occupation. When the academic affairs committee of the faculty senate reviewed this proposal, they decided to support it because of the actual and potential support it had within the student body. Faculty argued that demographic changes had left Jeffrey with a more diverse set of students, among whom were students of Asian descent who had a "need" for the program. This sort of logic is commonly cited by those who try to explain the emergence of new areas of study concerning identities. However, in this case it is clear that the logic of need followed student and faculty activism rather than standing alone as a justification for the establishment of a program. Those advocating for Asian American studies focused on the involvement of a variety of faculty and graduate students in the nascent program, thus limiting the need for new resources in establishing the program, and high student demand, with fifty students expected to enroll per year. Faculty and administrators were persuaded by this logic and approved the certificate program in 1999. However, they maintained the idea that Asian studies and Asian American studies were connected disciplines, and therefore the certificate as approved is a joint certificate in Asian and Asian American studies. Students must take courses in both areas, though they can concentrate in one or the other.

Those who were part of the process of establishing the Asian American studies certificate hoped that it would be the first step in a process leading to the development of a major, much as had been the pattern for women's studies. They continued to work for program expansion. Students attended regional Asian American studies conferences and particularly conference sessions on Asian American studies organizing. After the certificate was established, a tenure-track faculty member was hired to teach in the program. She left the campus in 2003 largely because of the lack of support and scholarly community for Asian American studies. Students demanded that she be replaced with two tenure-track faculty members and an office space for Asian American studies. These demands were not met, and today the program is coordinated by a non-tenure-track faculty member, though this faculty member has impressive academic credentials. Budgetary difficulties are often cited to explain the lack of hiring, though opponents of the program say that low enrollments are the reason for limiting the fiscal resources provided to the program.

Students have continued to be frustrated by the lack of resources, faculty, and curricular options in Asian American studies. Demand for courses continues to outstrip supply, with most Asian American studies courses filling to or beyond their capacity. While about 600 students enroll in Asian American studies courses each semester, only about eight students complete a certificate each year. Perhaps this is because the course offerings are so limited. But it is also likely that Jeffrey's heavy general education requirements and the fact that students are not required to earn a minor or certificate in addition to the major leaves students feeling that the certificate program would reduce their curricular flexibility when they have the option of simply enrolling the courses they want to take. Jeffrey has also moved away from some of the non-curricular reforms instituted in response to the building occupations by abolishing ethnic identity housing and special advising and orientation programs for students of color. As campus diversity continues to grow, racial issues remain contentious and unresolved.

"Running Out of Steam"

Queer student life at Jeffrey began early. In 1970, just a year after the Stonewall Riots and at a time when queer students on most college and university campuses remained closeted, students at Jeffrey chartered an organization known as the League of Homophile Students. But queer life on campus was not always rosy. Students had to content with spates of homophobic incidents. For instance, in the early 1980s, conservative students formed a campus organization that had as its goal reducing the presence and visibility of queer students on campus. Signs posted by the queer student group were defaced with homophobic slurs, anti-gay signs were posted all over campus, and a queer student dance was disrupted by a bomb scare. Later in the decade, the campus Republican group invited a virulently anti-gay speaker to campus. His presence served as a catalyst to queer activism on campus. It prompted the establishment of a faculty/staff group for queer people on campus as well as leading at least one untenured faculty member to come out.

It was around this time, in the mid-1980s, that the queer community at Jeffrey began to take major steps forward. Students demanded improved services and an improved climate for queer people on campus. A graduate student in education took the initiative to conduct a climate report on the queer experience at Jeffrey.

One of the 15 recommendations she made in the report was the establishment of queer studies. For the author of this report, queer studies was crucially important, as she believed the queer experience would never be taken seriously without academic legitimacy. In response to this report and to the homophobic incidents they experienced, students demanded the establishment of an office devoted to LGB concerns, the institution of heterosexism awareness training in all residential areas on campus, funding for student affairs professionals, and expansion of library resources on queer issues.

In response to the climate report and associated student demands, the administration agreed to fund a part-time staff member as well as to allow a few experimental queer studies courses that were generally offered for one credit. Though students were pleased with these developments, they were not satisfied. They continued to demand that more courses be offered. They also asked that faculty become more responsive to students who wanted to do research on queer issues and that better advising be made available to queer students. Eventually, they persuaded the administration to establish a queer student center with paid professional staff. As part of the center's activities, faculty groups began holding workshops on how to increase coverage of queer issues in the classroom.

Visible queer campus resources did not put a stop to homophobic incidents. In the 1990s, the conservative campus publication often printed anti-gay articles and editorials; anti-gay student groups continued to form as well. In the early 1990s the queer campus group was even stripped of its seat in the student government, resulting an increase in militant political activism on the part of queer students. They even held a kiss-in directed at the campus conservative group. While the administration always responded to homophobic events in ways that were publically supportive of queer community members, they did not provide funding or resources. More recently, the campus has come to be seen as a "politically correct" place, and so homophobic sentiments are expressed less overtly today. Though funding cuts eventually lowered staffing levels at the queer student center, the population of student organizations dealing with queer issues expanded and a residential option for those with an interest in queer studies was added. Jeffrey began to be a magnet for students looking for a queer-friendly university.

Initiatives to build on the early queer studies courses and develop a program began as a collaborative effort among area colleges in the 1990s. However, the faculty from these different campuses could not agree on an intellectual grounding or an organizing philosophy for the program and thus their efforts did not go far. On Jeffrey's campus, faculty meeting regularly as part of a task force on queer issues began compiling course guides listing those courses with a primary or secondary focus on queer issues. There were also plans to develop a certificate program in queer studies during this period, with the hope that it would eventually expand into a major. Students pushed for faculty hires in queer studies. It was really students who had an interest in a queer studies program, but they never developed a "critical mass" in calling for queer studies on campus. Instead, faculty members worked on the proposal. The administrative response was to allow students who attended an ongoing lecture series at the queer student center to earn one course credit.

As may be an unsurprising refrain by this point in the Jeffrey story, budget cuts again threatened the queer studies initiative. Those who were part of the initiative believed that queer studies could go forward in spite of these cuts, as there were many faculty members offering courses in their departments with significant queer content and others who might be persuaded to do so in the presence of a formal program. Students continued to express an interest in a queer studies program throughout the 1990s, and many more wanted to take queer studies courses. Those students who were active in pushing for queer studies never built a strong rationale, however. They primarily focused their claims on the fact that other identity groups had certificate or major programs and thus queers should too.

The initiative soon faced a series of stumbling blocks. First, many students with an interest in queer studies courses were reluctant to enroll because they did not want to have words like "queer," "lesbian," or "gay" appear on the transcripts they showed to family and to potential employers. Sometimes, this dilemma was solved by offering a course under an alternative title, but many instructors do not like going that route. Second, faculty working on queer studies had significant conflicts over what the academic focus of the potential program would be. Some faculty members wanted to build a program focusing on the lesbian and gay experience and incorporating the critical insights of queer theory, as did most of the undergraduates interested in queer studies. Other faculty members thought that the program should focus on sexuality studies and include a component on heterosexuality, which the students viewed as exclusionary. This division was never fully resolved. Thirdly, there were never sufficient faculty members involved. Those who did have an interest in queer studies were primarily untenured faculty without the time to become a "champion of queer studies." Other supporters of queer studies came from the women's studies program, but during the height of the queer studies initiative the women's studies department was caught up in its own efforts to establish a graduate certificate program. Graduate students also played an important role on the committee and at one point created a queer studies interest group for graduate students teaching in the writing program, but this was never formalized. Much of the initiative for queer studies continued to come from undergraduates and from non-academic staff, particularly student affairs professionals working in the queer student center. This led to difficulties with the University administration. The faculty senate has not been inclined to support programs unless they emerge from within the faculty body and come with a compelling academic justification. In an attempt to ameliorate this, a proposal was put forward to locate the queer campus affairs office jointly in both student affairs and academic affairs, but this proposal was not approved.

While many faculty members and students felt that the queer studies initiative was making progress, it fell apart as the new millennium began. Participants explain this by focusing on the role of state politics. A string of relatively centrist governors was replaced by a conservative governor who then appointed conservative members to the state governing board. At the same time, the state entered yet another budget crisis. While the governor, the state governing board, and the chancellor were clearly unsupportive of queer studies, the budget issues were probably more important in eroding the chances for queer studies. Additionally, this period was marked by an effort on the part of the University to improve its status among research universities. This process of status-seeking caused a devaluing of service and teaching activities and of innovation and caused faculty members to turn away from activities other than research. Faculty who were already fighting to preserve their jobs and their departments in the face of new research demands and significant budget cuts "ran out of steam" and simply were no longer interested in participating in additional committees or working on new curricular initiatives.

Today, the region in which Jeffrey University is located is seen as one of the most queer-friendly nationwide. In fact, the county in which it is located is among the top twenty nationwide in terms of the percentage of cohabiting couples who are same-sex. The queer student center is seen as a national model for other colleges and universities looking to find ways to respond to the growing presence and voice of queer students on their own campuses. Yet no queer studies program is available. Faculty and staff turnover in the mid to late 2000s have reduced burnout and have begun to lead to the beginnings of a new initiative, but budget crises are still looming. So far, all that has developed is a faculty seminar series. The non-academic staff hope that this seminar series will cause faculty to take ownership of a curricular initiative and move beyond seeing themselves as too busy to work for queer studies. This will take time, however, and in an environment where funding remains sparse it may be unlikely. The faculty did request a hire in queer studies, but one in women's studies took precedence. In order to spur faculty support, the student affairs professionals who are the main impetus behind current queer studies initiatives have been working to rebuild collaboration with other area colleges.

Out and activist queer students continue to show interest in a certificate or major program and in increasing course offerings and enrollments in the few queer studies courses that are offered remains high. Despite this interest, students are less involved than they were in the mid-1990s. Perhaps this is because there are a greater variety of queer political and social causes for students to participate in. Perhaps it is because fights to preserve campus resources and limit tuition increases have been taking up students' time. Perhaps it is because queer issues no longer seem as urgent in an era when several Northeastern states have legalized same-sex marriage. In the words of one student affairs professional at Jeffrey, "it is easy to get people together to fight an enemy, but hard to get people together to advance a vision." The campus climate for queer students at Jeffrey is good. There is much more inclusion of queer issues and support for research on queer topics from within mainstream disciplines. Perhaps students no longer feel that the development of queer studies is urgent.

"Someone Has Come Before"

Though analysts of higher education would not classify Jeffrey as a progressive or experimental university, it has consistently been an innovator in new curricular programs. It offered one of the first women's studies programs in the nation and created one of the first queer student centers anywhere. These changes were not adopted simply because Jeffrey had a commitment to curricular experimentation. The faculty did not simply adopt new programs because they felt like it; the administration did not respond to demographic changes or the innovative programs adopted by peers by pushing something new onto the campus. Rather, concerted effort by faculty, students, and sometimes non-academic staff lead to the changes that have occurred at Jeffrey.

What is particularly interesting about looking at the paths from the first initiative to the current situation for women's studies, Asian American studies, and queer studies at Jeffrey is the comparison between the three fields. Though advocates for women's studies got their start in the early 1970s while advocates for Asian American studies and queer studies did not become active until the mid-1980s, these three fields encountered a similar university with a similar history, a similar faculty, and a similar cultural context. In some ways, women's studies ought to have had a harder time. It was a pioneer in a discipline that barely existed, while Asian American studies and queer studies had been part of the landscape for years before students and faculty at Jeffrey became involved in them. Women's studies also emerged at a time when the University was just beginning to consider questions of faculty and student diversity, while Asian American studies and queer studies both entered a context where at least some administrators were committed to diversifying the University. Yet today, women's studies is a thriving department, while Asian American studies a certificate program that is barely surviving and queer studies does not even exist. What is the difference here?

There are a number of factors which might be important in exploring these differences. How did advocates for each discipline explain what they were trying to do? What strategies did they use? What was the balance of faculty, students, and non-academic staff in each initiative? How did those involved in each initiative relate to potential allies and competitors across the University? And how did the administration and the broader University community respond to each initiative?

In order to gain support for any kind of organizational change, advocates for that change need to explain to others what they are doing and why. Social movement scholars call such explanations frames (Benford and Snow 2000; Cress and Snow 2000) and specify that movements have three types: those that diagnose a problem, those that propose a solution, and those that motivate activism. While advocates for women's studies, Asian American studies, and queer studies all diagnosed problems that their fields of study were responding to and worked to motivate participants to push for programs, queer studies was never able to develop a frame that explained how the program would solve the problem. Women's studies and Asian American studies were. Women's studies advocates argued that women's studies would lead to women's empowerment by providing safe spaces for exploring women's issues and that women's studies would provide a location for women's ways of knowing that had been devalued in traditional disciplines. Asian American studies advocates pointed to the ways in which learning about one's own history helps one develop self-knowledge and deeper understanding. Queer studies advocates, in contrast, argued that everyone else had identity studies and they should too, and they could never agree on whether heterosexuality belonged inside or outside the program.

Framing is not the only thing that movements do to get their message across. They also choose strategies, sometimes disruptive ones. At the beginning, women's studies did not need to consider disruptive action because it was so easy to start new experimental initiatives. Later on—and this is where the difference in timing for Asian American studies and queer studies does matter—it became more difficult to start something new. As women's studies and Asian American studies advocates faced these constrained circumstances, they choose disruptive activism to make their voices heard. Student activists for Asian American studies occupied a building. Women's studies activists held teach-ins and made threats of more disruptive action; these threats never needed to be carried out, as the history of campus protest had made the administration aware of the disruptive potential of angry students. Queer studies activists never tried anything of the sort. Perhaps in a time when students are still disowned for coming out to their parents, there were reasons for that. But the Asian American students who participated in the building occupation had parental reactions to fear as well. And it very well may have been the disruptiveness of their actions that made the campus community and the administration take their demands seriously.

As noted above, the campaign for queer studies also suffered from the fact that non-academic staff were often its primary representatives, a problem that will recur in the story of queer studies at Sagebrush University, which will be considered in the next chapter. Students and faculty did care deeply about queer studies but were less willing to be the public face of the campaign. In the cases of women's studies and Asian American studies, both students and faculty were actively involved with the campaign from the beginning until the end. The balance of faculty and student participation was different for women's studies than for Asian American studies, however. In the case of Asian American studies, students were the primary activists with faculty playing a supporting—and declining—role. In the case of women's studies, the faculty were a driving force from the beginning, though they were always supported by large numbers of students. Perhaps the strong and enduring role of faculty in women's studies is what ultimately enabled the program to develop a major and a graduate certificate rather than remaining stuck with a minor.

Women's studies and Asian American studies also developed more significant alliances with other groups than did queer studies. Women's studies worked with Black studies to avoid competing for resources and to support each other's programs. Women's studies activists also included some non-academic community members, but because Jeffrey University in the early 1970s was a permeable and community-based campus, these community activists were not seen as outsiders. As one faculty member in the program explained, women's studies faculty know that someone has come before and that they can draw on that experience and knowledge. Asian American studies activists built common cause with students working for other ethnic studies programs. The campaign for queer studies did not build alliances and was unable to sustain a cross-campus working group; indeed, queer studies had even competed with women's studies rather than finding a way to work together.

Had queer studies faced the kind of university that women's studies did when the first advocates for women's studies came together, perhaps the story would have been different. Not all the blame can be laid at the feet of queer studies activists. Rather, there are important dimensions of the organizational context and of the University response that shaped what each group was able to achieve. These factors are not only about responsiveness to each individual program. In many ways, at least later in the campaign, less administrative and faculty hostility was expressed towards queer studies than towards Asian American studies and women's studies. Often more important is the overall receptivity of a college or university towards change. The campaign for women's studies emerged at a time when the University was quite open to new initiatives; though that openness declined over time, advocates for women's studies made sure to keep their foot in the door so they could grow their program larger and larger. Asian American studies did not experience such an open environment, but it took advantage of the temporary openness created by the building occupation to push the administration forward. In contrast, the strongest push for queer studies occurred in the context of a major budget crisis and a shift towards political conservatism on the part of the state governing board that occurred in the aftermath of the election of George W. Bush and of the terror attacks of 9/11/01. By the time these difficulties began to fade, queer studies advocates were already suffering from burnout and had moved away from the initiative. Both Asian American studies and queer studies advocates also had to deal with the increasing prestige and research focus of the University in the late 1990s and the 2000s, a factor that made faculty less willing to spend time on service and activism.

It is the complex interplay of movement strategy, movement membership, and the organizational context that makes change more or less possible. In the case of Jeffrey, the variation in these factors means that today women's studies is strong and vibrant and Asian American studies is just hanging on while queer studies activists wait to potentially regroup and try again. Some similar dynamics, particularly the role of varying combinations of movement membership and of considerations of university prestige, are important in the story of Sagebrush University that will be considered next.

Chapter 7

Fanning the Flames of Knowledge: Sagebrush University

At first, a visitor might not think that Sagebrush's campus holds a highly selective and prestigious research university. Filled with palm trees and just a few miles from the massive waves of the Pacific Ocean, it would seem to be a spot for beach bunnies and surfers. But this West Coast public university is ranked among the top 50 research universities. Its large campus holds 25,000 students, 80 percent of whom are undergraduates. Though the University invests heavily in faculty, the student-faculty ratio remains near 20 to one. While more than half of the students find housing in the surrounding suburban communities, a sizable number live in the modern dormitories available on campus.

About 95 percent of students at Sagebrush come from the state in which it is located, with about a quarter coming from the local area of the University. These students pay less than $10,000 in tuition and fees, though living expenses can easily double the cost of attendance. Those students who choose to come to Sagebrush from out-of-state will end up spending well over $30,000 a year on their educations. Despite the significant cost of tuition, only about half of students receive any financial aid from the University. Yet over 80 percent of all students who enroll at Sagebrush graduate within six years.

Not only is Sagebrush one of the most selective universities in the United States, it is also one of the most diverse. The heavy science and engineering focus of the University has meant that the student body remains under 50 percent female. Over half of all students are students of color with a particularly high concentration of Asian American students. Despite heavy and competitive academics, including a trimester schedule that squeezes courses into ten-week terms, students at Sagebrush have found time for organizational life and activism. Particularly notable were student demonstrations against the Vietnam War shortly after the University opened, as well as a system of student-organized co-ops that work to make campus life more affordable. Students have been active in protests when the administration has interfered with the co-op system.

Sagebrush University was founded in the middle of the 20th century to relieve pressure on an overcrowded state system of public universities as the baby boomers entered higher education. It opened with a unique organizational structure of distinct themed residential colleges that offered a framework for innovation and experimentation. Though the impact of that structure has diminished as the University has become just one among many elite research universities, students still experience different general education requirements depending on which residential college they choose. These colleges have distinct missions and values and have the capacity to offer courses outside of any academic department. Yet college enrollment does not affect students' choice of a major, and undergraduates can choose from over 120 different majors at Sagebrush that span the liberal arts and scientific fields. Graduate students as well can choose from a wide array of degrees spanning the liberal arts, with a concentration in scientific and professional fields. Today, the curricular options at Sagebrush include coursework in women's studies, Asian American studies, and queer studies. There is an undergraduate major in gender studies; within this major, students can choose to concentrate on the study of sexualities, though there is no queer studies program. Sagebrush also has a department of ethnic studies that offers an undergraduate major and a graduate program; while there are many Asian American studies courses, ethnic studies majors cannot choose to concentrate on only one ethnic group.

"A Chilly Climate for Women"

Sagebrush was located at the West Coast epicenter when women's studies programs started to hit the academic stage. Accordingly, it is not surprising that the first course that might be identified as women's studies was offered in the 1970–71 academic year, just after the first women's studies program was initiated at San Diego State University. By the mid 1970s, students began pushing for the creation of a women's studies program at Sagebrush and a student-run women's center was organized. This women's center publicized those courses focused on women's issues, those faculty and staff who were available to advise students with an interest in women's studies, and the method for creating a self-designed major. However, the campus newspaper pointed out that only nine courses on women's studies had ever been taught, and of those nine, two had been led by students. The auspicious start for women's studies might have led to a pioneering role in program development, including the adoption of a major program in the 1970s, but it did not.

The curricular change process at Sagebrush varies considerably depending on the type of changes desired. New majors and their associated departments must be reviewed and approved by the relevant academic affairs and budgeting committees, the faculty senate, the University administration, and the president of the entire state university system. On the other hand, new courses and minors are relatively easy to initiate. Particularly helpful in this regard is the college system. Individual colleges can develop and offer their own minors, providing an opportunity for new and experimental areas of study to emerge without having to be situated within a traditional academic department. Sagebrush has developed many minors of this type, and by 1981, a minor in women's studies was approved. Though the women's studies minor was not listed in the undergraduate catalogue until the 1983–84 academic year, there is no indication that the decision to offer a minor was controversial. Again, this easy adoption of a minor might have provided a starting place for the rapid development of a major, but this did not happen.

Instead, Sagebrush embarked on a decade-long period of contentious gender relations. Before the mid-1980s, women's issues at Sagebrush were rarely addressed. But in the mid-1980s, two women who worked in the office of the vice chancellor for undergraduate affairs set about conducting a women's needs survey. The survey asked questions about curricular issues as well as a wide variety of other issues facing women on campus. Though the survey had only a 30 percent response rate, students indicated a strong interest in more women's studies course offerings. The survey did not ask about student interest in a women's studies degree program, but some students wrote comments at the end of the survey attesting to the desire for a major in women's studies. Other students took a very different approach in the comments. They believed, like many members of the Abigail Adams College community, that feminism and lesbianism were conflated on campus.

Despite demonstrated interest in women's studies coursework—over 1,500 enrollments per year in women's studies—feminist activists on campus had another priority. Sagebrush's women's center was still a volunteer project run by a student organization in the early 1990s. Ultimately, students ran this women's center on $1500 a year and their own volunteer labor for 17 years. Other universities in the state system had long since created funded and professionally staffed women's centers. By this time, a number of the most prestigious universities in the state, both public and private, offered women's studies majors as well. Sagebrush was still offering only a minor. Classical models of administrative power and neoinstitutionalism would suggest that in a situation in which Sagebrush was clearly being left behind by its peers it would begin to copy them, yet no such event occurred. The administration seems to have paid no attention to the decisions other universities made regarding women's studies and women's centers. Rather, the campus activists who wanted to see women's studies and a women's center developed marshaled evidence from other campuses to press for administrative action. At first, they were not successful.

Students gathered 8,000 signatures from faculty, staff, and students on a petition asking for a women's center in the late 1980s. They gained the support of three vice chancellors before bringing their proposal forward. But the chancellor rejected the proposal, and the women's center was not established until 1996, quite a delay for a major research university. One of the reasons for this lack of success was that the women's center was a great source of controversy on campus. The controversy itself is rather telling when considering the difficulties that women's studies were facing in the 1990s. When the chancellor rejected the women's center, he wrote that "it would only service a special interest group." Women are still a minority at Sagebrush, and they were even more so then. As is clear from the chancellor's comments, the needs of women were seen as the needs of a small and marginal group, not as the needs of a core portion of the campus.

In fact, the chancellor was more favorably inclined to women's studies than to the women's center. At one point, he proposed establishing women's studies as an *alternative* to the women's center. Some faculty members had been in favor of developing strong ties between the two initiatives, while others were committed to keeping them separate. All supporters, however, wanted to see both initiatives adopted. One women's studies faculty member explained the problems with adopting women's studies in the absence of a women's center: it would require that women's studies "faculty act as a representative body rather than an intellectual one" and it would cut off women who were not participating in women's studies (such as students enrolled in heavy science-focused course loads) from being able to access women's resources and community. Feminist campus activists also pointed out that establishing women's studies without a women's center would ghettoize all women's issues into one small part of the University—the only part headed by a female vice chancellor.

Most feminist activists on campus were dedicated to ensuring that both women's studies and a professional women's center were available on campus as separate and autonomous entities. However, the same activists were working on both campaigns. The student group that ran the women's center was quite involved in increasing the visibility of women's issues on campus. They had meetings and conversations focused on their interest in women's studies; they also worked to locate faculty who would supervise women's studies independent study courses. More publically, they used their limited funding to sponsor several lecture series that brought notable feminist speakers to campus. They also worked with faculty on the campaign to develop a women's studies major. The faculty and students who wanted a major saw their goal as institutionalizing women's studies with a full-time faculty director. They also wanted to institute an interdisciplinary seminar on research on women at the graduate level as part of the process of increasing the respectability of women's studies in the research university environment.

All of these activities occurred in an environment that the Committee on the Status of Women called "chilly." In the early 1990s, Sagebrush was still without a campus day care service, pay equity for female faculty, or a sexual harassment policy. Though there was a small group of faculty committed to the initiative over the long term, many were worried about the impact that their involvement would have on their chances of tenure. This fear is one important factor in explaining why women's studies came so late to Sagebrush—the strongest push to create a program did not occur until after a few key faculty members had earned tenure.

Female faculty members' fears were based on concrete events that highlighted the second-class citizenship of women at Sagebrush. For instance, in 1992, the chancellor met with supporters of the women's center to tell them that the services they wanted to house in the women's center would be better spread across existing University departments. At the meeting, he told them that it was his wish that the numbers of female students would increase to such a level that they could be limited by law to 50 percent of the population, a situation he claimed was already the case in Cuba. This desire certainly foreshadows the current claims of some education pundits that affirmative action for men is needed to address the damaging situation in which women are the majority of college students (Jaschik 2006). In the years before women's studies became a public issue on campus, the hostility faced by women at Sagebrush was even worse. The stereotypes that women are not good at math and science led many at this science-focused university to believe that women on campus contributed nothing to the academic atmosphere. In one academic division in which fieldwork is often necessary for research, women were generally excluded from expeditions to field sites. One faculty member said that discrimination at Sagebrush was so common that it was openly discussed; men would simply state that they saw no problem with discrimination.

Women and people of color were only recruited to fill tenure-track positions after it was made clear to the University administration that the University faced government sanctions for their lack of affirmative action compliance. In response, the University developed new affirmative action policies and hired an administrator in charge of affirmative action compliance (policies that have since had their power dramatically curtailed). After a pregnancy leave policy was developed, many department chairs instructed female faculty members that they were not permitted to take advantage of the policy. And yet these changes did make a real difference for women at Sagebrush, who were now present in sufficient numbers to allow the development of core support for women's studies.

These new female faculty members wanted to organize an interdisciplinary space to do work on women. Some experienced ghettoization within their traditional academic departments, in other words clear expectations on the part of department chairs and colleagues that their work focus on women. Yet even these women hired for their expertise in research on women found little support for research and teaching on women. The new administrator working on affirmative action provided a space for women to talk about women's studies and worked to make women's studies an institutional concern. The new female faculty members were not only working on women's studies, however. They were also working hard to produce the scholarship expected for tenure at an elite research university. The excellent quality of their work eventually began to win them respect from the rest of the campus. Having delayed acting publically until after some key spokeswomen earned tenure also gave female faculty at Sagebrush a reputation for "political smoothness." Unlike women's studies activists at other colleges and universities such as Abigail Adams College and Jeffrey University, those in favor of women's studies at Sagebrush did not make threats, engage in demonstrations, or bring national news media attention to campus. Ultimately, however, the fact that women at Sagebrush began to succeed at the prestige game did not change the overall images and stereotypes that men on campus held about women. Instead, successful female faculty were grudgingly seen as examples of "female exceptionalism."

When women finally felt able to voice their demands for women's studies, they asked for a major program and the ability to make faculty appointments, much more than they thought they would get at the time. They did not present the united front that they might have a few years earlier. Many feminists on campus were more interested in pursuing other gender-related issues, such as pay equity.

Those who were committed to increasing curricular opportunities focused on women's issues were split between those who favored women's studies and those who favored gender studies. There were also continuing debates among women on campus as to whether women's studies actually offered a unique curricular perspective. Yet the proposal moved forward. In these final stages of the initiative, graduate students played an important role. Many were doing work on women in their graduate programs and were committed to the instructional potential of the discipline, despite the absence of a graduate component. In particular, one graduate student worked on the administrative aspects of proposal development and eventually served in an administrative position supporting program development. Additionally, a student rally held in May 1990 saw 125 students protesting racism and sexism on campus, as well as the lack of a gender studies program.

Twenty years after women's studies courses were first offered at Sagebrush, the women's studies major was approved by the academic policy committee. A few months later, in February 1992, the budget subcommittee of the academic senate granted its approval. This approval did not come easily. Though the budget subcommittee's mandate was to review only "resource concerns," as befitting its focus on the budget, it responded to the proposal for women's studies by questioning the degree to which the proposal defined an academic program, whether the program had a political agenda, whether the faculty involved were qualified, how well-conceived various individual courses were, and whether careers would be available for women's studies graduates. This last concern was particularly peculiar given the track record of women's studies graduates from other colleges and universities nearby in finding jobs for two decades. Ultimately, the budget committee suggested that an academic advisory committee of faculty continually review the program. It highlighted the complaint that "every social issue should not become a major." The chair of the committee on the status of women was able to respond to these concerns. She pointed out that students were already planning their majors in advance of program approval and that approval would "heighten the morale" of female students, faculty, and staff. In addition, she returned to the observation that other Universities with which Sagebrush compared itself already had majors. While the administration clearly did not seek out such information, it did at times respond when presented with it. Ultimately the program was allowed to go forward.

Female faculty members at Sagebrush today still find that their salaries are undervalued by administrators who do not believe women are competent scholars. Data from the Integrated Post-Secondary Education Data System (IPEDS) of the United States Department of Education shows that even in 2008, male full professors at Sagebrush made $17,000 more a year than did female full professors, while the salary differentials at the assistant and associate level were closer to $5,000 (National Center for Education Statistics 2010). These gaps have narrowed somewhat over the past half decade, but at least at the full professor level they are somewhat larger than gaps for universities comparable to Sagebrush within the state university system. Women are not only receiving lower salaries, they also continue to represent the minority of faculty members, with women making up only about one quarter of faculty at Sagebrush throughout the 2000s. Women's studies clearly did not make as big of a difference as some thought that it would.

Women's studies at Sagebrush quickly became more institutionalized and less radical. In the 1997–98 academic year, the women's studies major changed its name to gender studies as part of a process of self-legitimation. Campus actors feel that gender studies has more of an intellectual grounding than would a program in women's studies, and Sagebrush remains concerned first and foremost with academic prestige. A variety of factors were important in leading to this shift. Some faculty members felt that their interests were drifting beyond the confines of a program on women and wanted to expand their intellectual home to match their interests. There was also a generational shift in the theoretical orientation of the faculty, with younger faculty coming from a postmodern perspective more concerned with the dynamics of categorization than with the effects of inequality. At the same time, state-level politics shifted, leading to a strong anti-feminist and anti-difference movement on campus and throughout the state. These contextual difficulties led to increasing difficulties in student recruitment for the program. The name change thus was a way to bring in new ideas, more male faculty members, and a broader slice of the student body.

Within the past few years, graduate students at Sagebrush have been advocating that the gender studies program add a graduate component such as a certificate program. Faculty took up this charge as early as 2004, but little progress has been made. Even the idea of an interdisciplinary graduate seminar on women seems like a dream from another time, though many traditional social science and humanities departments do offer graduate students the opportunity to concentrate their work on gender. Enrollments in gender studies also remain limited, with only about five to ten majors graduating each year and about 500–600 students enrolling in courses, well below the levels found at other research universities like Jeffrey and Technopark. The program has become more institutionalized, however. In 2004, it was able to gain its first tenure-track faculty line, though the line is shared with another department. If the faculty member hired to fill this line is successful at winning tenure in both departments by meeting or exceeding the high and prestige-focused standards that Sagebrush holds, she will become a force ensuring some measure of permanence for a program now notable for the fame and quality of its affiliated faculty.

"For the Sake of the Program"

Sagebrush University was founded just before the massive social upheaval of the 1960s. It is therefore not surprising that students rapidly formed campus organizations of various sorts and that many of these organizations eagerly became involved in activism. The Asian American student organization was one of the first to be founded on campus. From the beginning it was politically involved, particularly with community issues. Early on, the group held conferences for Asian American high school students to encourage them to choose Sagebrush for their college educations. As Sagebrush is a large university with a large Asian American student population, the original Asian American student organization spawned many descendants. One of these descendants was founded in the wake of a statewide political controversy about college admissions for Asian American students. This organization's mission statement showed its explicit concern with the educational needs of Asian American students. Despite their organizing strength, the Asian American community did face controversy. For instance, in the late 1980s, a controversy plagued the entire state university system over an English language test that some claimed was favoring White applicants.

Throughout its early history, Sagebrush had some degree of difficulty in attracting students of color, apparently despite the best efforts of engaged students like those in the Asian American student organization. The University's focus on rapidly seeking prestige led it to discount the importance of social issues, particularly in comparison to some of the other campuses within the state system. Yet there were pockets of possibility. One of the undergraduate colleges on campus was founded in 1969 with an original mission of working with academically underprepared minority students; this college continues to have a curricular focus on multiculturalism. The curricular flexibility allowing for experimental courses on contemporary issues discussed above also allowed faculty and undergraduate colleges to explore ethnic studies early on.

Despite the early difficulties in recruiting students of color, the Asian American student population grew rapidly. In 1976, over a decade and a half after the University was founded, only 5 percent of students were Asian American. By 1986, 15 percent of Sagebrush students were Asian American, as were 10 percent of admitted graduate students. Today, the University is over one third Asian American, well above their proportion of the state population, but it continues to face difficulties in enrolling Black and Latino/a students. This increasing Asian American student population undoubtedly increased interest in Asian American studies coursework, but no one—not students, faculty, or administrators—ever claimed that Asian American studies was needed because of the numbers of Asian Americans on campus. Though there were sizable numbers of Asian faculty throughout the history of Sagebrush, most were foreign-born scientists and thus did not contribute to the development of interest in Asian American studies.

Asian American student organizations at Sagebrush also had a long history of interest in learning more about Asian American issues. A faculty member who served as an organization's advisor for a time recalls students getting course readers from friends who attended other campuses of the state university system where Asian American studies courses were already available and using these readers as the basis for informal discussion groups on Asian American studies topics. Students built on their social ties to work with a system-wide coalition of Asian American student groups. They hoped that students at campuses already offering Asian American studies might advise them on how to proceed in their quest to develop a program, but these connections turned out to be less helpful than the students expected. It seems that until more recently, when Sagebrush experienced a significant increase in prestige, students at some of the other campuses looked down at Sagebrush students. The organization also created an educational advocacy position within its slate of officers. Though the office-holder was expected to focus some attention on the role of remedial courses in the education of Asian American students as well as on language issues facing Asian teaching assistants, most of his energy was focused on advocating for Asian American studies. Among the strategies the educational advocacy officer engaged in were participating in the student affirmative action committee, a group in support of expanding ethnic studies opportunities more generally; the officer was also responsible for generating reports about the state of ethnic studies.

A minor in Asian American studies was first proposed in 1983. Members of the campus Asian American community met with the Sagebrush administration and presented a petition calling for Asian American studies. While the administration did not move forward on the minor at this time, the University did begin to take small steps in the direction of Asian American studies during the mid-1980s. A few experimental courses were offered, generally by visiting or adjunct professors hired especially for their ability to teach Asian American studies. A steering committee to guide the proposal process was also established. However, Asian American studies advocates met with continual resistance from the administration. While advocates frequently invoked the fact that other campuses in the state system already offered Asian American studies programs, the administration took no initiative in working on the program and was continually slow to respond to the steering committee. It eventually took the involvement of several state legislators and a member of the state higher education governing board to propel the administration to respond.

The formal minor proposal was submitted in November 1987. It explicitly focused on the fact that Sagebrush lacked a program while its peers in the same state already had programs. The minor proposal was molded after the women's studies minor and other interdisciplinary minor programs on campus. It asked for one full-time faculty hire as well as funds for part-time lecturers. In order to be adopted, this proposal faced approval by multiple academic senate committees as well as by the administration, but supporters brought with them an arsenal of strength. Thirty-eight faculty members, 13 community groups, eight notable community figures, and eight student organizations had signed on to the proposal. Again, the proposal was met with resistance within the Sagebrush community. An administrator in the social sciences division claimed that the program would be a misuse of resources because students would only enroll in basic literature and history courses rather than completing the entire minor program. Another administrator said that since enrollments were low in those ethnic studies programs that already existed on campus, Asian American studies should not be created.

A prominent figure in the community who occasionally taught on campus as a visiting professor explained how at another campus in the state system, demand for ethnic studies had increased dramatically when the campus instituted a general education requirement focused on diversity. In fact, many of the other campuses in the state system had already adopted such requirements, and there was some pressure to require them system-wide. Sagebrush did not adopt such a requirement because general education programs are in the hands of each individual undergraduate college. Students therefore began lobbying each undergraduate college to institute such requirements, but they met with limited success; today, some of the colleges have instituted such requirements while others have not.

Students took note of all of this talk about enrollments, however. They developed a strategy for increasing enrollments in courses to create the illusion of market demand and to satisfy critics who believed students would not take Asian American studies courses or earn an Asian American studies minor. At first, the Asian American student organization handed out fliers advertising courses and bombarded their membership with mailings to encourage enrollments. When these publicity campaigns failed to encourage sufficient numbers of students to sign up for courses, they came up with something much more innovative. They began to encourage students whose curricular requirements precluded their participation in Asian American studies, such as those with the heavy major requirements in engineering, to sign up for Asian American studies courses as overload over their normal semester's course requirements. These students would then attend class for the first three weeks. After the third-week attendance reports were due from the instructional faculty, students would drop the courses. This strategy resulted in course enrollments that were consistently high, with at least sixty students enrolling in each course. Because enrollment data was not collected again after the third week, it now appeared that the demand for Asian American studies was consistently high.

While they were organizing to effectively carry out the enrollment campaign, students had other drains on their time and energy. Students working towards Asian American studies expended considerable effort "putting out internal fires" as conflicts developed between students and faculty over strategy, the direction the program proposal was taking, and other matters. The student leadership asked other students to put conflict aside "for the sake of the program." While it took a lot of persuading on the part of the student leadership, they were largely successful at keeping the most problematic conflicts submerged. On the other hand, Asian American student activists struggled with the lack of Asian American consciousness among their classmates. This lack of consciousness was one of the reasons to support the development of Asian American studies in the first place. However, it also meant that few students were likely to be part of Asian American studies activism or to fully understand the rationale for developing a program. Activists understood that the consequence of this phenomenon was that they did not have the critical mass for assertive actions like those taken at universities such as Jeffrey. Instead, they choose to work within the system, play by the rules, and strategically create a market for their desired program.

In 1988, a year after the minor proposal had been submitted to the University, a minor was still not approved. However, the administration had approved the creation of one tenure-track faculty line in Asian American studies. The Asian American studies committee responded by collecting 400 faculty signatures on a petition that expressed appreciation for the one tenure line in Asian American studies but also asked for three more faculty lines as well as approval of the minor. About one quarter of the signatures on this petition were obtained by students who individually met with faculty members to urge them to sign. The academic affairs committee did review the minor proposal and found it to be intellectually sound, but it decided that a minor could not be approved without hiring to ensure adequate faculty for staffing courses.

The Asian American studies committee therefore set out to hire someone to fill the one allocated tenure-track faculty line, a person who would be prestigious enough to meet Sagebrush's standards and who would teach and do research in Asian American studies. Because there was no departmental home for Asian American or ethnic studies, this faculty member would have to be hired within a traditional academic department and would be subject to the hiring and tenure guidelines of that department. At first, the search seemed promising. A variety of scholars, all of whom were then or subsequently became big names in Asian American studies, expressed an interest in coming to Sagebrush to work in the nascent program. Any of these scholars would have performed well in the competitive and research-driven culture of this elite research university. But difficulties plagued the search process. Some of these difficulties were of the ordinary types that plague many faculty searches, such as desirable candidates getting earlier or better offers elsewhere. Others were specific to the Sagebrush situation. Candidates claimed that their candidacy was not being fairly evaluated by the departments in which they would work, various department chairs and administrators often did not support candidates who received support from other faculty in the hiring department, and most departments were reluctant to approve a hire because this Asian American studies specific hire might limit the ability of the department to hire to meet other needs later on. One department in the social sciences went so far as to tell an Asian American studies candidate that had been brought to campus that the department was not interested in developing expertise in "a narrow topic such as race and ethnicity," citing William Julius Wilson's book *The Declining Significance of Race* as evidence that such expertise was not needed in the department. Furthermore, the department avoided discussing the intellectual merit of the candidate's work and never held a departmental vote on whether to hire the candidate. This incident inspired the Asian American student group to write a report exposing the problems with hiring in general in this department, including its poor track record in hiring women for tenure-track positions. Today, these problems have been remedied somewhat, but the department in question remains about one quarter female and only about 15 percent faculty of color, with even fewer faculty of color born in the United States.

After experiencing continuing difficulties with various academic departments, the Asian American studies committee eventually approached an administrative department with the authority to approve academic hires. The hope was that this department would allow Asian American studies to bypass the unsupportive departments they had previously been dealing with, but it was already too late to hire a faculty member in that year. Just as administrators responded to requests for progress by agreeing to schedule more meetings, the social science department discussed above had "stalled Asian American studies out." The lack of progress finally encouraged allies to come forward. Faculty working in Black studies and in Latino studies expressed their concerns and their displeasure with the difficulties encountered during the faculty search process. Some of these faculty members came to the discussion from positions of institutional strength. For instance, one faculty member in Black studies who argued on behalf of Asian American studies held an administrative position in one of the colleges. But the new support was not altruistic. A major reason why Black and Latino studies faculty stepped forward was that they, along with Asian American studies, would benefit from the creation of ethnic studies as a stand-alone academic department with its own budgetary and hiring authority. It is worth noting that most of the faculty members engaged in supporting the Asian American studies and the ethnic studies initiatives held tenure prior to beginning involved, freeing them from some of the fears that their colleagues in women's studies had experienced.

Before Asian American studies ever had a chance to get off the ground on its own, the push for combined ethnic studies became a reality. A committee of deans and department chairs formed to draft a proposal for a department of ethnic studies with degree-granting powers. Despite the work that students had put into advocating for Asian American studies as well as other ethnic studies areas, they were shut out of this committee. One faculty member explicitly told a student activist that it was now "grown-up time." In 1989, an initial proposal for a department of "Comparative American Cultures" was floated to the administration. The rationale for this department was that graduates would be able to find jobs teaching the courses now offered across the country as part of new diversity requirements adopted by many campuses. This program would have allowed students the opportunity to concentrate on the experiences of a particular ethnic group, such as Asian Americans, while taking a group of comparative courses as well. Students were generally indifferent to this development. They were willing to support a combined ethnic studies department if faculty thought it was the right way to go, but were upset by their exclusion from the process. While the administration expressed some interest in the proposal, it suggested that reorganization and revision of the proposal was necessary. In particular, the administration believed that it was important to include plans for a graduate program in order to attract top faculty to the new department. The administration also saw ethnic studies as an ideal way to respond to the continuing demand for Asian American studies.

Though they were upset by the way the faculty were handling the campaign for ethnic studies, students became actively involved in pushing for the department and the major. Students wrote letters to the academic senate urging approval of the program, signed petitions, met with faculty members in the social sciences and humanities to educate them about the need for ethnic studies, and encouraged their parents and members of the community to write to the University's academic affairs office in support of ethnic studies. Even during those phases of the campaign when much of the impetus for progress came from the faculty, students did much of the legwork. They created publicity, provided logistical support for visiting speakers, filled the seats at lectures, and urged faculty members to sign petitions. Students supporting Asian American studies attended regional conferences on the Asian American student movement. When the focus shifted to ethnic studies, Asian American studies activists joined forces with students interested in Black and Latino studies to demand that the administration move forward on the proposal. In particular, these student activists demanded that the major have a programmatic focus on people of color in the United States, that the program be organized as a department, that the committee provide a seat for a student representative, and that the social sciences become more involved in the program. Students issued a written document outlining these demands; this document threatened "action" of an unspecified sort if the demands were not fulfilled by the end of the spring semester in 1988.

Even as support grew in some sectors of the campus, ethnic studies experienced opposition from others. For instance, a faculty member from anthropology complained that ethnic studies was not a discipline, that student interest in courses would not transfer into enrollments in the major, and that the whole thing was far too political. This faculty member was particularly troubled by the connections between ethnic studies and affirmative action and by the role that ethnic studies played in providing a forum for expressing views about and attacking marginalization. A faculty member in psychology commented on the ethnic studies proposal by saying that ethnic studies topics could not even provide a week's worth of lectures in the traditional disciplines, never mind an entire major. Even where issues might be of concern to traditional disciplines, the scholarship was insufficient. This faculty member additionally believed that learning about minority communities would not prepare students for life outside of college. Other campus actors saw the ethnic studies proposal as an opportunity to ghettoize everything interdisciplinary or radical on campus. Some urged that Jewish studies, urban studies, and women's studies be folded into the new ethnic studies department. This proposal is not as outlandish as it might seem. At New York University, programs in Africana studies, American studies, Asian American studies, gender and sexuality studies, Latino studies, and metropolitan studies were combined in the 2000s into one department called Social and Cultural Analysis that administers majors in each area as well as a combined major program and several graduate degrees.

Not all opposition was quite so reactionary. A faculty member from history believed that the creation of an ethnic studies program would amount to "letting other departments off the hook" and that the ethnic minority experience could not be fully understood without ample attention to the White experience as well. There may indeed have been good reason for faculty to be skeptical of the potential of ethnic studies. Sagebrush is and was a very academically focused university with a high number of course requirements. Students felt that it was a sacrifice to take any course which would not fulfill a requirement, and thus it represented a significant commitment to the field of ethnic studies when students enrolled in even a single course. Some students who enrolled in the early courses sacrificed their grades in other courses due to their commitment to ethnic studies. The ethnic studies major would at last provide students with an opportunity to enroll in a full program of ethnic studies courses instead of working to fit courses into one of a very few elective slots remaining in their programs.

The consolidated ethnic studies department was in fact approved over the summer and fall of 1988 despite the opposition. Just prior to this approval, in the spring of 1988, Asian American studies had gained official approval. As the committee worked to finalize arrangements for the program's commencement, it treated Asian American studies as one of the existing programs to be incorporated into the ethnic studies department. By 1990, the program was in operation. Sixteen faculty members in traditional disciplines were teaching ethnic studies courses, with an additional eight incorporating ethnic studies into their courses in a more limited fashion. Over 50 students had already declared majors in the program and over 2,000 students were enrolled in ethnic studies courses. Despite this progress, the program had not yet been fully implemented. In May of 1990, 125 students rallied to protest the lack of progress on establishing ethnic studies and gender studies, particularly the lack of departmental status, as well as racism and sexism on campus more generally. Students demanded the implementation of a diversity requirement, the integration of work on gender and race into existing curricula, admissions reforms designed to ensure greater representation of students of color, "retention and recruitment programs" for students and faculty of color, a commitment to diversifying the tenured faculty, reassessing definitions of academic excellence so as to increase the value of gender and ethnic studies, increased student involvement in decision-making in the academic senate, and divestment from apartheid South Africa. Few of these demands were ever met.

As specified in the planning process, the new ethnic studies department was intended to be explicitly interdisciplinary and comparative. The faculty moved away from the initial plan to allow students to concentrate on the experiences of one ethnic group. While students may still do this on an unofficial basis, it is not noted on their transcripts and there are requirements built into the program to force them to diversify their course choices. The major requires students to pursue comparative studies and prohibits them from taking all their courses on one ethnic group. The departmental mission is focused around the notion that "nondominant [*sic*] ethnic groups are never systematically studied in higher education in the way that dominant Euro-centric trends have flourished in the United States." In particular, the department aims to challenge the organizational foundations of traditional disciplines by working to "synthesize social and humanistic elements" and create an "understanding of coherent subcultures" that makes clear "common cultural associations in Western life." Yet Black studies and Latino/Chicano studies still retain separate minor programs for students who wish a more focused exploration of the Black or Latino/Chicano experience. Asian American studies came to the game too late to establish and maintain its own program. Native American studies, on the other hand, remains vastly underrepresented among the course offerings.

Diversity remains a problem on campus. A cross-cultural center was only founded in the 1990s after students stopped highway traffic in protest. Faculty members associated with the weak Black studies minor have had difficulty earning tenure. In 1999, students held a demonstration in response to the low numbers of Black students on campus; they also called for more female faculty and faculty of color and again for the establishment of diversity requirements. Even in the mid-2000s, faculty signed a petition claiming that there were continued problems with the lack of diversity in hiring. Some faculty continue to believe that the administration will only begin to care about such issues if a lack of action will cause them to lose funding, as was the case with the establishment of an affirmative action program discussed above.

Today, the ethnic studies department employs about a dozen tenure-track faculty members, as well as assorted visiting and temporary faculty, graduate instructors, and dozens of affiliated faculty with appointments in traditional departments who are available to teach or do other work in ethnic studies. The program offers a major and a minor program and runs dozens of courses every year. Approximately 25–30 students earn majors in ethnic studies each year. The department also offers a well-regarded graduate program offering master's and doctoral degrees. About 30 graduate students are enrolled at any given time, with two to four earning degrees each year; they go on to jobs at top colleges and universities in a variety of disciplines. In other words, ethnic studies at Sagebrush University is about as institutionalized as a department can be.

"Enough to Sate Their Interest"

Like the Asian American community at Sagebrush, the queer community has been involved in a variety of political issues both on campus and in the wider world. For instance, in 1998, students held a demonstration protesting anti-gay hate crimes in the aftermath of the Matthew Shepard killing. This came just months after a student coalition called Diversity in Action issued a set of demands in May 1998. The coalition was "an organization committed to the liberation and inclusion of people of color, women and children, the lesbian-gay-bisexual-transgendered communities and working class peoples" and also opposed to the corporatization and elitism of the state university system. Diversity in Action's demands related to a set of recommendations that came from a report issued by a campus diversity commission. In particular, the coalition asked the University to revoke Newt Gingrich's invitation to give a speech on campus and to use the $100,000 fee that Gingrich commanded to implement the recommendations of the diversity report. Queer student organizations on campus have maintained significant ties to national, regional, and system-wide queer organizations and have used these to intensify their activism. At one point, there was even a gay campus newspaper.

All of this queer activism did not really solidify until the early 1990s, when a group of people at Sagebrush wrote a queer campus climate report. This group was created through a grassroots initiative by non-instructional staff who sought to confront the difficult campus climate for queer people. They formed a campus queer organization and sought official approval and funding from the administration. The report, which was issued in 1992, focused primarily on the different student organizations that existed on campus, documenting their funding problems and highlighting the utility of creating a queer student center or some other form of organization that would centralize queer activities and services. It also discussed the emergence of queer studies coursework on campus, as the first courses were offered between 1990 and 1992. Though these early courses were offered in a few departments, most were sponsored by the English department, which enrolled a core group of students who were active in demanding courses focused on the queer experience. The committee who drafted the 1992 climate report believed that a six-course queer studies minor could be a reality within a year or two, though they noted that without donor funding for an endowed chair a major would be all but impossible. In the short term, the committee wanted to focus on hiring more openly gay faculty and more faculty with queer research and teaching interests. One of the primary recommendations the committee made in its report was the formation of a chancellor's committee on lesbian, gay, and bisexual issues, much like the committee on the status of women that had become the organizing nucleus for the recently-approved women's studies program.

Such a committee was formed in 1994. While it was primarily populated by non-instructional staff, it was open to and involved some faculty and students. Shortly after being formed, this new committee issued its own campus climate report. This 1995 report focused more attention on the experiences of queer employees. It advocated for expanding anti-discrimination statements to insure coverage of queer people, providing diversity training on campus, and implementing partner benefits for same-sex couples. But the report also paid some attention to student issues. It reiterated the need for a queer student center. The report also discussed the fact that other universities in the state system were expanding queer studies course offerings and suggested that Sagebrush needed more curricular opportunities in queer studies. Coverage of queer studies issues in the report included a discussion of faculty and student interest in queer studies courses as well as the importance of a tenure-track faculty hire in queer studies and the development of a campus conference and lecture series concerning queer experiences. This discussion of queer studies came about not because of the initiative of the non-instructional staff on the committee, but rather because a group of faculty approached the committee to ask that such a request be included in the report.

The faculty members who brought this request to the Chancellor's Committee represented a small group of faculty who had begun meeting in an attempt to broaden the queer curriculum at Sagebrush, but this group felt that there were not a sufficient number of faculty members or courses available to establish a minor at that time. Yet both faculty and students were exhibiting significant interest in queer studies. Students often complained to both faculty members and the administration about the fact that too few queer studies courses were available, particularly in comparison with other campuses of the state university system. Initially, faculty who tried to establish new queer studies courses were not provided with the resources necessary to do so, a fact that the faculty group construed as administrative discrimination. Later on, some resources for course development did become available, and faculty used them to create at least one interdisciplinary queer studies course. The resulting course was only offered once.

In 1997, the chancellor's committee issued a second climate report intended to monitor progress on the recommendations contained in the report from 1995. The report highlighted the progress that had been made in adding courses on queer topics. It listed six courses explicitly focused on queer issues as well as almost a dozen more with some relevant subject matter. However, the report also documented a number of enduring concerns. There was still no progress on developing a queer campus center, offering benefits for same-sex partners, or providing diversity training so as to reduce the harassment queer employees experienced on campus. In terms of the curriculum, the report noted that no queer-focused courses were yet offered in the history or psychology departments. The report documented high enrollments and waiting lists for queer studies courses as well as student demand for additional and especially upper-level courses and strong student attendance at queer-focused conferences. In addition, the committee argued that Sagebrush was behind the curve, as other campuses in the state system already offered queer studies minors. In a return to the eternal concern at Sagebrush that arose in discussions of both women's studies and Asian American studies that no program be limited to any particular group on campus, the report's authors explained that many students with an interest in queer studies coursework were in fact heterosexual.

Though employment issues were more of a priority for the staff members who made up the chancellor's committee, they were eager to form issue-by-issue coalitions with faculty and students to deal with curricular and other campus issues. These did not have much of an impact on the effort to advance queer studies on campus. Despite strong student interest, the demand for queer studies remained a minority position. In the words of one committee member, "there was not enough critical mass" to advance the campaign. The number of queer faculty, especially those willing to be openly involved in the initiative, remained very low. In particular, untenured faculty were very reluctant to go to the meetings at which the chancellor's committee presented its reports or to advocate openly for queer studies in any way. It was the untenured faculty, however, who were the most interested in the potential for a program. Faculty who were interested in queer studies also found it difficult to build common cause with other faculty holding similar views.

As seen in the discussions of women's studies and Asian American studies at Sagebrush, many faculty and administrators saw students as having only a limited role in curricular change and campus politics. Many involved in queer studies believed it would be expecting too much of students to ask them to get involved in the campaign. It is therefore not surprising that students played a marginal role, mostly constraining their activities to simply asking for more. Faculty could have mentored students to help them understand the Sagebrush bureaucracy and how to maneuver within it, but faculty members did not see such mentoring as their role. One member of the chancellor's committee argued later on that student activism would have significantly increased the potential for a queer studies program.

While progress on queer studies remained limited, change occurred in other areas of queer life on campus. A queer student center was founded in 1999; a large facility with offices, meeting spaces, and a library was built in the mid-2000s. Queer student affairs professionals such as those staffing the center formed a network across the state system that they used to share information in an attempt to maintain consistent and high levels of resources and services for queer students at all of the campuses. Similar networks were forming nationally in the early 2000s as well.

After the women's studies program changed its name to gender studies in 1997–98, gender studies added a concentration in sexualities. Though this move brought some queer studies faculty into the gender studies program, the sexualities concentration is not the same as a queer studies program. Few of the courses are explicitly focused on queer experiences, though many include some discussion of queer issues. More common are courses about the body, reproduction, and sex in historical literature. Yet this move led some faculty members newly involved in gender studies to become quite committed to expanding coursework on queer studies within the existing curricular framework. Newer faculty have reopened the discussion about the proper place for queer studies, but the debate has not taken on the character of the debate between queer and sexuality approaches that the one at Jeffrey University did.

Many students have remained committed to the idea of a stand-alone queer studies program and enrollments in queer studies courses remain high. Graduate students have also begun seeking the opportunity to enroll in interdisciplinary queer studies coursework. Sagebrush has won a series of grants enabling more systematic explorations of queer studies, including an endowed annual lecture, a series of lectures on sexuality and location, and a dialogue series where interdisciplinary groups of faculty and graduate students come together to discuss queer issues. These initiatives represent the commitment of some members of the Sagebrush community to increase academic dialogue on queer issues. The chancellor's committee drew on this interest to again push for a queer studies program in 2004, and the academic advisory board passed a recommendation supporting the creation of a minor program in queer studies. Again, however, the program did not move forward. Like women's studies and Asian American studies, queer studies has faced opposition. Many people at Sagebrush feel that all such programs are not self-sustaining and that they do not enroll sufficient undergraduate students to justify the funding outlays they require, particularly given stiff competition for funds between the many interdisciplinary programs and traditional departments. In fact, even some advocates of queer studies worry that moving forward with a program would be detrimental to gender studies, ethnic studies, and other interdisciplinary minors on campus.

According to a queer student affairs professional at Sagebrush, there were by 2005 at least thirty faculty members with some interest in queer issues, while about a dozen have research and teaching interest in queer studies. Additionally, there are adjuncts and more transient junior faculty who could support queer studies. Some of the faculty interested in queer studies have now earned tenure and would be more comfortable speaking up than in the past. Yet students in the mid-2000s were not clamoring for a queer studies program any longer. Unlike in the past, the campus climate for queer people is now supportive and open. Most of the policies queer campus activists fought for have been implemented. A large number of students seem to feel that the few queer studies courses offered through the sexuality concentration are "enough" to sate their interest in the subject. A queer student affairs professional believes that without student activism, a program will never develop. This staff member takes a long view of the process of program development, noting that even the approval process in the academic senate takes two to three years. If a queer studies program were to emerge on campus, in this staff member's opinion it would be because a tenured faculty member took up the cause as his or her own and stimulated interest and excitement among students that would then inspire student activism. However, as in the case of Asian American studies, campus activism around such issues would be a sacrifice for contemporary academically-focused Sagebrush students. Furthermore, the state university system of which Sagebrush is part has experienced considerable financial difficulties resulting in many cuts to campus programs; new initiatives are not on the horizon as long as budget difficulties remain. It seems, then, that queer studies at Sagebrush University is unlikely to become a reality any time soon.

"The Pursuit of Prestige Above All Else"

In just half a century, Sagebrush University has gone from being the newest stepchild of a large state university system to being one of the most elite public research universities in the United States. It has made that climb due to a relentless focus on the pursuit of prestige, a pursuit that is obvious from the most perfunctory perusal of its webpage. The "About Sagebrush" section of the campus web site highlights the lofty performance of the University and its component programs in national rankings, highlights its preeminence in research, and lists national and international honors earned by Sagebrush faculty. Far from their roots as local students with an interest in community activism, today's Sagebrush students are academically driven and top of their class.

Neoinstitutional models of organizational change argue that it is exactly organizations like Sagebrush was in the 1980s that ought to be copying their peers—those who are not yet at the top of the heap but are desperately clamoring to reach it. Yet Sagebrush administrators again and again avoided adding academic programs that were already available at many of Sagebrush's peers. Women's studies majors and Asian American studies programs were offered at many other campuses in the state university system as well as other universities with which Sagebrush compared itself long before they were adopted at Sagebrush; queer studies programs can be found elsewhere in the state but not at Sagebrush. So if it is not institutional isomorphism that explains why the pursuit of prestige mattered so much in shaping curricular change at Sagebrush, what is it?

The pursuit of prestige defines much of life at Sagebrush, particularly the organizational context within which change decisions are made. While it is quite easy for individual new courses to be taught by tenured faculty and even by tenure-track or temporary faculty so long as some department or administrative body is around to provide funding, the establishment of any more formal program is quite difficult. The University is eager to capitalize on innovation that can build its prestige, but is reluctant to formalize that innovation without assurances of the academic merit of new programs. This has had important consequences for the framing strategies that advocates of women's studies, Asian American studies, and queer studies used. Potential academic programs at Sagebrush have to be discussed in terms of intellectual excellence and be supported by clear academic justifications; proposals must include some argument that will convince administrators that these new programs will clearly add to Sagebrush's prestige. These justifications might include the ability to attract noteworthy faculty, the likelihood of graduating superior students, or the fact that Sagebrush might be left behind as other prestigious universities move forward. Yet being left behind, as noted above, has not always convinced Sagebrush administrators to act. In fact, in the case of both women's studies and Asian American studies, change was partially spurred only because of pressure from outside the University. In the case of women's studies, this was threats from state authorities about the dire consequences that might result from the failure to adopt an affirmative action policy; in the case of Asian American studies, this was pressure from elected officials to move forward on a program proposal. This external support—particularly for Asian American students—was only gained through the concerted efforts of campus activities to reach out to potential supporters beyond the campus borders.

Formal changes to the curriculum are also stymied by the multiple levels of approval required for program adoption, just as they were at Technopark. Programs require approval by various committees and administrators within the University as well as by the state system president. The low teaching load, with some faculty teaching just two courses a year, and the hefty administrative requirements at Sagebrush mean that offering even a minor program is likely to lead to budgetary conflicts. Furthermore, most faculty members at Sagebrush are primarily concerned with protecting their own research, reputation, and resources to the end. This makes them less likely to engage in the activism necessary for new initiatives, as well as much less likely to mentor and motivate student activists.

Just as was the case at Jeffrey, it seems that at Sagebrush faculty initiative can go a long way but will not result in the establishment of a new program without some student role.

Students themselves have not always played the role that they could have in curricular change initiatives, and this too reflects the prestige-seeking culture at Sagebrush. In the first half of Sagebrush's existence, roughly until the late 1980s and early 1990s, students were often involved in campus activism of various sorts. In more recent times, faculty members have recused themselves from sponsoring student activism. More importantly, they have at times actively discouraged or prevented students from engaging in activism, as was the case at the beginning of the ethnic studies proposal-drafting process. The fact that Sagebrush operates on a trimester system also limits students' availability for activism. Students who are themselves pursuing prestige and academic excellence in compressed terms requiring an intense degree of focus have little time for anything else. According to one student affairs professional on campus, today's Sagebrush students are not likely to get involved in campus activism or activities because of their academic schedules, which do not even leave much time in between terms to catch up.

The Sagebrush story is not only about the pursuit of prestige. Another important aspect of this story is the importance of connections between curricular changes and other issues on campus. Sagebrush has historically not been supportive of gender, race, or sexual orientation diversity. On some level, this may be a reflection of the pursuit of prestige, as the organizational focus remains fixated on excellence in academics rather than on equity. But prestige is not the only issue. Indeed, Sagebrush actively avoided hiring excellent candidates for tenure-track faculty positions in Asian American studies, candidates who would have contributed mightily to the prestige of the campus; it also limited the resources and support available to female faculty members and thus limited the intellectual contributions that they could make. Though there has been some progress, Sagebrush still employs a faculty more White and male than the average American university faculty despite being located in a region more diverse than average. Today's students may know less of these difficulties, but they are certainly aware of the disparities in enrollments of Blacks and Latino/as. The problems that students, faculty, and staff have faced on campus have lead to a variety of initiatives for change beyond academic programs. There have been campaigns about non-discrimination, about affirmative action, about campus resource centers, and about staff benefits. Many of these campaigns have been deeply connected to campaigns for curricular change. Indeed, both academic and non-academic change initiatives at Sagebrush have been rooted in broader movements for social change at the University and in the world, reflecting the roots of women's studies, Asian American studies, and queer studies as new knowledge movements.

Connections between curricular change initiatives and broader social movements can be seen in many of the case studies discussed so far, especially Abigail Adams College and Jeffrey University. There are other similarities between events at Sagebrush and events at Jeffrey, particularly regarding the queer studies dilemma. At both Sagebrush and Jeffrey, activist groups of non-instructional staff organized to pursue queer studies. While faculty and students were involved to greater or lesser degrees in these campaigns, the main initiatives remained with non-instructional staff, particularly those housed in student affairs. For research universities committed to academic prestige, the student affairs division is a poor site for the emergence of an academic initiative. Research universities may respond to student activism, but they want faculty figureheads to take on the responsibility of ensuring that programs are grounded in strong intellectual justifications. Non-instructional staff at Sagebrush and Jeffrey worked hard and made many changes in their universities, but without faculty sponsorship and student activism neither could achieve a queer studies program. Why were faculty and students so absent from these initiatives? For faculty at research universities, the pursuit of prestige and their own worries about tenure, teaching loads, and reputation-building activities are often more important than curricular change, no matter how committed they may be to the program in question. For students, the lack of time may matter. But another factor to consider is the lack of an enemy. When students mobilized for women's studies and for Asian American studies at both Jeffrey and Sagebrush, they were mobilizing in the face of universities and local communities that made their lives difficult in some sense or that embodied policies they saw as problematic and discriminatory. By the time that activism for queer studies reached its zenith at both Jeffrey and Sagebrush, being queer on campus was easy. Both are seen as great universities for queer students; both now boast visible populations of out queer faculty and offer some access to queer studies coursework. From the perspective of students who have many demands on their time and care about many political issues, why fight if there is no enemy?

Perhaps things will change one day and Sagebrush will eventually come to offer a queer studies program. Perhaps the gender studies program will finally be able to establish the graduate component that students have wanted for decades. Stranger things have happened. Places less hospitable to innovation have seen curricular change come their way. The College of Assisi, where we will travel next, is just such a place.

Chapter 8

Understanding Human Experience:
The College of Assisi

Nestled in a quiet residential neighborhood just a few miles from the center of its post-industrial New England city, the College of Assisi's tightly packed campus serves as home base for approximately 5,000 undergraduate and graduate students. These students live and study surrounded by the crosses that attest to Assisi's Catholic identity. The College was founded in the early 1900s by a conservative order of friars to educate Catholic young men. While its mission has expanded considerably over its century-long history, Assisi remains committed to the conservative Catholic teachings that guided its founding. Unlike at some Catholic colleges and universities, clergy at Assisi remain deeply involved in administration and teaching.

Assisi retained a focus on educating men until the 1970s, and as at many traditional liberal arts colleges, the decision to pursue coeducation was a difficult one. However, the campus had hosted female students long before it became formally coeducational. Its earliest female students were women religious (a term many prefer to the oft-used "nun"); later, laywomen were able to earn degrees through an extension program. Today more than 50 percent of students are female, a typical number for colleges like Assisi.

Though Assisi was originally founded to educate young men from the local area, its reputation has grown and now in-state students make up only about a tenth of the student body. Tuition and fees of approximately $40,000 in 2010 (room and board can easily add another $15,000), coupled with a somewhat lower endowment and thus financial aid budget than other New England liberal arts colleges, means that Assisi's students are predominantly of middle and upper class backgrounds. Assisi has also struggled to attract students of color; currently, only about 10 percent of students come from non-White backgrounds, and the College is actively pursuing student diversity by seeking international applicants. One thing that Assisi students do share in common is their academic ability; the College accepts well less than half of its applicants, making it more selective than the vast majority of colleges and universities in the United States even as it has not breached the top tier. The high graduation rate—over 80 percent of first year students go on to graduate from Assisi on schedule—and the student/faculty ratio of under 15 to one attest to the academic excellence of the campus as well. Students major in a wide variety of liberal arts and professional fields, with graduate training available in business, education, and religious studies. Though no courses or programs are available in Asian American studies or in queer studies, the College recently began offering an interdisciplinary major in women's studies. This new major draws on a well-established minor that had been founded a decade and a half earlier.

Everything is not about schoolwork, however. Assisi students follow their sports teams closely and like their parties. Since juniors and seniors may be permitted to live off campus, which about a fifth of students do, some of those parties occur away from the watchful eyes of administrators who have grown increasingly concerned about alcohol consumption on campus (though not concerned enough to shut down the campus pub). This active social life has not been matched by as active of political engagement, though the campus has occasionally been host to controversies over social issues.

"The Unity of the Human Family"

Interest in women's studies at the College of Assisi was present from the beginning of coeducation in the 1970s. During the transition to coeducation, the College formed a committee designed to ease the process of integration. Shortly after women arrived on campus as full-fledged members of the community, this committee formed a subcommittee to consider curricular issues. One of its first actions was to conduct a survey of students to gauge the level of interest in women's studies courses or programs as well as the current treatment of women in the general curriculum. However, the survey had a low response rate. Those students who did respond demonstrated demand for women's studies courses and for integration of women into the curriculum, as well as a small but significant interest in a women's studies certificate program. Perhaps the most notable survey finding was that many students complained about the erasure of women and women's experiences from the Western civilization courses required as part of the general education curriculum. Students were not interested in a major or in joining the curricular subcommittee at that time.

Beyond the survey of students, the curricular subcommittee also surveyed female faculty, who had been part of the campus community for several years before the student body became coeducational, and met with departments. The faculty survey had a higher response rate than did the student survey. About half of the female faculty on campus thought a women's studies program would be a good idea, and most were willing to teach in such a program. One faculty member, in explaining her support for women's studies, wrote that the benefits of the program would include female students "receiving adequate support and encouragement to make equal (though not necessarily the same) contributions to society as men."

Some faculty members were quite opposed to women's studies and suggested that it would serve to limit the integration of women into the campus community. The subcommittee's tour of academic departments also uncovered limited support. Many departments believed that increasing course offerings related to women was a good idea, particular as departments sought to attract female students as majors.

However, they also worried that a stand-alone women's studies program would lead to separatism and would undermine the idea of the liberal arts.

Though the subcommittee's explicit goal was the integration of women into the curriculum, it came to argue that a women's studies program could serve as a first step in that direction. When it completed its report, it noted that many of Assisi's peers, both Catholic and local non-Catholic colleges, already offered women's studies courses, while a few offered programs. Furthermore, it took the step of showing how women's studies could fit with the Catholic mission of the College, in particular by emphasizing "the personal autonomy of women" rather than "women's liberation." Yet despite their care in couching women's studies in Catholic terms, the subcommittee faced significant opposition to women's studies from many quarters of campus, and support was only lukewarm. Therefore, the subcommittee tabled the notion of a women's studies program and instead focused its resources on building a speaker's program. In addition, it developed women's studies pedagogy workshops and encouraged departments to offer more courses on women. The only notable curricular change resulting from this process was that a course on the history of women began being offered in the continuing education division. Though the speaker's program did get off the ground, the subcommittee seems to have disbanded soon after it began. Most of the energy around women's issues on campus became tied up in work on affirmative action and career services.

By the early 1980s, female students had become full-fledged members of the campus community and had started working to reshape the College according to their needs and interests. Their particular focus was on building a campus women's center. The center would have been fully staffed by students, and many on campus believed that its presence would have aided the continuing efforts to recruit more female students. However, there was significant opposition to this plan. Some opponents simply believed that a women's center was unnecessary and pointed to the various resources already available on campus, such the availability of women's literature in the library as well as services for women provided by the counseling center, career center, and health center. Others remembered the lack of interest in women's initiatives in the 1970s and suggested that this women's center initiative would suffer from a similar lack of interest. But the most notable opposition came from those who believed that a women's center would have negative consequences. These individuals argued that a women's center would promote female separatism, abortion, and birth control, and suggested that female students' needs would better be taken care of by women religious working on campus. The women's center was not established at that time.

By the early 1990s, things were a bit different. The first course that might be considered women's studies in the regular curriculum was listed in the 1990–91 course catalogue, though given the time delay in publishing catalogues at the College of Assisi it is likely that it was offered several years earlier. In addition, there were a number of courses in the early 1990s that included substantial women's studies content. Though course titles and descriptions did not always make their focus clear, students with an interest in women's studies knew where to go.

Faculty with an interest in women's studies worked hard to find students who might be receptive to their message. On this conservative campus populated with middle class Catholic youth, few had heard of women's studies. Few had even thought seriously about intellectual or political questions around the issue of gender—unless one counts the strong opposition to abortion and homosexuality that comes along with being a Catholic college. However, in the small number of courses in which the issue of gender surfaced, Assisi students began to do serious intellectual work on women. Faculty nurtured this spark and drew on it to create a yearly symposium in which students presented course papers and independent research on women. The students that presented at these symposia had no formal training in women's studies, but they worked hard to make the symposia successful. Students who presented at the symposia also helped to plan and run them, and they faced harassment from male faculty and students opposed to women's studies for doing so. The quality of the academic work presented was quite high, and the faculty who were involved in advocating for women's studies used this student work as proof that women's studies had the intellectual rigor necessary to exist as an academic program. An issue of the student newspaper published in the spring of 1993 suggested that the symposium was a key event in generating interest in and verifying the need for a women's studies major.

The symposium and the courses touching on women's issues worked to increase student interest in women's studies. In the winter of 1992, students and faculty came together to begin the process of planning a minor. They drew on what had come to be known as the "unofficial women's studies concentration," a group of eight courses that were taken by students with an interest in women's studies. Coupled with three courses then in the planning stages, this unofficial concentration spanned the disciplines, with courses in art, sociology, religion, politics, literature, business, and psychology. The planning committee originally intended to develop an interdisciplinary program based on the structure of the American studies program at Assisi. They were particularly interested in learning how to draft a proposal that would show that women's studies was not a threat to Catholicism. Towards that end, they researched women's studies programs at other Catholic colleges and universities. When a Catholic college in a nearby city held a conference specifically on women's studies curricula and Catholicism, the planning committee sent three faculty members to it. This conference helped the women at Assisi draft a proposal which framed women's studies in explicitly Catholic terms. They conceived of their program not as feminist but rather as womanist.

Womanism is a model of gender equality that emerges from a Black tradition of concern for the whole group (men *and* women) that "affirm[s] connectedness to the entire community and the world, rather than separation" (Walker 1983:81). Womanism thus rejects the White middle class feminism that seeks escape from domination in the home through satisfaction at work and instead asserts a unique emphasis on the history and experiences of Black women (particularly southern Black women) in which the home and the gender-integrated family is an escape from subjugation in the outside world. This tradition resonated with the values and mission of the College of Assisi because of its emphasis on gender integration and the centrality of the family, but it is still quite interesting to observe the claiming of a Black philosophical tradition by this White, northern, privileged college. With womanism as a starting point, the committee planned a program with a particular emphasis on women's spirituality, the history and achievements of women, and "the unity of the human family." The committee continued to work throughout the spring and over the summer of 1992, soliciting additional information from Catholic peer colleges and universities as well as starting a new lecture series on women's studies topics. The first session of this lecture series was called "Student Perspectives on Women's Studies."

"The Best Interests of Women"

The women's studies minor proposal was formally presented and debated in a faculty meeting in the spring of 1994, the second step in Assisi's short curricular change process, which requires proposals to be approved by the academic affairs committee, the faculty senate, and the president. Various faculty members had expressed concerns about the program, many of which echoed the criticisms of women's studies that had been put forward on campus since the earliest days of coeducation. Such claims included the fear that a women's studies program would lead to separatism, that it would isolate its students, and that it would jeopardize the campus reputation of its students. But the committee members were prepared. They responded by saying that a women's studies program would provide resources to help departments integrate women into their curricula, an argument that rehashes the claims of the earliest women's studies advocates (both at Assisi and across the United States) that the discipline might outlive its usefulness when gender was properly integrated into the rest of academia.

Further opposition came from a faculty member who stated that a culture cannot be understood without incorporating the experiences of both men and women. Of course, the Assisi curriculum had gone along for decades without incorporating the experiences of women at all, but some faculty believed that giving even a small part of the curriculum to women's perspectives would damage students' understandings of Western civilization—a key focus of the Assisi curriculum—irreparably. A more grave challenge came from those who believed that the women's studies program might, even if unintentionally, become a platform for "extreme views of feminism" that might undermine the central values of the College. In fact, as noted above, the faculty who had drafted the women's studies proposal had worked hard to keep it centrist in ideological orientation and thus to avoid the radical feminism which had characterized the early roots of many women's studies programs. This work was supported by a Catholic theologian who discussed feminism in

Catholicism at the very faculty meeting at which women's studies was debated. Faculty also emphasized the excellent academic work that students had presented at the symposia, and a student due to graduate in 1994 presented to the faculty meeting about the student need for a women's studies program.

Ultimately, this push was successful, and a women's studies minor was approved in the spring of 1994. The administration saw this approval as "throwing a bone" to the women on campus; the program's establishment, after all, was not asking much of them. A small grant from a local corporation with headquarters in the community as well as other funding initiatives helped finance the beginning of the program. The grant was part of a larger scholarship fund for female students and students of color, and in particular it helped fund a semi-annual forum on women and business that provided a key access point to women's studies for the many business majors on campus. The minor started with seven students and seven faculty participants. By 1996, it was cited as "the fastest-growing minor on campus."

Students had worked alongside the faculty women's studies committee by forming a women's student organization. This organization maintained close ties to the women's studies program, meeting in its office and co-sponsoring many events. The organization was founded particularly to help build the program, and in fact had support for building women's studies as an explicit part of its mission statement. A letter to the editor in the campus newspaper in 1993 stated that the organization was needed *because* of the lack of women's studies. When students first organized the group, its constitution stated that that it would "act in accordance with the missions and goals of the College if they [were] in the best interests of women." The clergyman with authority over student affairs did not approve this constitution, however, and required the group to delete the reference to women's interests. Unlike women's student groups on many campuses, this women's organization was open to men, and in fact a few male students took on leadership roles and functioned as spokespeople for the group.

Students in the group lobbied hard for the women's studies minor proposal and for its passage through the faculty senate. Additional curricular activities included exposing gender biases in the curriculum. But the group did not constrain itself to academic matters. In more recent years, it has become quite political. The group sponsored Take Back the Night rallies (part of a national series of events protesting sexual assault of women and calling for women to be able to walk at night without fear) and highlighted the high number of sexual assaults on campus, which were not taken as seriously as they might have been. These activities were met with verbal and physical harassment from other members of the campus community. The student group also performed *The Vagina Monologues* on campus, at least until they were shut down because "the overall tone of the *Monologues* did not fit in with the school's mission statement."

Alongside this increased student activity, the women's studies program continued to grow. By 1997, students were creating self-designed majors in women's studies through a program that allowed them to take a full complement of women's studies courses alongside a major in a traditional discipline. Some faculty began to consider creating a special curricular focus in Black women's studies, but that initiative did not take off. In 2003, the faculty sought to hire a full-time equivalent faculty member in women's studies, but they were unable to win approval. However, there are now two dozen faculty members involved in the women's studies program, of whom seven have formal joint appointments.

In 2006, there were five students completing self-designed majors in women's studies, enough that faculty who had never dreamed it possible realized they might be able to go ahead with a major proposal. Yet at the same time, women's studies was not yet fully accepted on campus, particularly among students. In the words of one women's studies faculty member, students "pay for it with their peers" when they take women's studies courses. Despite the lack of acceptance, faculty were able to point to strong student interest and the cumbersome self-designed major process to win approval for a major in spring 2007, 14 years after the minor was introduced. About ten women's studies courses are offered each semester, almost all of which are interdisciplinary—to be included in the women's studies program, a course need only devote half of its content to women's issues. But the focus remains squarely on women, and the faculty continue to believe it is important to avoid turning the focus back towards men.

Challenges remain. There are some limits on course content, with discussions of birth control not possible in the curriculum. While issues of homosexuality and transgender identity are discussed, instructors avoid mentioning them in course descriptions or on syllabi. Incoming students remain conservative, in keeping with the traditions of the College, and despite lingering gender inequity, the administration remains convinced that a gender equity study is unnecessary. However, women's studies faculty with many years of service at Assisi are proud of what they have accomplished. In less than two decades, their campus has gone from one almost entirely hostile to the study of women to one with a full-fledged major.

"To Respect and Understand"

The process of attaining a women's studies program at the College of Assisi was long and slow, but the program does exist and seems to be—for the time being— on solid footing. Asian American and queer communities on campus have not attained such outcomes. Their experiences have differed in significant ways.

Less than three percent of students at the College of Assisi come from Asian American backgrounds, and the campus does not have a long history of responding to racial issues. The first program in "multicultural awareness" was not developed on campus until 1990 (many other colleges and universities had started engaging in such activities in the late 1960s or early 1970s). In the early 1990s, campus energy around race, ethnicity, and the curriculum was primarily absorbed by issues related to the exclusion of people of color from the mandatory Western civilization curriculum. More recently, the College administration has sought to increase racial diversity on campus, but has found it challenging to do so.

Though Asian American students are quite active in multicultural programming on campus, they have not pushed for Asian American studies. A large percentage of Asian American students at Assisi do identify as panethnically Asian American. However, many others, particularly those from Southeast Asian refugee communities, continue to identify with their specific ethnic origins. These students appear to be quite satisfied with the curricular opportunities available in Asian Studies. Asian Studies offers an interdisciplinary minor program which has attained considerable support on campus, and even a recent series of articles in the student newspaper about diversity issues on campus has focused little attention on the Asian American community. It is thus fair to say that a major reason why Asian American studies cannot be found at the College of Assisi is because there has been no sustained effort to create it.

Queer students on campus are another story entirely. Given Assisi's identity as a conservative Catholic college, it may seem at first that there is little to discuss about queer studies there. In fact, the dynamics of lesbian and gay student lives at Assisi are quite interesting, and perhaps rather illuminating to discussions of campus change. As in the case of women's studies, the climate for queer students today is quite different from what it was like several decades ago.

Throughout the 1990s—and undoubtedly in earlier periods as well—students at Assisi found it rather difficult to even engage in consciousness-raising around issues of sexuality. For instance, even though at least one Assisi alum has made a career in AIDS research, students were forbidden to discuss safe sex as a means of AIDS prevention or even to publish in the student newspaper a letter from Magic Johnson that mentioned safe sex. The campus environment for lesbian and gay students, especially for gay men, was quite hostile. Students were openly homophobic and some gay students felt that they were forced to move off campus to avoid harassment.

Despite—or perhaps because of—the hostile environment, students had wished for and tried to build a queer student group beginning in the early 1990s. A comparative study of other Catholic campuses showed that a number had approved such groups, though this was particularly likely in situations in which lawsuits or assertive student movements forced the administrations' hands. Yet the Assisi administration continued to fear that a queer student group would recruit students into homosexuality, serve primarily as a venue for locating sex partners, and open the campus to outside opprobrium. While students at some colleges and universities are able to form student organizations without official administrative approval so long as they do not seek funding, Assisi's student organization policies prevented unrecognized groups from so much as hanging fliers on campus. Despite administrative disapproval and restrictive organizational policies, there was an underground queer student group in the mid-1990s.

In the early 2000s, students again sought formal approval for a gay-straight alliance organization. Earning approval for a new student organization at the College of Assisi is a two-step process. First, the prospective organization must win approval from the student government; then, the administration must approve the group. While the student government was eventually persuaded to approve the gay-straight alliance, administrative approval was more difficult to attain. The administration required that the gay-straight alliance devise a constitution that would not "promote the homosexual lifestyle or deem it morally permissible." Students worked with the clergyman in charge of student affairs over the summer of 2001 to draft an acceptable constitution, and in the fall students collected more than 200 signatures in one week in support of the organization. Ultimately, it was approved.

Yet even these narrow parameters for action provided the group with an important mission on campus. It would work to educate the campus that even if Catholic doctrine was opposed to same-sex sexual relations, it also did not approve of homophobic harassment and attacks. Thus, as the gay-straight alliance began to organize itself, it focused its attention on stopping homophobia and restoring dignity and tolerance while arguing that it was nevertheless important to "respect and understand" those who have a "moral disagreement with the homosexual lifestyle." As might be expected, Assisi still does not include sexual orientation in its non-discrimination statement, and lesbian and gay students still face harassment on campus. But now they have a source of support to make their time on campus more tolerable, and they have a way to educate other segments of the campus community about the impact of homophobia.

Because of Assisi's Catholic mission, even women's studies faculty find it difficult to include much discussion of queer experiences in their courses. Of twenty courses currently listed in the women's studies program, not one mentions sexuality issues in the course description. While official Catholic doctrine teaches that homosexuality is a sin, Assisi's foundation in a tradition of Catholic education that emphasizes the roles of argumentation and diversity does allow room for considering the dynamics of homophobia as well as "alternative ways of defining human experience." However, these discussions always must be pursued without casting aspersions on Catholic teachings. As noted above, faculty members do not mention discussions of sexuality on their syllabi even when some such discussions may arise as part of class sessions.

A few faculty members are supportive of increasing coverage of sexuality issues in courses, and a curricular program that emphasizes preparation for public service careers employs a flexible curriculum that allows students with an interest in homophobia or sexuality issues to pursue these interests. One alumna said she thinks that it is possible that the curriculum could become more objective in relation to issues of sexuality, but that even this small change would require the persistence of key students and faculty members. Of course, formal consideration of queer studies topics in the curricula of Catholic colleges and universities is rare (though Catholic DePaul University does offer a minor in LGBT studies), even among colleges and universities founded in more liberal Catholic traditions than Assisi's. Yet given Assisi's traditions and mission, the fact that the campus today offers a queer student group and a few courses in which homophobia can be discussed objectively is worth noting.

Assisi stands out in some ways as different from the other five colleges and universities we have considered. Each presented its own unique obstacles to curricular change—students spread too thin by the responsibilities of school, home and work; faculty whose sense of propriety is offended by the intrusion of new areas of study into the curriculum; combative organizational politics; and all the other issues faculty and students at the five colleges and universities faced in trying to get their programs off the ground. The movement for women's studies at Assisi may have faced the most significant obstacle of all—at the start, the organizational ethos at the College of Assisi was deeply opposed to the mission of women's studies. Here, it was not that a few powerful faculty members could not abide transformations in what is considered academically meritorious, it was that they saw women's studies as contradicting the very underpinnings of their College's value system. Yet somehow, faculty and students committed to women's studies found a way to build a minor and then a major in their field. How was this possible? What enabled them—and all the program supporters who did so at the other five colleges and universities—to succeed? This question will be answered in the chapter that follows.

PART III
Analysis

Chapter 9

Moving Curricular Change: The Process and Product of Change Campaigns

Women's studies activists at the College of Assisi made a major impact on their campus. They emerged when the college had only just opened to women and was hostile to any initiative that suggested feminism; today, they've created a vibrant and institutionalized women's studies program that participants are proud of. On the other hand, queer studies activists at Jeffrey University operated on a campus that some see as a Mecca for queer students and that has a history of openness to new and experimental academic initiatives. Yet after years of organizing and activism at Jeffrey, no queer studies program was developed, and in fact the queer studies initiative has probably taken several steps backwards from where it was a decade ago. These two cases—women's studies at the College of Assisi and queer studies at Jeffrey University—represent just two of the potential outcomes of movements for curricular change at colleges and universities.

Given the three areas of study and the six colleges and universities considered in this book, there were eighteen potential instances of curricular change. In four of these instances, no campaign for curricular change developed; in four, curricular change was sought but did not materialize (three involved contentious politics, while one relied only on the normal shared governance approach); and in the remaining ten, new programs were developed (see Table 9.1 for a summary of these outcomes). Students played a role in all ten of the cases in which curricular change did occur; students were also involved in three of the four cases in which campaigns for curricular change did not produce new programs. Faculty played a role in all fourteen campaigns—a point that is a notable corrective to those who believe that faculty participation is unimportant in campus social movement activism (Bayer 1972; Lipset 1976). The case studies presented in Chapters 3 through 8 demonstrate, however, that the extent of student involvement, the dynamics of that involvement, and the role of faculty in these campaigns varied considerably—as did the outcomes of these campaigns for curricular change.

All thirteen of these cases involved organized campaigns of contentious politics directed at achieving a particular goal and utilizing actions that went beyond or outside institutionalized means in an attempt to achieve this goal. Thus, though definitions of social movements vary, I believe that all 13 qualify as social movements. This chapter, then, will examine the variation between the 13 cases in which movements for curricular change were active (excluding the one case, Asian American studies at Technopark, in which change was—unsuccessfully—sought

Table 9.1   Outcomes of Curricular Change Efforts across the Six Cases

	Women's Studies	Asian American Studies	Queer Studies
Abigail Adams College	Major	Certificate	Minor
Promenade University	Minor	No Campaign	No Campaign
Technopark University	Major (recent)	No Program—shared governance approach only	Campaign, but no program
Jeffrey University	Major	Minor	Campaign, but no program
Sagebrush University	Major	Ethnic Studies only	Campaign, but no program
The College of Assisi	Major (recent)	No Campaign	No Campaign

by non-movement actors) and will use this variation to explain why the outcomes of these campaigns were so different.

Insider Activists and Insider Activism

Though movements aimed at changing organizations often consist of outsiders looking in at organizational practices and using tactics like boycotts and publicity campaigns as bargaining chips (Burstein et al. 1995) to encourage change, as in the animal rights movement and the anti-sweatshop movement, movements also occur *inside* organizations. In these cases, the shape of activism may be quite different from what social movement analysts have come to expect. Most theoretical models of social movements are based on an understanding of movement activists as outsiders without access to the power resources of the states that they are targeting and of movement strategy as relying on non-institutionalized tactics such as protests and demonstrations. However, insider activists do have access to some of the power resources of the organizations they target, at least some of the time, and frequently do rely on institutionalized tactics.

There are important differences between insider activism as part of social movements or social-movement-like campaigns and what one could call "reform from within." Santoro and McGuire, in their work on insider activism within the state, explain insider activists as

... social movement participants who occupy formal statuses within the government and who pursue movement goals through conventional bureaucratic channels. Institutional activists are polity members in that they have routine, low-cost access to decision-makers ... Unlike traditional movement actors, institutional activists experience pressure to engage solely in institutional tactics ... [They] hold formal positions within the polity and use their offices' resources to affect policy change. (Santoro and McGuire 1997:504–6)

Santoro and McGuire's model suggests that insider activists will be more important when those individuals with the potential to act as activists are more prominent within their organization, when there is general hostility within the organization to the goals of the activists, and when the activists' goals are highly complex. Insiders, to Santoro and McGuire, are those who have access to structural power within the organization, such as a highly-ranking executive in a corporation. In contrast, where insiders exist, but where goals are simple and relatively acceptable to the organization, change can be enacted through the "reform-from-within" process, or what Katzenstein calls "unobtrusive mobilization" without resort to contentious activism in which "institutional routines are disrupted and the norms of an organization contested" (1998:9).

There are, in fact, two types of insiders within organizations. One is the type that Santoro and McGuire describe: the insider who has access to structural power within the organization, such as elected officials in state-based movements or a highly-ranking executive in a corporation. The other is the regular rank-and-file insider—an insider who is structurally marginalized and thereby "excluded from important institutional decisions" (Grossman 2010).[1] Though lower-level bureaucrats could perhaps serve this function in state-based movements, in so far as their jobs give them routine access to information about the inner workings of government, this type of insider is much more common in movements targeting organizations. The study of labor movements could perhaps be seen in this light, notwithstanding the often large gap between the study of labor movements and the study of other forms of collective behavior—individual workers, particularly in smaller workplaces, know quite a bit about the internal dynamics of their organizations, and in some cases do have routine (if not low-cost) access to decision-makers. Katzenstein (1998) further suggests that we can determine the degree to which activists count as insiders by exploring their accountability to the organization in terms of finances (whether activists are funded by the organization

---

1 Even though faculty members do have significant decision-making authority in terms of the curriculum at most institutions, this research has shown that the normal shared governance process did not play a significant role in enabling the curricular changes discussed here. Instead, the faculty members who advocated for women's studies, Asian American studies, and/or queer studies often did feel structurally marginalized within the decision making apparatus of their college or university. This issue will be taken up in more detail in the Conclusion.

in some way), organizational authority and structure (whether activists are in some way subject to the authority of the organization), and discursive elements (whether activists identify with the organization).

Insiders and outsiders often work together. Insider activists may face structural limitations on what they can ask for or accomplish, while outsiders may maintain significant political strength. Working together in a situation of trust and good communication (Eisenstein 1996), insiders and outsiders can limit their vulnerabilities and maximize their strengths as part of a strategic organizational process to maximize outcomes. Essential in this process are mediators, who Kelly Moore defines as "individuals who are members of a movement and also professional members of an institution ... mediators are likely to occupy marginal positions with respect to institutional membership, movement membership, or both" (1999:104). These mediators are able to translate movement claims into organizational action. At the same time, however, Moore notes that though organizational professionals appear to have the most organizational power, it is only through a combination of the activities of mediators and the employment of "innovative and disruptive action" (1999:114) that movements targeting organizations can make a difference.

Social movement theory is thus beginning to understand the importance of considering movements that target organizations. Scholars have taken some noteworthy steps towards developing an understanding of how such movements work, including Raeburn's work on lesbian and gay workplace rights (2004), Katzenstein's work on feminist movements in the Church and the military (1998), Binder's study of efforts to promote creation studies and Afrocentrism in the schools (2002), Rao and Sivakumar's study on the emergence of investor relations departments in large corporations (1999), Rao's broader study of movements targeting markets (2009), Epstein's work on HIV activism (Epstein 1996), Rojas's work on African American studies (2006), Wilde's study of Vatican II as a social movement (Wilde 2004), Meyerson's work on tempered radicals in the workplace (Meyerson 2001; Meyerson and Scully 1995, 1999; Meyerson and Tompkins 2007), and Yamane's study of student movements for multiculturalism (2001). Armstrong and Bernstein have developed the multi-institutional politics perspective to consider movements targeting social institutions, a perspective that leaves room for exploring the roles of culture, strategic choices, and insider activists (2008)— indeed, Armstrong and Bernstein argue that challengers are *often* insiders and that "challenges by those outside of the institution being challenged are expected to be less frequent than challenges by insiders or those with a semi-marginal position" (p. 92). But despite these advances in the scholarship of movements targeting organizations, we are still left without a clear framework for understanding how and when such movements are able to make an impact on the organizations that they target.

The Organizational Mediation Model

The organizational mediation model responds to several of the limitations of existing schools of social movement theory. It is a model designed to explain how and why social movements targeting organizations are able to have an impact on those organizations. The organizational mediation model draws on the strengths of political mediation theory (Amenta and Caren 2004; Amenta et al. 2005; Amenta, Halfmann, and Young 1999), which is designed to explain the outcomes of movements targeting the state, but the organizational mediation model incorporates several modifications to make the theory applicable to movements that target organizations. Like political mediation theory, the organizational mediation model argues that movements will be more likely to have an impact when their strategic choices align with the context in which they operate. However, the organizational mediation model alters the conception of context (here called "organizational context" instead of "political context") to take into account the particulars of organizations; incorporates an understanding of framing and insider activism into the conception of strategic choice; and incorporates an understanding of institutionalization into the measurement of impacts, given the fact that innovations in organizations are often temporary in nature.

The organizational context consists of two primary elements: first, the favorability of the organizational mission to the proposed changes, and second, administrative openness and flexibility. Additional secondary aspects of the organizational context may include aspects of organizational structure and control and organizational resources; these, however, do lead to a significant complication of the model and thus for parsimony's sake I will focus only on the primary elements of context. Movement strategy consists of three primary elements: whether strategies are assertive or assimilative in nature, whether activists position themselves as insiders or as outsiders, and the types of framing strategies and audiences for frames that are selected. The organizational mediation model argues that when movements make strategic choices that conform to the elements of organizational context outlined above, they will have a greater chance of achieving their goals. Table 9.2 outlines the predictions that the organizational mediation model makes about the alignment of strategy and context that is most likely to produce a movement's desired outcomes.

Organizational Context

While the organizational mediation model as described above is a general model that could be applied to a wide variety of social movements targeting organizations, the model needs to be further specified before it can be used in any particular set of circumstances. In other words, the particular details of the organizational context that are important for a given social movement must be clarified before analysis can begin. Given this book's focus on social movements with the goal of establishing new curricular programs in women's studies, Asian American

Table 9.2   Aligning Strategy with Context in the Organizational Mediation Model

Organizational Mission

		Favorable	Unfavorable
Administrative Openness/Flexibility	Open	I: Assertive tactics; framing that resonates with core constituency	II: Assimilative tactics; framing that resonates with core constituency
	Closed	III: Assertive tactics; framing that supports core mission	IV: Assimilative tactics; framing that supports core mission

studies, and queer studies, the organizational context here includes the college or university mission and the openness and flexibility of the upper administration of the college or university.

There are several key elements of the organizational mission that contribute to its overall degree of favorability to any given change attempt. The first element is whether the college or university's primary academic mission is centered in the liberal arts or is focused on vocational and professional training. Those colleges which place the highest value on graduating students with specific marketable credentials and skill sets will be favorable to curricular changes that increase the marketability of their graduates, but are less likely to be favorable to curricular changes that emphasize the liberal arts. The second element is the degree to which the college is favorable towards interdisciplinarity and other challenges to the established organization of knowledge in the academy. Some colleges and universities structure themselves to make innovations that go beyond the historically-entrenched disciplinary structure quite difficult (Klein 1990, 1996; Lattuca 2001; Peterson 2009), while others create openings for such innovations. Finally, colleges have varied values and ideologies. Particularly important for the cases considered here are religious affiliations, values around diversity, and commitments (or the lack thereof) to social justice work. Such values and ideologies can shape organizational priorities quite significantly, and can in turn alter the calculus an organization engages in when considering claims made by social movements.

Most colleges and universities are required by their accrediting agencies to craft and make available a mission statement that addresses some or all of these dimensions of favorability, but this statement may not line up with the lived reality of organizational mission. As Amitai Etzioni has written,

... the *stated* goals of an organization can serve as a clue to the actual goals of the organization. But a researcher cannot uncritically accept the stated goals of the organization as its actual sociological goals, since organizations tend to hold 'public' goals for 'front' purposes. Nor can he elicit this information from the top elites of the organization, since they may not be free to communicate these goals to the researcher. (Etzioni 1975:104)

Therefore, instead of relying on statements of organizational mission, the researcher must consider the ongoing process of the production of organizational goals and the perspective of organizational insiders.

The degree to which a college or university exhibits administrative openness and flexibility consists of two interconnected factors. Most importantly, openness depends on administrative willingness to consider input from non-administrative organizational insiders, particularly students and faculty members. Colleges and universities which are willing to consider such input may demonstrate this by including students and faculty on key committees and as part of other governance structures, by allowing students and faculty to select their own representatives rather than being subject to administrative appointments for committee service, by allowing non-members to attend and speak at meetings of governing boards, and by providing other similar opportunities for formal consultation and participation. There are also more informal ways in which administrators may demonstrate their willingness to listen to students and faculty, such as by being generally accessible on campus or holding open office hours. The second element here is the element of flexibility. Flexibility may be constrained by rigid and hierarchical organizational structures, state-mandated articulation agreements, financial crises, and other similar factors. Where flexibility is constrained, it is harder for change to occur—though, of course, it is not impossible. Table 9.3 lays out four ideal types of organizational context representing the intersections of mission and openness/ flexibility to demonstrate the potential variation in organizational context that could occur.

Movement Strategy

Social movements targeting organizations, just like other social movements, are faced with a variety of strategic decisions that shape the way they approach their targets. Primary among them is the consideration of how assertive tactics should be. The assertiveness of tactics that movements use against their organizational targets can be judged in much the same way that it would be for social movements targeting the state: petitions and letter-writing campaigns are non-assertive tactics, while building occupations and violent demonstrations are highly assertive. In between are all manner of other tactics seen in movements targeting organizations: teach-ins, mass meetings, peaceful demonstrations and rallies, and other tactics. The organizational mediation model argues that more assertive tactics will be necessary for movements to make an impact when they

Table 9.3   Ideal Types of Organizational Context in the Organizational Mediation Model

Organizational Mission

		Favorable	Unfavorable
Administrative Openness/Flexibility	Open	I: Interdisciplinary liberal arts focused; democratic leadership	II: Vocational or religious; community-centered governance structures
	Closed	III: Interdisciplinary liberal arts focused; hierarchical or inflexible leadership	IV: Vocational or religious; authoritarian governance structures

face *more* favorable contexts, while more assimilative tactics will be necessary in *less* favorable contexts. This prediction is the opposite of that made by the political mediation model (Amenta 2006; Amenta and Caren 2004; King 2008), but the political mediation model was developed to apply to formally democratic states. In democratic states, the sanctions that can be applied to activists are typically circumscribed (imprisonment and other legal sanctions are often the most severe penalties available, and where freedom of speech and assembly are preserved, these are limited to the most assertive and disruptive protests). In organizations, on the other hand, the penalty of permanent exile from the organization remains available to organizational leaders as a tool of repression, and organizational leaders can also call in the repressive force of the state to intervene on their behalf. Activists in unfavorable contexts have, of course, greater reason to fear the application of such sanctions—and even minor job sanctions such as negative comments on a performance evaluation can play a significant role in stifling dissent (Katzenstein 1998), which highlights the degree to which perceptions of risk affect organizational activism. Using highly assertive tactics in situations with unfavorable organizational contexts also might further reduce the likelihood of having your voice heard (King 2008), especially when organizations retain power over exile and over intra-organizational communications. On the other hand, where the context is open and favorable, movements that do not engage in assertive tactics simply may not be heard above the fray of others articulating their own interests and demands.

The degree of risk borne by participants, then, can be used as a proxy for assertiveness. Organizational outsiders can choose highly assertive tactics without fear of reprisals, and in fact may even be "compelled" to use such tactics, while organizational insiders are subject to reprisals and at the same time able to shape their strategic choices in such a way as to make them conform to the norms, procedures, and practices of their organizations (Grossman 2005). Alternatively, organizational activists may choose to break norms—where activists targeting the state would break laws—as away to disrupt "long-settled assumptions, rules, and practices" (Katzenstein 1998:7). On average, however, activists inside organizations will use somewhat less assertive tactics than activists targeting democratic states might; the risk of severe sanctions like exile is much higher within organizations. Instead, the tactics directed at organizational targets aim to create a situation in which "institutional routines are disrupted and the norms of an organization contested" (Katzenstein 1998:9); it is this disruption that then enables movements to have an impact (King 2008; King and Pearce 2010). One example of this type of tactic—one that is assertive and disruptive within an organization but which might not be seen as such in a different type of context—would be the "baby-in" that feminist activists held at the University of Illinois Chicago to demand access to campus child care (Gardiner 2002; Strobel 2000). Similarly, Sucheng Chan refers to her practice of "guerrilla warfare"[2] inside the university in which backstage pressure on administrators forces capitulation to activists' demands (2005:174). Specific features of individual organizations, however, will influence the degree to which particular tactical choices are viewed as assertive or assimilative. In some organizations, a rally might be quite an ordinary occurrence (think of how many protests of various sorts have occurred across the last five decades at the University of California Berkeley), while at others, even a petition campaign would be out of the ordinary.

Movements targeting organizations, unlike movements targeting states, have to grapple with the additional question of whether to engage in activism as insider activists or as outsider activists. This is actually quite a complex question. All organizations include some individuals who are complete insiders, such as high-level executives or administrators. All organizations also circumscribe some individuals—including those who might participate in a social movement targeting that organization—as complete outsiders (this is particularly the case for those who lack a legitimate or formalized relationship to the organization, such as employee, student, or customer). But most potential movement participants will fall somewhere between these two poles. In the cases considered in this book, these movement participants include students, faculty, and staff; all three of these groups are dually situated as insiders and as outsiders. Depending on the specific details of the organizational context and on the strategic choices made by a movement, students, faculty, and staff can slide back and forth along the spectrum between insider and outsider status. The organizational mediation model predicts that activists will be

---

2   Chan's *In Defense of Asian American Studies* (2005) offers an unusual look at the tactics behind Asian American studies activism by providing primary source documents she wrote over her many years as an activist for and teacher and administrator of Asian American studies in the University of California system. Her words are wonderful source material for readers who want to see how the tactical framing process works and hear the first-person words of someone involved in contentious insider activism.

more likely to have an impact when they act as insiders, though some organizations may be willing to consider the claims of outsider activists as well.

The third element of strategic decision-making relates to framing issues, which are of increased importance for movements targeting organizations (Davies 1999; Rojas 2006). Social movements have broad latitude in shaping and deploying frames. However, in order to match their strategic choices to the organizational context, they must choose frames that conform to the organization's mission and self-perception, and these frames must resonate with movement participants as well as with conscience constituencies (Jenkins 1983; McCarthy and Zald 1977) and other organizational insiders. More specifically, movements must develop diagnostic frames that clearly specify a problem that others within the organization agree is problematic. They must develop prognostic frames that propose a solution that fits with the mission and values of the organization and which seems possible. And they must develop motivational frames that convince potential movement participants and conscience constituents that the problem is important, enduring, and worth devoting time to and accepting risk for. Successful frames use "the vocabularies and conceptual schemes" of the organization, "forcing credentialed experts to deal with their arguments" and using "pre-existing lines of cleavage" within the organization (Epstein 1996:335–6) as well as translating demands into "official institutional language" (Grossman 2010:660).

Each particular college or university is unique, and therefore the ideal framing strategies will conform to that particular college or university. For instance, at a university concerned with prestige, framing strategies ought to emphasize the ways in which the desired reforms will enhance, or at least not detract from, that prestige. Or at a religious college, framing strategies might need to demonstrate how the desired reforms will conform to the religious mission. Despite the context-specific nature of framing, there are some broader arguments that the organizational mediation model can make about the shaping and deployment of framing strategies. In contexts that are marked by administrative openness and flexibility, framing strategies are best targeted at the movement's core constituency and should resonate with them in order to help build mobilization and support; this corresponds to Guigini and Yamasaki's argument that movement impacts often occur through movements' creation of public opinion and alliances (Guigini and Yamasaki 2009). The types of frames used in open and flexible contexts, then, might include arguments about how the proposed innovation would benefit members of the constituency personally or help them to achieve their own broader goals. In contrast, movements which face contexts that are closed and/or inflexible need framing strategies that conform more closely to the organizational mission in order to ensure that they are heard by organizational administrators. These types of frames might include arguments about how the proposed innovation supports or even is made necessary by the organizational mission or discussions of how the innovation would support financial or prestige gains by the college or university; these frames might include those drawing on a market-based or neoinstitutional logic for change. Framing can additionally be used as a "public relations" strategy to appeal to broader audiences

(King 2008; King and Pearce 2010) and thus gain greater organizational support for movement goals (Guigini and Yamasaki 2009).

Testing the Model

The analysis here relies on the thirteen instances of attempted curricular change in which there was some sort of initiative by students and faculty outside of the normal shared governance process to push for a particular curricular change (of the fourteen instances in which change was sought, one—Asian American studies at Technopark University—did not include any such contentious politics and is thus excluded from this analysis). Each of the six colleges and universities included in this book are classified in Table 9.4 as to their positions in terms of mission favorability and administrative openness and flexibility; these classifications are further discussed in the text, along with the strategic choices made by and the outcomes of each movement.

Table 9.4   Classifying the Cases by Organizational Context

		Organizational Mission	
		Favorable	Unfavorable
Administrative Openness/Flexibility	Open	I: Jeffrey; Abigail Adams (late)	II: Technopark
	Closed	III: Sagebrush; Abigail Adams (early)	IV: Promenade; Assisi

Favorable Mission and Open/Flexible Administrations

Two out of the six case study campuses display favorable organizational missions and open and flexible administrations: Jeffrey University and, after a presidential change in the mid-1980s, Abigail Adams College. Jeffrey University has a long history of support for interdisciplinarity, first offering students the opportunity for self-designed majors in the 1960s and providing a variety of interdisciplinary academic programs and experimental courses. Jeffrey emphasizes the undergraduate liberal arts component of its educational program to a greater extent than do many other public flagship universities, and it has a strong commitment to student diversity. Students have a formal role in campus governance and both undergraduate and graduate students have been able to create their own academic courses. New academic initiatives have found homes in the continuing education division before they were ready for formal administrative approval. Faculty have felt able to speak out on campus issues without fear of reprisals, though the increasing prestige focus of the university has caused some faculty to limit political involvement in more recent years.

Abigail Adams College is deeply committed to women's undergraduate liberal arts education, student leadership in curricular and other campus affairs, and diversity of all kinds. Though it does not have as extensive of a history of interdisciplinarity as Jeffrey University does, a variety of interdisciplinary programs do exist on campus. Students have a formal role in curricular and other campus governance; an Abigail Adams faculty member told a national news publication that students might have more power than faculty on campus, despite the faculty senate that maintains control over curricular decision-making. Though faculty members have sometimes faced warnings that activism could affect tenure prospects, the campus has become more accepting of faculty involvement in contentious politics. Furthermore, the small size of the campus has meant that faculty, students, and administrators know each other and are available to one another.

The organizational mediation model predicts that movements in favorable and open/flexible contexts have the greatest chance to make an impact if they choose assertive tactics and develop frames that resonate with their core constituencies. Of the five movements located in such organizational contexts, two chose the assertive and constituent-directed strategies expected to result in impacts—the movements for women's studies and Asian American studies at Jeffrey University. Both of these movements made an impact. Women's studies activists held a teach-in and were able to credibly threaten a shut-down of the university with building takeovers. They began their campaign with a "feminist studies" frame that resonated strongly with their core constituency, but later broadened to a "women's studies" frame that used the trappings of a conventional discipline and arguments about resource allocation to convince a wider audience of the necessity of women's studies. These activists were able to obtain a major program in women's studies well before such programs were established on other campuses. While the campaign for Asian American studies at Jeffrey began with assimilative tactics, activists later occupied a building for six days, an action that drew national attention. Activists developed framing strategies that focused on the importance of learning one's own history for understanding one's experiences, claims that resonated with their core audience, while simultaneously arguing that Asian American studies was a legitimate object of academic inquiry. The Asian American studies program at Jeffrey was approved just two years after the building occupation.

Two movements, those for Asian American studies and queer studies at Abigail Adams College, chose assertive tactics but used framing strategies that were not constituent-directed. Though both had small but real impacts, they did experience some unique circumstances that may explain their deviation from expectations. Asian American studies activists primarily relied on lectures and conferences rather than assertive tactics, though they did support students at another campus who engaged in a building takeover at a nearby college by engaging in a sympathy walk-out. On a small campus where individual students' actions are noticeable, a walk-out is a fairly assertive tactic. Activists engaged in little framing activity directed towards either administrators or constituents. Though a certificate program was approved, it relies heavily on nearby colleges for courses and faculty and thus has made a limited impact on Abigail Adams itself. Queer studies activists began by using assertive tactics such as a rally early in the campaign, though later activists primarily used assimilative techniques. This pattern supports Linders's observation that "new outcomes can and do unfold long after the active involvement of movements have ceased" (2004:376). Framing strategies concentrated on campus need; they were more clearly resonant with the Abigail Adams's mission than with the activists' primary constituency. However, because women's studies faculty eventually developed an interest in queer studies and the ability to revise their own curriculum, student activists were less dependent on a wide campus hearing than they might otherwise have been. Ultimately, the queer studies program was developed as part of the women's studies program.

The movement for queer studies at Jeffrey University did not choose the strategies that organizational mediation model predicts would lead to impacts, and it did not result in curricular change. While some of the tactics queer studies activists used were novel and innovative, such as the development of one of the first GLB campus climate reports in the nation, none were disruptive or assertive in any significant way. In addition, the movement was unable to develop a coherent and resonant framing strategy—faculty could not agree on a common intellectual grounding for a program, and students claimed that queer studies would resolve campus problems for queer students but never explained how. A queer studies program thus was never developed at Jeffrey University.

Unfavorable Missions and Open/Flexible Administrations

Technopark University displays an unfavorable mission coupled with an open and flexible administration. Though Technopark does value education in the liberal arts, other aspects of its mission predominate: science, technology, and professional education, preparing students for professional futures, local economic development, and emerging areas of graduate study. The American studies program has served as a focal point for interdisciplinary academic innovations on campus, but is limited to working in areas in which its own faculty members have interest and expertise. Though Technopark is somewhat constrained by the many hurdles erected by the state governing board for approval of new majors, minors are not so constrained. Students have formal roles in campus governance and participate in a strong and active student government. Despite its size, students, faculty, and staff have retained easy access to deans and other administrators. Faculty—including adjuncts—have felt able to engage in campus activism without endangering their careers and have maintained significant academic freedom; though one early women's studies supporter was denied tenure, this was likely due more to her involvement in non-academic activism than her involvement in women's studies.

The organizational mediation approach predicts that movements targeting open and flexible administrations in organizations that nonetheless have unfavorable missions will have the greatest likelihood of making an impact if they choose assimilative tactics and develop frames that resonate with their core constituency. The movement for women's studies at Technopark did just this and had an impact, while the movement for queer studies chose assimilative tactics but lacked resonant framing strategies and thus did not have an impact on the campus curriculum. The main push for women's studies came through backstage negotiations rather than assertive tactics, though some of the same activists used assertive tactics in other movements in which they were involved. Framing strategies emphasized the role that women's studies would play in the lives of female students and faculty, and thus resonated with the core constituency. Women's studies activists were able to create a certificate program and ultimately a major despite the difficult curricular change process at Technopark. Queer studies activists also relied on backstage negotiations. Despite the fact that these meetings were private and covert and never involved an active or direct challenge to the administration, some faculty did feel that participating in them was a career risk—not because activism was looked down upon, but rather because Technopark was a hostile environment for queer people. The campaign never developed much of a framing strategy, something which means that activists had little support on campus even though they were working with an administrator supportive of a potential queer studies program, and the campaign ultimately died out without developing a program.

Favorable Missions and Closed/Inflexible Administrations

Two of the six case study campuses exhibit favorable missions but closed and/ or inflexible administrations: Sagebrush University and the earlier (pre-1980s) Abigail Adams College. Sagebrush offers many interdisciplinary programs, and these programs are facilitated by an organizational structure that offers opportunities for academic innovation. Though the university as a whole emphasizes science, graduate education, and the pursuit of prestige, the residential college structure provides spaces where interdisciplinarity, undergraduate liberal arts education, social justice, and diversity remain valued and cultivated. However, this favorability and indeed flexibility coexist with a climate (for faculty) that "hammers any nail that sticks out," encouraging faculty to focus on their careers as they face a grueling tenure process. Even some tenured faculty have worried that their involvement in contentious politics might undermine their reputations, and untenured faculty have felt entirely unable to be involved. Students are able to act publically with less fear of reprisals, but administrative officials are distant, constrained by state educational policy, and not particularly interested in what students have to say. Even faculty involved with curricular change campaigns have taken the opportunity to shut students out of serious discussion—for instance, a faculty member told an Asian American studies student activist that it was now "grown-up time" and the student's involvement was no longer needed. In fact, some campus administrators think that non-academic staff are the only group able to be granted an administrative audience, but non-academic staff are rarely seen as a credible voice around issues of curriculum.

While Abigail Adams exhibited many of the complexities discussed above during this earlier period, the administration was much less open and flexible before the change in presidential administrations in the mid-1980s. The College was deeply committed to an educational mission of providing women with opportunities equal to those granted men, and while other definitions of equality are possible, Abigail Adams defined equality as sameness. Coupled with a strong presidential presence that lent a hierarchical feel to campus administration, it is easy to see how innovation was discouraged during this period. In fact, faculty members at Abigail Adams at the time worried that if they became publically associated with activism, it would be disastrous. These fears were not overblown, and in fact faculty members involved in feminist and women's studies activism were denied tenure or reappointment.

The organizational mediation model predicts that movements in favorable contexts faced with closed or inflexible administrations will have the greatest likelihood of making an impact if they choose assertive tactics and develop frames that correspond to the organizational mission. Of the four movements that experienced this configuration of organizational context, two chose assertive tactics and mission-based framing strategies: the movements for women's studies at Abigail Adams College and for Asian American studies at Sagebrush University. Both had significant impacts. Women's studies activists at Abigail Adams mounted, in Moore's terms, a "disruptive, wide-spread, long-term" (1999:99) campaign. They combined assimilative tactics like conferences, lobbying, an electoral campaign, and a research program with more assertive tactics like a week-long workshop, an armband protest at commencement, and a picketing campaign. Student activists developed a variety of framing strategies that relied heavily on the connection between women's studies and the Abigail Adams mission; activists believed that women's studies would provide the necessary link between academic work and social change and used all the intellectual tools at their disposal to demonstrate this connection to their campus audience. The campaign resulted in the development of a strong and institutionalized women's studies major program. Asian American studies activists at Sagebrush also combined assimilative tactics like informal study groups and petition campaigns with more assertive and innovative tactics like manufactured enrollment statistics and strategic threats of disruptive action. They utilized framing strategies based on market and neoinstitutional logics to convince administrators of the merit of ethnic studies in a context in which many faculty and administrators were skeptical; in the end, a well-respected ethnic studies program offering undergraduate and graduate studies and substantial coursework in Asian American studies was developed.

The movement for women's studies at Sagebrush University utilized mission-based framing strategies coupled with assimilative tactics and was nevertheless able to have an impact; however, it took considerable time for this to occur. Women's studies activists primarily relied on backstage negotiations, though students also sponsored campus events to raise awareness about women's studies. They relied on mission-based framing strategies that emphasized the potential for prestige-focused Sagebrush to be left behind as other universities adopted women's studies. While the organizational mediation perspective would not have predicted assimilative tactics to result in the development of a strong women's studies major, they did. Perhaps this is because even in the absence of what we would typically see as assertive tactics, the faculty activists for women's studies at Sagebrush were taking quite a risk. Few female faculty members were employed on campus, and even fewer held tenure. Pervasive gender stereotyping and a culture of discrimination made many female faculty members feel that they could not take the risk of associating with women's studies. After some of the first feminist faculty members to arrive on campus earned tenure, they used their new status to push women's studies forward. In the end, it took Sagebrush a long time to move forward on women's studies, and perhaps the lack of assertiveness may be an explanation for the delay.

The movement for queer studies at Sagebrush University also utilized mission-based framing strategies and assimilative tactics, and it was unable to create curricular change. Activism for queer studies occurred almost entirely under the auspices of a staff LGBT group; others did work to create academic lectures on queer studies, but given the availability of outside funding and the prestige-seeking culture at Sagebrush, such events were well within the confines of normal actions on campus. Queer studies activists never chose tactics that challenged the normal order of things, and those who were involved did not feel they were taking on any risk from their involvement. Activists did use mission-based framing, including emphasizing market-based and neoinstitutional logics. But given the lack of strategic assertiveness, no queer studies program was developed and even individual courses in queer studies remain rather rare.

Unfavorable Missions and Closed/Inflexible Administrations

The remaining two case study campuses exhibit both unfavorable missions and closed/inflexible administrations: Promenade University and the College of Assisi. Nevertheless, women's studies programs were developed at both campuses—a small one at Promenade University and a strong one at the College of Assisi. This shows that if effective strategies are found, change is possible even in circumstances which might seem rather hostile. Though Promenade's culture emphasizes diversity, its academic goals focus primarily on professional and skills education. Promenade students tend to work to put themselves through schooling designed to increase their marketability rather than spending time in liberal arts coursework. In fact, the administrative structure at Promenade specifically forecloses possibilities for interdisciplinarity, as all programs—including minors—must be housed within an existing department or division. In order for the women's studies program to move forward, it had to create a summit meeting just to find an organizational home. The hurdles would be even greater for a major program. Though students at Promenade have at times been involved in political activism and can make their voices heard at the University, the responsibilities of school, work, and family combine to make it difficult for students to become involved. A much higher percentage of faculty are part-time at Promenade (two thirds at Promenade compared to 20–40 percent at the other five campuses), limiting their input into campus affairs, and full-time faculty often feel their voices are not heard in the campus governance structure. Some female faculty in the late 1980s and early 1990s were so uncomfortable with gender dynamics on campus that they left the University. The flip side, however, is that faculty (and students) have generally felt free to speak their minds without fear of reprisals.

The College of Assisi's mission is rooted in its conservative Catholic faith. Catholic theological education and interdisciplinary Western civilization courses form the centerpiece of its rigid and intensive general education curriculum. While this curriculum does include interdisciplinary opportunities and a strong focus on the liberal arts, a large number of Assisi students earn their degrees in professional disciplines like business, and in fact many of the interdisciplinary degree areas available (like policy studies) are themselves professionalized. Assisi makes student activism extremely difficult—there are strict guidelines on what sorts of activities student organizations are permitted to engage in, and students need administrative approval even to post a flier calling for an organizational meeting. Many people believe that those students who are involved in campus governance are hand-picked to best represent the mission and values of the College. The few students who do become politically involved face hostility and ridicule from their peers, contributing to a climate in which students generally do not feel comfortable contributing to change efforts. Faculty, on the other hand, can argue for change as long as they do so by using "official institutional language" (Grossman 2010:660).

The organizational mediation model would predict that social movements targeting organizations with unfavorable missions and closed or inflexible administrations would be most likely to have an impact if they use assimilative tactics and develop frames that correspond to the organizational mission. Both of the movements that experienced such contexts—the movements for women's studies at Promenade University and at the College of Assisi—chose assimilative tactics and mission-based framing strategies, and both were able to have an impact, though to different extents. Activists at Promenade University circulated petitions and organized backstage; their most assertive tactic was the engineering of a summit meeting at which they brought together administrative personnel to force a minor confrontation about the future home of the program. Though this meeting was a disruption of the normal governance procedure, it was in no way an assertive move. Framing strategies focused on helping the university stay up-to-date and on the role that women's studies could play in helping students find their voices.

These frames resonated strongly with the university's mission. Promenade activists were ultimately able to develop a women's studies minor. While a minor makes a much smaller impact on a campus than a major does, given the administrative inflexibility at Promenade, it is a major accomplishment indeed.

Women's studies activists at the College of Assisi used a variety of innovative tactics, including mentoring and the development of research symposia, along with an institutional research project. Students formed an advocacy group; while it did not employ assertive tactics, it was notable on a campus where feminism was generally invisible. Activists used a complex set of framing strategies that emphasized student need, the actions of Catholic peers, and womanist philosophy. These framing strategies strongly resonated with Assisi's mission, and they contributed to the fact that the College of Assisi was able to develop a women's studies minor that ultimately developed into a major program.

Insider versus Outsider Strategies

The assessments of each movement's strategy above have ignored one dimension of strategic choice—the choice of using insider versus outsider strategies. But these strategic choices are not simply determined at one point in time. Rather, they can vary across the lifespan of a movement, and indeed activists can work strategically to manipulate their effects. Katzenstein (1998) argues that insiders can be detected by examining the patterns of financial, organizational, and discursive accountability that they have to the organization. Using Katzenstein's three criteria, this section of the chapter considers why (Armstrong and Bernstein 2008) social movements choose to use insider or outsider strategies and what the consequences of such decisions might be.

In four of the 13 movements considered in this chapter (queer studies at Jeffrey University, Sagebrush University, and Technopark University and women's studies at the College of Assisi), almost entirely insider strategies were employed. In the cases of queer studies at Jeffrey and Sagebrush, the most visible activists were non-academic staff; the realities of their work lives meant that they were financially, organizationally, and discursively accountable to the university administration. While queer studies activists at Technopark included a greater faculty presence, their activism was carried out under the auspices of an administrative sponsor, keeping them accountable as well. Women's studies activists at Assisi were not as directly responsible to administrators, but they worked to position themselves discursively as insiders, speaking from a deep commitment to the College and to its values; organizational and financial accountability came from faculty use of College grant support and from the formal recognition policies for student clubs.

In three cases (women's studies and Asian American studies at Abigail Adams College and Asian American studies at Sagebrush University), predominantly insider strategies were employed, though some elements of outsider activism were present. In all three cases, activists worked from a commitment to their campus and drew on organizational and financial resources from within it. However, in each case, some challenge drew the activists slightly outside. At Abigail Adams, a popular professor denied tenure used the opportunity of students' anger about this personnel decision to argue forcefully for a program. She spoke as an outsider, or at least as an insider forcibly evicted from the organization and the community, and this moment proved to be a rallying point for students. In the other two cases, activists developed strong alliances with those beyond the campus—activists at other colleges in the movement for Asian American studies at Abigail Adams, and local community activists and politicians in the movement for Asian American studies at Sagebrush.

The campaigns for women's studies at Jeffrey University, Sagebrush University, and Technopark University and for queer studies at Abigail Adams College were marked by the transition over time from outsider to insider strategies. Many early women's studies activists at Jeffrey University were community activists with only weak ties to the university, and autonomous financial resources (such as the self-funding continuing education program) were used by these activists. As the program began to develop, activists' discursive identification with the university grew, and strategic decisions "brought the outside in" as activists shifted towards more insider strategies and become organizationally and financially accountable to the university. Similarly, women's studies activists at Technopark began as outsiders with strong connections to other women's liberation and social justice issues, such as economic equality, anti-discrimination work, and child care issues. Their use of outsider strategies did not pay off; a key early participant was denied tenure due to her connections with these other activist groups, and later activism— which had a greater impact—employed insider strategies. In the cases of queer studies activism at Abigail Adams College and women's studies activism at Sagebrush University, early activists faced quite hostile climates that limited their ability to claim insider status. As activists worked to improve the general campus climates for queer people and for women, respectively, they were able to transition to being insider activists for the academic programs they desired.

The remaining cases, Asian American studies at Jeffrey University and women's studies at Promenade University, involved more heavily outsider strategies. Women's studies activists at Promenade may have relied on institutionalized and assimilative tactics, but these tactics were situated in a broader outsider politics. Women's studies activists included women who were not yet employees of Promenade, giving them little accountability to the university structure. In addition, the difficulty in understanding where a women's studies program might be housed limited organizational accountability, and the climate for female faculty at Promenade was somewhat hostile at the time that the program was being developed. Asian American studies activists at Jeffrey University were even more clearly situated as outsiders; as one former professor put it, the University seemed to rely on a notion that the modern world was "post-ethnicity," a notion that devalued Asian American students' experiences. Though activists did claim discursive accountability through their argument that their experiences belonged in the University, their strongly assertive tactics and their connections to many outside groups highlighted their position as outsiders. In addition, almost all of the Asian American studies activists at Jeffrey were students—a more disproportionate ratio than in most of the cases considered here—and Jeffrey is a university which does not insist on closely supervising or limiting students' political involvement. This means that organizational and financial accountability were further diminished.

The analysis presented here suggests that when activists targeting organizations are able to choose insider strategies they generally will, and when the option presents itself but is not immediately chosen (such as in the cases of women's studies at Jeffrey University and Technopark University) an early awareness that outsider strategies are not paying dividends may convince activists to turn inwards. Though both the women's studies activists at Promenade and the Asian American studies activists at Jeffrey did not have the option to conceive of themselves as true insiders and therefore used an outsider strategy throughout their campaigns, they were still able to make impacts. However, these two programs remain among the most vulnerable and least institutionalized of all the programs considered here (along with Asian American studies at Abigail Adams College). The fact that these activists were forced into outsider strategies may be in part a reason why. This question will be explored in further detail below in the discussion of outcomes and institutionalization.

What's Special about Queer Studies?

In considering the distribution of strategic choices and movement outcomes among the three areas of study included in this book, it is clear that queer studies stands out. Women's studies and Asian American studies activists used strategies that varied from quite assertive to quite assimilative. But in the case of queer studies, assertive strategies were used only at Abigail Adams College, and even then only quite early in the movement. Despite the lack of progress experienced by movements for queer studies, they never moved on to assertive strategies (as, for instance, the Asian American studies activists at Jeffrey University did). This analysis cannot explain why activists did not develop assertive strategies. However, it is worth considering the fact that even in organizational contexts supportive of interdisciplinarity and of queer campus issues, queer studies may be challenging in a way that goes beyond the challenge presented by women's studies or Asian American studies. Queer studies remains highly politicized on a societal level; students even worry about whether having queer studies courses appear on their transcript might harm them in some way. At Technopark, the registrar pushed the women's studies program to change course names so that students would stop complaining when issues of sexuality appeared on their transcripts. In the earlier phases of queer studies activism, activists faced additional risks simply by "coming out" as advocates of queer studies and as potentially queer-identified themselves (Taylor and Raeburn 1995).

Perhaps, then, activists felt that they were being assertive simply by proposing academic work in such a politicized and radical arena. Indeed, queer-identified faculty—and their allies—have often faced considerable personal and professional risk simply from being open about their identities and interests; activism for queer studies only increases this risks. In 1992, for instance, 43 percent of the lesbian, gay, or bisexual faculty Taylor and Raeburn studied reported that they had experienced professional bias related to their sexual identity (Taylor and Raeburn 1995). These distinct challenges faced by queer studies show that it is not a simple matter to compare multiple movements within one organizational context. However, even if queer studies activists faced higher hurdles, queer studies is still possible. As the methodological appendix shows, 10 percent of a group of 523 colleges and universities considered for this study offer queer studies programs. The Abigail Adams queer studies movement shows that a college can move from being a place where queer faculty fear for their careers to one offering a formal concentration in queer studies.

Outcomes and Institutionalization

The particular type of innovation being considered here involves the creation of a new program with a new organizational structure. Such structures can be temporary and informal, or they can be institutionalized in such a way as to make them fairly enduring within the social system (Arthur 2009; Clark 1968). When social movements targeting organizations first have an impact, this impact is likely to come as a sort of restricted trial of the proposed reform (non-institutionalized); institutionalization comes with full adoption. Though the differences between a restricted trial and full adoption vary depending on the particular type of organization and type of reform proposed, a consideration of the trajectory of women's studies at Jeffrey University might be illustrative. Early in the history of women's studies, activists were able to develop a small certificate program drawing on courses offered through the continuing education division. This program had to fund itself, relied on no permanent faculty or staff, and did not gain legitimacy as a normal academic program. Today, however, the program is a full-fledged department with seven tenured and tenure track faculty members that offers well-respected undergraduate and graduate training to its students. When it was part of continuing education, women's studies at Jeffrey was in the restricted trial stage; today, it is fully institutionalized.

Many scholars emphasize the importance of departmentalization as an indicator of institutionalization. Departmentalization provides access to increased budgetary resources, increased discretionary authority (especially in terms of personnel decisions), and increased organizational legitimacy, though it may come at a cost of reduced authenticity and de-politicization (Hu-DeHart 2004; Kimura-Walsh 2009). However, given the varied organizational contexts, procedures, and structures of colleges and universities in the United States, departmentalization is not the only indicator of institutionalization. Table 9.5 provides a more detailed metric for evaluating whether a program should be considered institutionalized or not. It draws on the work of Boxer (1998) and Astin and Parelman (1973:390) on women's studies programs in order to represent the spectrum of difference across which new curricular programs may vary. By examining any particular program across the full set of dimensions outlined in Table 9.5, we can understand the degree to which it is institutionalized.

Table 9.5   Elements of Institutionalization

Element	Institutionalized	Non-Institutionalized
Program Goals	Traditional academic goals: research & theory that meet academic qualifications; program names more broad (e.g. "gender")	Ideology, activism, and consciousness-raising are part of program goals; program names specific (e.g. "women")
Legitimacy-Seeking	Focus on defending place of the discipline in academe, quality of work, etc.	Justification for program focuses on prior exclusion and need for change in academe
Ideological Standards	Those teaching should hold standard academic qualifications	Those teaching should be activists and/or ideologically committed to program goals
Role of Non-faculty	Teaching and program administration should be done by conventionally qualified faculty, perhaps with student representatives to a committee	Democratic program administration which involves the full community of faculty, staff, and students is used; community members/activists and students valued as teachers with their own expertise
Program Organization	Stand-alone department (courses may be offered by other disciplines)	Interdisciplinary program (courses primarily offered by external departments)
Degree Programs	Established major; where college or university offers graduate work, established M.A., Ph.D., or graduate certificate	Minor, certificate, 2nd major, or self-designed major; if graduate courses exist, they are not organized into a program
Role of "Outsiders"	Faculty and students who do not hold an identity relevant to the program are incorporated and encouraged	Generally excluded from teaching; legally cannot be excluded from courses, but ignored or thought of as problematic
Relationship to Community	Minimal, or only through formal service-learning programs	Assumption that students will connect their lives to their classes; existence of low-cost continuing education for community members; close ties between to community
FTEs and Funding	At least one FTE faculty member with sole appointment in the program; stable funding	No appointments in the program; discretionary funding

As can be seen from the case studies presented in Chapters 3 through 8, some new programs remain in the restricted trial or non-institutionalized stage for quite a long time, or even permanently (this of course does not include the programs which never get off the ground in the first place, like the queer studies programs at Jeffrey University, Sagebrush University, and Technopark University). In particular, the Asian American studies programs at Jeffrey University and Abigail Adams College and the women's studies program at Promenade University remain non-institutionalized programs. While each has adopted academic program goals, ideological standards, roles for non-faculty and other "outsiders," and relationships to the community that are in line with institutionalization, these moves toward institutionalization have not been reciprocated by the college or university administrations. All three programs continue to engage in legitimacy-seeking behavior that highlights their exclusion from the mainstream curriculum; all three remain interdisciplinary programs with budgetary problems and no full-time equivalent tenured or tenure-track faculty members; and none are able to offer majors or appear likely to be able to do so in the future. This lack of institutionalization persists despite the fact that all three programs are now approaching a decade or more in age.

A more ambiguous position is held by queer studies at Abigail Adams College, as was the case for women's studies at the College of Assisi and at Technopark University until the end of the 2000s. As recently as 2006, the women's studies programs at Assisi and Technopark still lacked the authority to offer majors to their students, despite the fact that the Assisi program was over a decade old and the Technopark program over two decades old. Both programs continue to have limited budgetary authority and control over their own hiring and faculty practices. However, both programs carefully worked towards institutionalization and now are able to offer majors, a significant step in the direction of institutionalization. The situation is somewhat different for queer studies at Abigail Adams, where the program has institutionalized goals, engages in legitimacy-seeking behavior, and maintains academically-oriented ideological standards, attitudes about the role of non-faculty and outsiders, and relationships to the community. However, it is organized as a concentration within a major, giving it a non-institutionalized organizational structure and no major-granting authority, and it has no full-time faculty of its own. These factors mean it would be extremely easy for the program to disappear, a hallmark of non-institutionalized status.

The remaining four programs, women's studies at Jeffrey University, Abigail Adams College, and Sagebrush University and ethnic studies (with its Asian American studies component) at Sagebrush University, are squarely on the institutionalized side of the spectrum. Though the women's studies program at Jeffrey began as a restricted trial, it is now institutionalized in almost all respects and in 2009 underwent a name change indicating an even more institutionalized perspective. The other three programs institutionalized more rapidly and qualify as fully institutionalized across all of the dimensions in Table 9.5 with one exception, which is that there are no faculty with sole appointments in the women's studies program at Sagebrush University.

It is worth noting that all four of the fully-institutionalized programs were established at colleges or universities that (at least more recently) have missions favorable to the innovation, though these campuses vary in terms of administrative openness and flexibility. Favorable missions may then be an important factor for the facilitation of institutionalization. On the other hand, the missions of Technopark University and the College of Assisi were *not* favorable, and both are at least well on their way to institutionalization. As noted earlier in this chapter, the case of the College of Assisi demonstrates that extensive change is possible even in environments that seem quite hostile to an innovation.

Where Movements Don't Develop

Out of the 18 possible combinations of campus and discipline, five did not involve movements for curricular change; four of these do not demonstrate any evidence of any initiative to create the discipline in question. At the College of Assisi and Promenade University, the Asian American students on campus are predominantly immigrant or first generation students from traditional families, many of whom see themselves in terms of their ethnic ancestry rather than in panethnic Asian American terms. There are also few—or even no—faculty members on each campus with an interest in Asian American studies; at Promenade, even Asian area studies is a new field of study.

In contrast, there are faculty and students interested in queer studies topics at Promenade University; courses on such topics are offered on occasion. But the climate at Promenade is quite hostile to queer studies. Faculty feel free to do research and to teach in such areas if they wish, but the campus culture is traditional and influenced by conservative religious traditions that stigmatize queer identities on campus. Students have had difficulty maintaining a queer student group and have given it a name that does not disclose its purpose. They feel that enrolling in queer studies coursework could 'mark' them on campus. The dynamics at the College of Assisi are similar. Assisi is grounded in conservative Catholic traditions that depict homosexuality as sinful and unnatural. Conservative faculty on campus portray homosexuality quite negatively. More liberal faculty will occasionally address issues of sexual difference, but only in a way that protects them against claims that they are betraying the campus mission and its Catholic values. These are serious charges in an era in which a prospective dean at a Catholic university could have her employment offer rescinded on the basis of her sexuality-related scholarship (Dillon 2010) and they are likely to make faculty think twice before bringing queer studies content into the classroom. Only in the past few years have students even been able to form a campus gay-straight alliance—under particularly restrictive conditions—and the founding members think it unlikely that positive portrayals of homosexuality will ever extend beyond the few most progressive departments on campus.

What about Asian American studies at Technopark University? Faculty members there tried to build a program through the normal shared governance procedure, based on perceptions of market and demographic need when they observed the skyrocketing numbers of Asian American students on campus. No students or faculty developed the organizational structures to sustain involvement or activism. Instead, faculty members within the established American studies program sought to incorporate Asian American studies into their curriculum to respond to their perceptions of need. Though they hired an adjunct faculty member who began offering such courses, interest from other faculty remained non-existent, and students did not take up the cause. Students were somewhat active for a time in demanding an Asian area studies program, but even this demand has been rejected. According to a Technopark graduate from the mid-2000s, the student body is quite apathetic about most issues and has become focused on curricula that ensure speedy graduation and well-paying jobs, factors that make a renewed campaign for Asian American studies unlikely.

Assessing the Organizational Mediation Model

The analysis of the outcomes of these 13 movements for curricular change supports the predictions of the organizational mediation model. Where strategy is aligned with organizational context—assertive tactics with constituency-based framing for favorable and open/flexible contexts; assimilative tactics with constituency-based framing for unfavorable but open/flexible contexts; assertive tactics with mission-based framing for favorable but closed/inflexible contexts; and assimilative tactics with mission-based framing for unfavorable and closed/inflexible contexts—movements are most likely to be able to make an impact on the organization that they target and thus enable the development of the changes they desire. Where strategy is *not* aligned with the organizational context, movements are less likely to be able to have such an impact.

Of the 13 cases presented in this book, ten strongly conform to the predictions of the organizational mediation model. The other three, women's studies at Sagebrush University and Asian American and queer studies at Abigail Adams College, deviate from the predictions of the model in small ways. Both movements at Abigail Adams were able to make small impacts at their college despite not making the strategic choices that the organizational mediation model predicted that they should have used. In particular, neither movement utilized constituent-directed framing strategies. Asian American studies activists gained a certificate program, but the program offers few courses and no new faculty were hired; in queer studies, a concentration was added, along with several new courses, but within the confines of an existing women's studies program. However, the impacts that both of these movements made were facilitated by unique organizational structures. Asian American studies was implemented through the actions of and by using the resources of a multi-campus consortium, while the development of the queer studies concentration required only funding and support from the existing (institutionalized and well-funded) women's studies program. The use of such organizational structures made it much easier to enact these particular innovations than it would have otherwise been, and thus it was less important for activists to make the best possible strategic decisions. However, it is also possible that use of strategies more clearly adapted to the organizational context might have enabled the movements to have a larger impact on their college.

The case of women's studies at Sagebrush University presents a greater challenge to the organizational mediation model. Women's studies activists faced an organizational context marked by a favorable mission but a closed and inflexible administration. The organizational mediation model would predict that activists in such a context would be most likely to make an impact if they chose assertive tactics and framing that resonated with the organizational mission. While Sagebrush women's studies activists did utilize mission-based framing, their tactics were assimilative in nature. Yet they ultimately were able to develop a strong and fairly institutionalized women's studies program. Perhaps the career risks that female faculty at Sagebrush perceived themselves as taking by becoming involved in activism there mean that their tactics should in fact be seen as more assertive, or perhaps the intensely sexist and frequently discriminatory environment for women at Sagebrush means that the mission—despite its favorability to interdisciplinary liberal arts and social justice education—should be seen as unfavorable. In addition, as noted above, the development of this program took a long time, and key activists had to earn tenure before the program was developed. It is possible, though far from certain, that more assertive activism by faculty and/or students might have lead to earlier impacts.

In summary, then, the cases considered in this chapter show that the organizational mediation model is a useful way to understand the impacts of social movements targeting organizations, and furthermore that these social movements were key actors in the organizational change process. Social movement activism was at least in part responsible for the development of all ten curricular changes that did occur among the six colleges and universities studied—whether directly or through the swaying of opinion and alliance structure (Guigini and Yamasaki 2009)—and in those cases where the strategy fits the organizational context, the outcomes movements desire are more likely to occur. This model therefore provides a corrective to the conspicuous absence of theoretical models explaining movements that target organizations (Van Dyke et al. 2004). It shows how movement strategy and organizational context interact to product changes in organizations—in other words, movement outcomes.

Chapter 10
Curricular Change and Collective Action: A Conclusion

In the middle of the 1980s, as students at Sagebrush University pushed on in the long fight to bring Asian American studies to their campus, they realized that their university was not listening to arguments about the intellectual worth and social merit of the discipline they wished to study. In consultation with a faculty advisor from another campus of their state university system which had already adopted an Asian American studies program, they realized that the message that the Sagebrush administration would hear was a message about dollars and bodies in seats. The students who were active in the movement for Asian American studies on campus therefore embarked upon a campaign to increase enrollment in the few classes already being offered, generally taught by adjuncts or visiting lecturers. They mass-mailed the Asian American student body. They handed out fliers all over campus. But they ran into a problem. The tight curricular structure and strong science focus of their university meant that many of their peers—no matter how supportive of Asian American studies in principle—simply did not have room in their class schedules for an elective that would not even count towards their general education requirements. But the students came up with a solution. They convinced their friends who studied science and engineering to sign up for the courses anyway on an overload basis. Their friends dropped the courses shortly into the term, after only attending a few weeks' worth of classes, but they stayed enrolled until after the enrollment reports were finalized.

The consequence of this innovative strategy was that almost every Asian American studies course offered on campus filled to capacity or beyond. A casual observer might easily assume that Sagebrush University adopted Asian American studies because there had been a significant increase in the number of Asian American students on campus, or because these students took advantage of a small opportunity to enroll in Asian American studies courses to vote with their pocketbooks for more such courses, supporting a market-based analysis. A more careful observer might note that other campuses in the state university system had already adopted Asian American studies, and therefore point to a neoinstitutional explanation for why Sagebrush chose to adopt Asian American studies—though it had been over a decade since other campuses initiated their programs. But in considering this tale, another explanation seems more likely: students engaging in innovative and strategic social movement activity, working with faculty to create joint insider activism campaigns, convinced the administration to finally give in to the pressure for Asian American studies in 1988.

A Changing Curriculum in a Changing World

The findings of this study suggest correctives to some of the stories of doom that pundits like to tell about contemporary higher education. Though the corporatization of the university is clearly proceeding apace in many ways, ranging from the creation of biotechnology spin-offs to public-private partnerships for developing distance learning and workforce training programs (Bok 2003; Kirp 2003; Slaughter and Rhoades 2005), and though the liberal arts account for declining percentages of student enrollments (Brint et al. 2005), perhaps the situation is not as dire as some analysis would suggest. There are still efforts to bring unheard voices into the curriculum. In the first years of the 2000s, these have included the push for a renewed focus on class, the development of fat studies (Ellin 2006), and studies of children and of the relationships between animals and society. Even in times of budget cuts, programs in ethnic studies, women's studies, and queer studies have continued to expand. For instance, even in the tough budget times of 2009 and 2010, Salem College, the College of Charleston, and Butler University initiated women's studies majors; Barnard College, Louisville Seminary, the University of Illinois Chicago, and the University of Texas Austin built new programs in ethnic studies; and the University of Oregon, San Diego State University, and Brooklyn College began offering programs in queer studies. Yet even as new programs continue to emerge, the fact that advocates of curricular change face significant opposition and must work hard to demonstrate the intellectual merit of their fields and the fit between the programs they propose and the colleges and universities they are part of shows that these new disciplines are not simply running roughshod over the curriculum with no supervision or restraint.

The case studies presented in this book also serve as a corrective to commentators' frequent decrial of college student apathy. While some of the movements considered here occurred in the early 1970s on the coattails of the 1960s student movement, others continued and even expanded during the 1990s and early 2000s, periods often considered low points in the trajectory of student political engagement. Despite the fact that today's college students are overscheduled, career-focused, often working while attending school, and increasingly experience family responsibilities that take time away from their involvement on campus, students still do become involved in issues that matter to them. They still care about receiving an education that is relevant to their lives, and they are still willing to become involved in activism to demand such an education.

College curricula remain today at the center of countless debates. A small sampling of current controversies might include those concerning the teaching of intelligent design, the resurrected cannon wars, the inclusion of ethics training in business education, the role of general education curricula in vocational programs, the degree to which law students should engage in hands-on training, and the balance of pedagogical and content-area coursework for education students. Some of these debates are best understood through the lenses of the market, neoinstitutionalism, or faculty and administrative leadership. But others—most especially the first two—are best understood through the lens of contentious politics. College curricula speak to our values and our identities. They play a major role in shaping the intellects of those who will become community, corporate, organizational, and national leaders. The importance that curriculum has in defining who we are and what our future will look like (Rudolph 1989) reminds us of the importance of studying curricular change.

Competing Explanations for Curricular Change

As detailed in the introduction to this book, analysts of organizational change have provided four broad sets of explanations for how such change occurs: the market, neoinstitutionalism, leadership and initiative, and contentious politics. Most commentators focus on one of the first three; contentious politics has rarely been seen as a major source of organizational change. But the findings of this study challenge these conventional notions of how organizations operate. The evidence suggests that women's studies, Asian American studies, and queer studies programs have not emerged through market pressures, neoinstitutional forces, or leadership and initiative by faculty and administrators and have instead developed as a result of social movements targeting colleges and universities.

Market-Based Explanations

Market-based explanations for organizational change suggest that organizations change when they have reason to believe that such changes would enable them to increase the number of paying customers or to decrease costs. In the curricular change context, this would mean that colleges and universities adopt new programs in order to attract more paying students (Tierny 1989) or when such programs would provide for a decrease in expenditures. Though the specific ways in which the market affects colleges and universities may vary, with prestigious and prestige-seeking campuses implementing changes when necessary to increase selectivity and draw while other campuses change based on perceptions of student need (Brewer et al. 2002), market-based explanations always propose that change occurs in response to economic forces of some kind. Had the market-based explanation been correct, cases of successful curricular change would be observed when potential college students make decisions about where to enroll (or perhaps whether to transfer) based on whether a college or university offers courses or programs in women's studies, Asian American studies, or queer studies, or when colleges and universities find that such programs result in a significant cost reduction. Administrators would thus sponsor new programs by explaining their potential to attract more students to the college, and once the new program was adopted, rapid enrollment growth would follow.

While the faculty members at Technopark University who were considering the development of an Asian American studies program, an initiative that did not get off the ground, did use such logic, none of the campaigns that resulted in actual curricular change did. Students did not threaten to transfer if such programs remained absent from the curriculum, and there is no evidence that prospective students avoided enrolling because these programs were not available. Indeed, most prospective college students have not been exposed to these fields of study prior to enrollment and thus are unlikely to make enrollment decisions based on their availability. In addition, while humanities and social science fields like women's studies, Asian American studies, and queer studies are low-cost and to some extent may result in financial benefits to the larger college or university budget (Johnson 2009), their implementation is not understood as a cost-saving measure, particularly since new programs often require the hiring of new faculty or at least the provision of reassigned time to program coordinators. External funding did not spur the creation of these programs; while it was available to the nascent programs in women's studies at Abigail Adams College and the College of Assisi as well as to the unsuccessful campaign for queer studies at Sagebrush University, programs were not founded due to the initiative of outside funders and in fact the Abigail Adams administration even rejected funding that would have supported women's studies. It is clear that market-based models do explain many instances of contemporary curricular change, like new programs in nursing or in homeland security administration, but the evidence in this study suggests that they are not helpful for explaining the emergence of women's studies, Asian American studies, and queer studies programs.

Neoinstitutional Explanations

Neoinstitutional explanations for organizational change would predict that over time there would be increasing homogeneity across similar types of organizations (Lounsbury 2001) or among organizations which are dependent on one another (DiMaggio and Powell 1991). In particular, the neoinstitutional model suggests that organizations which face similar environmental constraints will alter themselves in similar ways (DiMaggio and Powell 1983). This process, called institutional isomorphism, can occur via three distinct pathways: coercive isomorphism, in which external agents of control such as the state or accrediting agencies force organizations to undergo change; normative isomorphism, in which organizational change occurs as part of bringing an organization in line with norms of professional practice; and mimetic isomorphism, in which organizations respond to environmental uncertainty by copying what other successful organizations are doing through a process of diffusion (DiMaggio and Powell 1983).

The adoption of curricular programs in women's studies, Asian American studies, and queer studies clearly did not occur through coercive or normative isomorphism. Accrediting agencies and state regulatory boards do not require college and universities to offer such programs, and professional organizations like the American Association of Universities and the Association of Governing Boards do not devote resources to encouraging them as part of normal professional practice. Mimetic isomorphism makes more sense as an agent of such curricular change. If mimetic isomorphism was the best way to understand the emergence of these programs, the cases of successful curricular change would be those in which organizational actors made decisions while steeped in knowledge about what decisions their peers had made. Administrators, alongside those faculty who were particularly concerned with seeking or maintaining prestige, would make decisions by explicitly comparing their own curricular offerings to those of their peers or those of the most prestigious colleges or universities they could imagine. This decision-making process would demonstrate a distinct concern with the degree to which proposed changes would be necessary or useful for maintaining or increasing prestige and social position. After program adoption, the neoinstitutional model would predict that the college or university would join networks of other colleges and universities offering similar curricula and additionally that administrators would devote resources to ensuring the success of their new program.

The evidence presented in this book does not support mimetic isomorphism as an explanation for curricular change. Administrators did not seek out information on what their peers were doing with respect to women's studies, Asian American studies, and queer studies. Indeed, when activists presented evidence about program adoption at other colleges and universities to administrators at Sagebrush University, Abigail Adams College, Promenade University, and the College of Assisi, administrators often ignored the evidence entirely—exactly the opposite of what they would have done if their actions had been driven by a neoinstitutional logic. Once programs were initiated, it often took many years for them to become institutionalized (when they have been institutionalized at all), and during these early years programs struggled with insufficient budgets and faculty resources. Administrative decisions to withhold resources from new programs prevent these programs from reaching their potential and from contributing to the development of prestige for the campus, again something that contradicts the predictions of the neoinstitutional model.

Leadership and Initiative

The organizational structure and leadership culture varies across colleges and universities (Tierny 2008), and thus the parties with primary responsibility over curricular decision-making vary as well. On some campuses, faculty have little decision-making responsibility or power and instead administrators make decisions about curricular offerings (Hefferlin 1969). On others, a rich tradition of shared governance grants the faculty primary control over the shape and content of college curricula (Bryson 2005; Cohen and March 1974). Even where faculty have official control over academic matters, some higher education analysts argue that faculty are not the center of innovation but instead are a body that exercises its rights to decide over proposals created by others (Kerr 1995).

In the cases included in this book, change did not occur through administrative initiative. Despite their ability to exercise leadership in other areas, administrators are predominantly positioned as reactive agents when faced with curricular issues; they respond to demands and pressures for change from below with apathy or with outright hostility, and they seek ways to contain contention and avoid radical change. In some cases, certain administrators did function as key conscience constituencies by supporting the demands of organizational activists or by providing them with space to organize their campaigns, but even in those cases where administrators have been extremely supportive of curricular change initiatives, they have been unable or unwilling to implement such changes without prolonged activism from below. It may be that administrators work by waiting for social movements to emerge so that they can be blessed at just the right moment, thereby allowing administrators to enable change without having to take full responsibility for it[1]— but even if social movements are nothing more than squeaky wheels, those wheels had to squeak effectively and loudly in order for change to occur.

Similarly, many analysts from within and outside of the higher education system see colleges and universities as places of unfettered faculty power, places where radical faculty can revolutionize the curriculum with little oversight by or interference from administrators, state governments, or more traditional faculty members (see, for instance, the frequent diatribes on this subject by David Horowitz and his supporters). The analysis presented here shows instead that faculty are quite constrained in their ability—or perhaps desire—to implement curricular change (Rudolph 1989). Among the fourteen attempts at creating curricular change that are presented in this book, only one (queer studies at Abigail Adams College) was able to proceed through the shared governance process without encountering serious obstacles along the way. This case was quite unique in being able to draw on the resources of a supportive and already-institutionalized department; in addition, a history of contentious action relating to queer issues within the college preceded the final push to implement queer studies in campus. In many of the other cases, faculty encountered real or perceived risk when they sought to advocate for the new programs they desired, and even where they did not encounter risk, they encountered other obstacles, such as administrative reticence to provide the funding that would be necessary for program establishment.

Contentious Politics

The contentious politics explanation for organizational change proposes that change occurs due to the pressure created by activists' demands and their participation in organized contention. This contention, and the disruption it creates, may function as "bargaining chips" (Burstein et al. 1995; King 2008) that lead those in power to believe it would be easier to approve new courses and programs than to continue facing protest; alternatively, the persuasive power of contentious action and strategic framing may lead decision-makers to come to support activists' demands (Guigini and Yamasaki 2009; King and Pearce 2010). The contentious

---

1   I want to thank Mitchell Stevens for suggesting this line of reasoning.

politics approach would predict that curricular change would occur where active, disruptive contention on the part of organizational insiders (particularly students) within the college or university creates sufficient pressure on those in power to encourage them to make the changes activists desire. Indeed, the instances of curricular change explored in this book occurred through the activism of students, faculty, and staff.

These activists are not the irrational actors of classical social movement theory as applied to the university. Rather, they are educated and strategic thinkers with sophisticated understandings of how the disciplines for which they are advocating can make substantial changes in the organizational structures and cultural practices of their colleges and universities. The case studies included in this book, in other words, demonstrate that contention within organizations is a primary factor in creating organizational change.

The Organizational Mediation Model

Social movements inside organizations are able to have a greater impact when their strategies—particularly their framing strategies and the degree to which their tactics are assertive and/or based on their position as insiders—are most closely aligned with their organizational contexts—particularly the organizational leadership's openness and flexibility and the degree to which the organization's mission is favorable to the interests and demands of the movement. Where movements face an open and flexible administration with a favorable mission, they are most likely to have an impact when they utilize assertive tactics and framing that resonates with their core constituency. Where they face an open and flexible administration with an unfavorable mission, they are most likely to have an impact when they utilize assimilative tactics and framing that resonates with their core constituency. Where they face closed and/or inflexible administrations with favorable missions, they are most likely to have an impact when they utilize assertive tactics and framing that supports the core organizational mission. And finally, when they face closed and/or inflexible administrations with unfavorable missions, they are most likely to have an impact when they utilize assimilative tactics and framing that supports the core organizational mission. The analysis presented in Chapter 9 demonstrates that the organizational mediation model is a useful way of understanding what makes it possible for movements to have impacts on the organizations that they target. The model is able to predict which of the movements included in this book will have strong impacts on their colleges or universities and which will not.

The organizational mediation model has broad implications for the study of social movements and organizational change. The literature on social movements that target organizations has grown substantially over the past decade. This literature advances the argument that organizations play an increasingly important role in our lives. Today, we are born in hospitals, educated in formal schools, work in corporations or other bureaucracies, spend our free time in clubs, live out our final years in nursing homes, and return to hospitals to die. These organizations are also looming larger in the global environment; some multinational corporations now control economies bigger than those of many nations. Social movements targeting organizations, therefore, are taking on greater significance as ways for groups to address grievances that the state cannot or will not address (Rao 2009).

While the growing literature on social movements that target organizations has highlighted the emergence of, strategic and organizational choices made by, and cultural meanings part of such movements, this literature (like that of social movement theory more broadly) has focused less attention on what makes it possible for such movements to make an impact. At the same time, social movement theory developed to apply to movements that target the state cannot be brought to bear on movements targeting organizations without modification (Van Dyke et al. 2004). The organizational mediation model, therefore, provides a way to systematically study the actions that make impacts possible for movements targeting organizations. It demonstrates that there is not one right set of strategic choices that movements targeting organizations must make in order to have an impact. Rather, movements make strategic choices in varying contexts, and they are able to make an impact on the organizations they seek to change when they select strategies and tactics that are aligned with these contexts.

The organizational mediation model can be applied to movements seeking a variety of other forms of curricular change, such as other ethnic studies disciplines (Black studies, Chicano/a and Latino/a studies, Native American studies, Irish studies, contemporary Jewish studies, Arab American studies, etc.); contentious scientific disciplines like environmental studies; and conservative academic movements like those for intelligent design and cannon revisionism. It will not be useful for explaining the emergence of professional fields like business that are clearly connected to economic incentives for both students and universities, nor will it explain those technological and scientific fields that emerged due to knowledge growth or human need, though it might explain the inclusion of science itself in the college curriculum (Rudolph 1989; Slaughter 1997).

The organizational mediation model is not limited to campaigns for curricular change. It can also be applied to other social movements within a variety of educational and non-educational (religious, economic, social, etc.) organizations. The particular aspects of organizational context that might matter in these varied organizations would themselves vary. Colleges and universities are unique organizational forms with a particular type of leadership structure and cultural orientation (Tierny 2008), and even within colleges and universities, movements for curricular change are a specific type of movement with attributes that may not reflect all movements targeting colleges and universities. Yet the organizational mediation model will be useful in many situations. A sampling of such situations might include efforts to create sexual harassment, non-discrimination, or family leave policies in universities or corporations; movements for divestment from Sudan or South Africa and other campaigns for corporate social responsibility;

efforts to expand gender and sexual orientation equality within religious denominations; contemporary labor campaigns in situations in which unions have been denied National Labor Relations Board protections; and movements around environmental issues like power conservation and the use of local food supplies within colleges, corporations, or housing developments.

Further research would help to refine the organizational mediation model and thus increase its analytical utility. In particular, such research could focus on three aspects of movement strategy and structure that were not fully developed in this study: timing, resources, and movement organizational structure. In many of the cases outlined in this book, there was a significant time lag between the height of activism and the achievement of the ultimate outcome; in some cases, very little or no activism occurred in the interim. The curricular change process at most colleges and universities is, of course, quite lengthy; the time from the development of a new idea to the implementation of that idea, even under the best circumstances, can take five years or more—as did the fastest campaigns in this study (women's studies at Promenade University and Asian American studies at Sagebrush University). But the slowness of curricular change procedure is unlikely to be the only factor explaining the time lags that occurred in these cases. The extent to which a movement can sustain protest, or at least advocacy, over a considerable time period (Moore 1999), despite personnel—especially student—turnover (Dugger 2000) and temporary setbacks, and in particular the extent to which the movement can keep its claims in the public eye, are an important part of movement strategy. Several of the initiatives which were not able to have a major impact, such as the movement for queer studies at Jeffrey University and the early wave of activism for women's studies at the College of Assisi, experienced prolonged periods of quiet during which advocates were not pushing for their discipline. More detailed attention to how timing functions in enabling or preventing desired changes from coming to fruition would enrich the explanatory power of the model. A starting place might be the counterfactual question of whether activists such as those pushing for queer studies at Jeffrey University might have been able to make a greater impact if they had sustained their activism.

Resource mobilization theory, in recent years, has expanded the notion of resources to include a variety of non-financial and non-tangible resources like skills, labor power, and social and cultural capital (McCarthy and Zald 2002) as well as the idea that resources can be increased through movement "resourcefulness" (Ganz 2000). These types of resources, which are vested in people power rather than financial capital, can be referred to as "human resources" (Edwards and McCarthy 2004). In addition, conscience constituencies—individuals or groups who will not be beneficiaries of the movement but who nevertheless support it (Jenkins 1983)—can be resources as well. Unlike earlier resource mobilization formulations, models that consider human resources and conscience constituencies do not make the simple prediction that more human resources equal a greater likelihood of movement impacts. Instead, the degree and type of resources needed varies according to the specific movement under study, a prediction that is a better fit with the organizational mediation model. The movements considered in this book had access to a variety of types of resources. Several had access to outside financial support;[2] all drew on human resources like administrative support, insider knowledge, and teaching skills; and most drew on conscience constituencies from among administrators, faculty, and organizational outsiders. Future research could untangle the connections between such resources, organizational context, strategic capacity (Ganz 2000), strategic choice, and movement outcomes.

Movement organizational structures vary as well. "Strong" organizational structures may help movements to choose strategies and take decisive actions (Andrews 2001; Ganz 2000). Again, however, the particular structures that are seen as making organizations strong vary among theorists and across movement types or contexts. The cases of activism considered in this book vary considerably in their organizational structure. In some cases, faculty and students worked together in loose, often student-driven coalitions; in other cases, faculty did almost all the organizing from within formal task forces and delegated only certain strategic tasks to students. Indeed, prior research has suggested that student movements are quite likely to be supported by faculty (Riesman 1973); students, similarly, are likely to support faculty change initiatives whenever those are related to student interests. However, the balance of faculty and student activism does not seem to correlate with outcomes in this study. Rather, those movements with the most enduring and institutionalized outcomes are those in which both students and faculty participated vocally.

So while the balance of faculty and student involvement is not an element of organizational structure with important predictive power, there may be other elements that are important. Charles Tilly's notion of WUNC (1999)—worthiness X unity X numbers X commitment—may be a fruitful avenue for the consideration of organizational structures. WUNC can be manipulated strategically, particularly through the use of framing strategies that emphasize the worthiness of the cause and those advocating for it. Yet many of the movements considered in this book involved a rather small number of individuals in colleges and universities with thousands of members. These movements, therefore, could not depend on their numbers as a persuasive tool or an element of organizational strength. They could develop otherwise strong organizational structures that would allow them to demonstrate unity and commitment (while worthiness might be better seen as an element of framing strategy rather than organizational structure). For instance,

---

2   Financial support may play a significant role in sponsoring the creation of new academic disciplines (Rojas 2007). However, though financial support was provided by grant funding from local or national foundations for women's studies and queer studies at Abigail Adams College, for women's studies at the College of Assisi, and for queer studies at Sagebrush University, in none of the cases considered in this book did a foundation directly fund the development of a new program. In fact, funding at Abigail Adams College was accepted partially to forestall the creation of a women's studies program without entirely ignoring research and teaching on women.

Asian American studies student activists at Sagebrush University expended considerable energy cooling conflicts that arose between students and faculty participating in the movement so that it would continue to look unified to the campus community at large.

Brayden King's work on movements targeting corporations has suggested another corrective to the political mediation model when it is applied to the organizational sphere. He studied the impact of boycotts on corporate policy, theorizing that boycotts have an effect on corporate policy through their "ability to damage corporate reputations" (King 2008:413). King finds that boycotts of corporations are much more likely to result in corporate change when they target firms that have experienced a reputation decline; firms that have experienced gains in their reputation are less likely to take the threat of a boycott seriously. Reputation is much harder to measure for colleges and universities. While *US News* rankings are often used as a measure of prestige, these are only available on a consistent basis beginning in 1991; in addition, the rankings methodology has frequently been revised, meaning that figures (especially for those below the top 25 colleges and universities) are not strictly comparable. Depending on the year, only the top 25–100 colleges and universities in each *US News* category are ranked, while others appear only in rough tiers, and many lower-prestige campuses (like Promenade University) never appear in the rankings at all. These factors mean that *US News* rankings can be an important way of measuring reputation for a small subset of colleges and universities over the past two decades, but they do not let me systematically analyze the role of reputation for the impacts of the social movements considered in this book.

As proxies for reputation, then, I considered the relative size of the full-time-equivalent faculty (1984–99), the total undergraduate enrollment (1984–2008), and the inflation-adjusted value of the endowment (1988–2008) for the six campuses considered here (National Center for Education Statistics 2010), but found them inconclusive. While these figures are available for all six colleges and universities and over a larger time range and are more directly comparable across campuses and years than are the *US News* rankings, they still do not cover the time during which the movements for women's studies at Abigail Adams College, Technopark University, Jeffrey University, Sagebrush University, and the College of Assisi first organized, and they are only rough proxies for reputation. Furthermore, because reputation according to these measures was either increasing or holding fairly steady across all six cases during the time periods when movements were active, I cannot test King's hypothesis on this data. However, I expect that a study which included colleges and universities experiencing a reputation decline would be able to observe the interaction of reputation and movement impacts. In addition, a better measure of reputation might incorporate specific data about faculty out-migration which is not available in this study.[3]

3　Thanks to Brayden King for suggesting this measure.

Concluding Thoughts

In his study of curricular change in the mid-1960s—a period of relative calm before the storm—Hefferlin (1969:18) wrote that "changing the curriculum, it has been said, is like moving a graveyard. In both cases, for better or worse, the content is generally lifeless." While many educational pundits—and indeed college students themselves—might agree with Hefferlin's sentiment, the stories relayed in this book make it clear that the curriculum is very much alive. Students, faculty, and other members of college and university communities are active in reshaping the curriculum to ensure that it remains relevant, socially engaged, and representative of the interests and identities of those who participate in it. Curricula have varied considerably across time—from the Harvard of the 1600s with its set program of recitations in Latin and Greek to the College of the Atlantic today where students can major in sustainable food systems by taking courses in activism and "emarketing"—indeed, Hefferlin himself found that colleges and universities on average add one program and drop one program every 15 years, and that the annual rate of course adoption and deletion is 4.4 percent. Curricula vary considerably across the landscape of colleges and universities today, from St. John's College and its four-year program of required courses focusing on the great books to Brown University where students can graduate without fulfilling a single specific course requirement. Curricular foci vary from the progressive and experimental Hampshire College, where students do not earn grades, to the politically and theologically conservative Liberty University, which requires almost two semesters of courses in Christian theology and philosophy of all students and offers a major in Worship.

A curricular landscape as varied and changing as this produces quite a lot of discussion and debate. Indeed, the content and purpose of the curriculum is a major topic for educational commentators. Should the curriculum emphasize the Western canon or make room for multiculturalism? Are progressive educators who teach courses on feminism, sexuality, and Marxism poisoning our youth or helping them learn critical thinking skills? Would students best be served by spending their time in college learning marketable vocational skills or being immersed in the world of the liberal arts? These questions have raged for generations, and they continue to rage today. But the words of commentators themselves don't shape the content and structure of the curriculum. And unlike in nations such as France, there are no national policies in the United States that dictate or even guide curricular decision-making. Rather, curricula are shaped on the local level, by state system governing boards and even more importantly by individual colleges and universities themselves. Such curricular decisions may be shaped or propelled by a variety of factors, including market demand, pressure from peers or outside agencies, the interests of administrators or faculty senates, or indeed by social movement activism.

In a world in which the protests of the 1960s have become a memory, we might tend to forget the role of activism in shaping the curricular experience. But that role is not only a historical one. Students and faculty continue to mobilize for curricular change, and they continue to make an impact on their colleges and universities. These social movements are only one type of movement targeting colleges and universities—in recent years, activists on campus have targeted tuition rates, privatization of campus services, labor policies, the choice of campus speakers, gun rules, and of course the perennial issue of dining hall food (though now it is more likely to be the source rather than the flavor of such food that draws protests). Colleges and universities are only one type of organization targeted by social movements—contemporary social movements target organizations of all types, from corporations to religious denominations, from hospitals to sports clubs. And movements targeting all kinds of organizations have taken on greater significance in our contemporary world as organizations themselves play a greater role in shaping social, economic, and political life. This book, then, provides a window into such movements. It shows how such movements manage to make an impact on the organizations that they target. And it provides a theoretical model for analyzing what makes these impacts possible—a theoretical model with broad applicability to all sorts of social movements that target organizations. Organizations are constantly changing, and social movements are among the forces shaping those changes. If we do not understand what makes their impacts possible—if we constrain our study of movement impacts to movements that target the state and our study of organizational change to those changes produced by neoinstitutional, market, or leadership-based forces—we are missing, it seems, the aspect of contemporary organizational life that is the very most alive.

Methodological Appendix

The analysis presented in this book is drawn from a larger study of the emergence of women's studies, Asian American studies, and queer studies programs in higher education in North America. This methodological appendix describes how the case studies presented here were developed and conducted and contextualizes them within the methods and findings of the broader study.

The larger study from which the analysis presented here was drawn involves a original large-scale dataset of 1251 colleges and universities in North America. This dataset includes a variety of information about the demographic makeup, institutional characteristics, and curricular offerings of each college and university drawn from a variety of sources that include college and university websites, the Integrated Post-Secondary Data Analysis System of the United States Department of Education (National Center for Education Statistics 2010), the Carnegie Commission (Carnegie Foundation for the Advancement of Teaching 2001), and the CollegeSource Online database (CollegeSource 2009).

The dataset was created in three phases. First, a random sample of sixty colleges and universities was drawn from those included in TheCenter's (Lombardi, Craig, Capaldi et al. 2002) list of all colleges and universities that had received at least one dollar of federal research funding over a five year period in the late 1990s, after discarding any colleges and universities that did not offer a four-year undergraduate degree in liberal arts and sciences fields. In the second phase of the research, these sixty colleges and universities were each asked to provide a list of other colleges and universities that they considered to be their peers, yielding a list of 523 colleges and universities. Finally, this sample of 523 colleges and universities were each asked to provide *their* peer colleges and universities, yielding a total sample of 1251 (after graduate-only campuses were removed).

The resulting sample is reasonably representative of American colleges and universities in terms of region and control. 45 percent of the colleges and universities in the sample are public, while 53 percent are private not-for-profit institutions; the remaining 2 percent are for-profit. 36 percent are religiously affiliated. As among colleges and universities more generally, the largest numbers are concentrated in the East, particularly the mid-Atlantic region. 8.9 percent are located in the northeastern states, 17.8 percent in the mid-Atlantic states, 12.6 percent in east north central states, 11.4 percent in west north central, 17.4 percent in the south Atlantic states, 8.1 percent in east south central, 9 percent in west south central, 4.4 percent in the mountain states, and 9.4 percent in the Pacific region (U.S. Census Bureau n.d.). Twelve universities, or 0.9 percent of the sample, are not in the United States—most of these are Canadian universities. The sample is less representative of American colleges and universities in terms of Carnegie classification (Carnegie

Foundation for the Advancement of Teaching 2001). The dataset over-represents four-year colleges and universities and under-represents community colleges and other two-year colleges as well as specialized institutions. This is by design, as the original dataset did not include any 2-year colleges, institutions that granted only graduate degrees, or other colleges or universities that did not offer bachelor's degrees in liberal arts and sciences fields (such as exclusively theological or engineering colleges). Excluding these types of colleges and universities, the sample is representative of the distribution of American colleges and universities across Carnegie 2000 classifications. This data is presented in Table A.1: while the percent of the sample in each Carnegie classification category is dissimilar to the percentage of all institutions classified by the Carnegie Commission that is in each classification category, it is similar to the percentage of colleges and universities in each category once associate's colleges and specialized institutions are removed, though baccalaureate general colleges (those awarding less than 20 graduate degrees per year and which award less than half of their baccalaureate degrees in liberal arts fields) continue to be somewhat underrepresented.

Table A.1   Distribution of Carnegie Classifications in Sample and Overall

Carnegie 2000 Classification	Percent of Sample	Percent of Classified Institutions	Percent of Classified Institutions, Excluding Associate's & Specialized Institutions
Doctoral/Research Extensive	11.4	3.8	10.2
Doctoral/Research Intensive	7.5	2.8	7.5
Master's I	31.6	12.6	33.7
Master's II	5.7	2.9	7.8
Baccalaureate Liberal Arts	14.2	5.8	15.5
Baccalaureate General	16.4	8.1	21.7
Baccalaureate/Associate's	1.7	1.4	3.7
Associate's	6.3	42.3	n/a
Specialized/Other Institutions	5.3	20.1	n/a

Case Studies

The six case studies presented in this book were selected from the original sixty-case sample. While they were not selected randomly, the randomness of the sixty-case sample from which they were drawn ensured that researcher bias could not overly influence the selection of cases. The six cases were selected to maximize diversity in college or university type, geography, size, selectivity, and other factors: they include both public and private universities; those in the Northeast, mid-Atlantic, Southeast, and West; highly selective and less selective campuses; small liberal arts colleges and major research universities; and both a Catholic college and a women's college.

Research into each case study involved site visits, archival research, and interviews. The first phase of research into each case involved a two to three day visit to the college or university in question. Prior to and during each visit, I discussed my research with the college or university archives staff. I then reviewed all available archival materials that might touch on curricular change; any attempts to establish women's studies, Asian American studies, and/or queer studies programs; the records of any such programs that did exist; records of student organizations focusing on issues around gender, race, and/or sexuality; records about student protest and contentious politics; and where appropriate, records of curriculum committee and other administrative deliberations. At each site, I viewed all issues of the student newspaper over the time frames of any applicable curricular change campaigns as well as issues of the course catalogue to see when courses related to these disciplines began being offered (some of these materials have been digitized).

As the quantity and quality of archival information available differed from campus to campus, I left the sites with between four and 18 pages of typewritten notes, as well as photocopies of key documents. Some of the colleges and universities had a clear commitment to preserving all the details of their historical records. At Abigail Adams College, my time in the archives uncovered even such ephemera as one-sentence memos sent between administrators and sign-in sheets from student meetings; similarly, many articles about the College from the national or local press had been preserved in the files. Not all colleges and universities have the resources to engage in such preservation. At Promenade University, the archivist and I had to sort through a cluttered and disorganized storeroom in hopes of finding the documents I sought; archives staff at Technopark University told me that some of the documents I was interested in seeing had recently been discarded because of space limitations.

Despite these obstacles, I was able to uncover one key resource at all six colleges and universities—names. The names of faculty members, non-academic staff members, students, and others who were either involved in or well acquainted with the curricular change campaigns had been preserved in the archives of all six campuses. I collected all the names I could find and sought out those individuals for interviews about the curricular change campaigns they had witnessed or participated in. Not all individuals could be located—some people with common names who were involved in curricular change campaigns of 30 years ago are lost to history at this point. However, attempts were made to contact 100 individuals. Of those 100, 73 were successfully located, and 53 participated in complete interviews. A few additional individuals provided small amounts of information but did not participate in formal interviews. Respondents were given the choice of participating in an interview via email, over the phone, or in person where possible; telephone and in-person interviews lasted between 15 minutes and one hour, depending on how much information the respondent was able to provide. Interviewees were reached from as far away as Norway and Australia. The number of interviews completed again varied according to the campus in question, from a low of four to a high of 16.

The six colleges and universities included in this study are referred to by pseudonyms to protect the identities of those who participated in these interviews. A number of the interviewees are current faculty members at the colleges and universities in question and their participation would easily be identifiable by colleagues and administrators if the identity of their college or university were to be disclosed. Some were worried that providing critical but accurate information about their program's history might imperil future attempts to expand it. Several interviewees disclosed details about their employment or personal histories that might be problematic if connected to them personally. Campus pseudonyms respond to all of these concerns.

On the basis of the archival and interview data, I was able to construct narratives of the curricular change campaigns that developed on each of the six campuses. These narratives serve as the basis of the case studies presented in Part II of the book. They also serve as the basis for the analysis that is presented in Chapter 9. The data gathered from the archival materials and from the interviews were analyzed through process analysis (Mahoney 2003); in this methodological strategy, the researcher explores hypotheses across cases, then looks within each case to determine which mechanisms link necessary and sufficient precursors with eventual outcomes and allows the researcher to test the implications of the hypothesis against the within-case evidence (Mahoney 2004). This approach allows the researcher to develop a detailed knowledge of each case in comparison to the others, thus making it possible to illuminate small differences between cases that may have large consequences for the theoretical explanation. It's important to note that the cases cannot be conceived of as independent (Valenzuela 1998)—all six cases coexist in the same national and temporal context, and to whatever extent neoinstitutional and diffusion pressures have affected program adoption in any one of the cases, that case may very well have been affected by one of the other cases in this study.

Quantitative Results

The broader dataset of 1251 colleges and universities has been utilized in a series of separate analyses, which are ongoing. Given the unavailability of specific data about internal organizational dynamics for such a large-scale dataset, it cannot be used to explore the appropriateness of the organizational context approach or the presence of leadership or contentious politics as explanations for curricular change. However, and especially given the inclusion of data on peer relationships, this dataset has allowed for the testing of market-based and neoinstitutional hypotheses regarding curricular change. Variables in the dataset include those measuring structural factors like college or university location, 2000 Carnegie classification (Carnegie Foundation for the Advancement of Teaching 2001), religious affiliation, and control; demographic factors like percentage of faculty and percentage of students female or Asian American, total enrollment, and percentage of students attending part-time; peer variables including the percentages of colleges and universities in the same state, Carnegie classification, and among those defined by a college and university as its own self-selected peers that offer a program; and outcome variables measuring whether each college or university offers any women's studies program, a women's studies major, any Asian American studies program, an Asian American studies major, and any queer studies program. Among the 523 cases included in the phase of the research that has already been completed, 74 percent offer some women's studies program, 38 percent offer a women's studies major, 11 percent offer some Asian American studies program, 4 percent offer an Asian American studies major, and 10 percent offer some queer studies program (queer studies majors are too rare to document using quantitative research methods). Hypothesis testing has been conducted using logistic regression analysis and network graphing. As the quantitative research is ongoing, finalized results are not available as of this writing. However, some illustrative results from analysis of the 523 case dataset are presented here.

Table A.2 shows that structural variables, particularly regional location, play a significant role in predicting where programs emerge, and that these structural factors have the strongest predictive value for women's studies programs. However, many key variables are excluded from the models presented in Table A.2. Because the dataset contains only 523 cases, there is a limit to the number of variables that can be included in each individual model without reducing cell sizes to a point too small for further analysis.

Table A.3 presents the results of a regression model drawing on factors that neoinstitutional researchers often suggest are important—selectivity and Carnegie Classification, in particular. These models have generally increased predictive power over the models presented in Table A.2, but few variables are significant.

There is a significant relationship between several Carnegie classifications and women's studies, but not the other fields; total enrollment has a significant but negligible effect for all five dependent variables. Only selectivity has consistent and measurable predictive power in these models.

Table A.4 presents the results of regression models drawing on demographic characteristics. Again, total enrollment is significant with a negligible effect size. Total enrollment and status as a single-sex campus do have significant predictive power for women's studies, while the percent of students who are Asian American has predictive power for Asian American studies (it is not possible to develop variables measuring the demographic composition of students or faculty as relevant to queer studies, so this field is excluded from Table A.4). An increase of 1 percent in the percentage of Asian American students enrolled at a college or university increases the probability that the college or university will offer Asian

Table A.2   Regression Coefficients (and Standard Errors) for Structural Variables

Variable	Women's Studies	Women's Studies Major	Asian American Studies	Asian American Studies Major	Queer Studies
New England	1.391 (0.731)	0.247 (0.450)	-1.511** (0.539)	-3.072** (1.109)	-0.938 (0.544)
Mid-Atlantic	0.266 (0.477)	-0.585 (0.132)	-2.039*** (0.509)	-2.485*** (0.744)	-1.888*** (0.551)
South Atlantic	-0.206 (0.463)	-0.480 (0.223)	-2.889*** (0.683)	-20.122 (4075.770)	-2.119*** (0.631)
East North Central	1.896** (0.709)	0.418 (0.289)	-1.810*** (0.512)	-3.521*** (1.080)	-0.684 (0.467)
East South Central	-0.158 (0.553)	-1.560** (0.584)	-20.368 (5651.285)	-19.957 (5712.041)	-20.019 (5811.946)
West North Central	-0.228 (0.483)	0.263 (0.422)	-2.221*** (0.697)	-2.903** (1.089)	-2.253** (0.805)
West South Central	-1.443** (0.484)	-1.768*** (0.538)	-2.755*** (0.805)	-2.903** (1.089)	-2.862** (1.077)
Mountain	-0.263 (0.635)	-0.063 (0.516)	-1.248* (0.610)	-2.575* (1.095)	1.756* (0.828)
West (excluded category)	—	—	—	—	—
Private	-0.599 (0.361)	0.545* (0.271)	0.144 (0.391)	-0.262 (0.681)	0.719 (0.379)
Protestant	-0.529 (0.438)	-1.280*** (0.400)	-19.697 (4639.170)	-18.643 (4450.557)	-1.790* (0.716)
Evangelical	-2.738*** (0.585)	-21.561 (6935.565)	-20.304 (6614.327)	-19.384 (6469.679)	-20.374 (6660.084)
Catholic	0.514 (0.621)	-1.248** (0.448)	-0.434 (0.648)	-18.495 (6370.267)	-2.378* (1.070)
Hispanic-Serving	0.558 (0.694)	-0.593 (0.625)	-0.442 (0.857)	-18.986 (8803.427)	-19.294 (8955.174)
Historically Black	-3.672*** (0.648)	-2.772** (1.038)	-17.894 (6278.577)	-16.264 (5737.147)	-17.946 (6388.221)
Cox & Snell R-Square	0.288	0.205	0.130	0.100	0.122
Nagelkerke R-Square	0.420	0.278	0.265	0.374	0.252

Note: *P < .05; ** P < .01; ***P < .001

Table A.3   Regression Coefficients (and Standard Errors) for Neoinstitutional Variables

Variable	Women's Studies	Women's Studies Major	Asian American Studies	Asian American Studies Major	Queer Studies
Selectivity	0.087*** (0.017)	0.031* (0.012)	0.104*** (0.025)	0.089* (0.039)	0.077*** (0.022)
Highest Degree Offered	-0.625 (0.354)	-0.146 (0.300)	0.436 (0.463)	-16.932 (3434.668)	0.447 (0.443)
Specialized	-20.995 (23165.772)	-20.622 (23200.390)	-17.276 (22477.760)	-33.530 (22127.002)	-18.402 (22683.616)
Associates/ Associates Baccalaureate	-1.590 (1.732)	-20.616 (19880.250)	-16.302 (17624.945)	-65.061 (19104.318)	-17.385 (18315.500)
Baccalaureate General	-.202 (1.090)	-2.909* (1.167)	-16.542 (6197.341)	-50.014 (9001.686)	-17.732 (6342.335)
Baccalaureate Liberal Arts	2.178* (1.089)	0.914 (0.614)	1.495 (0.892)	-33.873 (6869.335)	1.165 (0.836)
Master's 1	0.262 (1.074)	-0.879 (0.790)	-16.745 (9306.961)	-34.015 (9869.886)	0.503 (1.233)
Master's 2	0.295 (0.888)	-1.017* (0.418)	0.692 (0.645)	-17.685 (3434.668)	-0.975 (0.759)
Doctoral Intensive	-0.417 (0.863)	-0.759* (0.382)	-0.655 (0.823)	-17.865 (4951.647)	-0.758 (0.700)
Doctoral Extensive (excluded)	—	—	—	—	—
Total Enrollment	0.000*** (0.000)	0.000*** (0.000)	0.000*** (0.000)	0.000*** (0.000)	0.000* (0.000)
Cox & Snell R-Square	0.372	0.299	0.207	0.091	0.148
Nagelkerke R-Square	0.573	0.402	0.399	0.321	0.292

Note: *P < .05; ** P < .01; ***P < .001

Table A.4   Regression Coefficients (and Standard Errors) for Demographic Models

Variable	Women's Studies	Women's Studies Major	Asian American Studies	Asian American Studies Major
% Tenured Faculty Female/ Asian American	-0.002 (0.016)	0.016 (0.016)	-0.110 (0.081)	0.007 (0.122)
% Faculty Female/ Asian American	0.002 (0.20)	0.004 (0.019)	0.051 (0.085)	-0.003 (0.137)
% Students Female/ Asian American	0.000 (0.014)	-0.011 (0.013)	0.187*** (0.032)	0.178*** (0.039)
Single-Sex Enrollment	21.177 (14882.648)	2.317* (0.928)	—	—
Total Enrollment	0.000*** (0.000)	0.000*** (0.000)	0.000*** 0.000	0.000*** (0.000)
Percent Students Undergraduates	0.023** (0.008)	0.000 (0.007)	0.017 (0.013)	0.022 (0.021)
Cox & Snell R-Squared	0.259	0.165	0.203	0.107
Nagelkerke R-Squared	0.379	0.224	0.413	0.397

Note: *P < .05; ** P < .01; ***P < .001

American studies by 2 percent and increases the probability that it will offer an Asian American studies major by 0.7 percent. It is possible that this result is due to a threshold effect. When campuses with less than 5 percent Asian American students are removed from the analysis, significance disappears for Asian American studies programs (though it remains for Asian American studies majors). In addition, there are no Asian American studies programs among colleges and universities with fewer than 2 percent Asian American students (and few with between 2 and 5 percent Asian American students) and no Asian American studies majors among colleges and universities with under 5 percent Asian American studies. In contrast, there are many colleges and universities with over 20 percent Asian American students who do not have an Asian American studies program of any kind, never mind a major.

Table A.5 presents the results of regression models drawing on the peer network variables. Except for Carnegie classification peers for the Asian American studies major, all are significant; though the overall effect sizes of the models are stronger than for the prior models, each individual variable has only a small effect size.

Table A.5   Regression Coefficients (and Standard Errors) for Structural Network Models

Variable	Women's Studies	Women's Studies Major	Asian American Studies	Asian American Studies Major	Queer Studies
Percent of Institutions in State Offering Program	0.039*** (0.008)	0.051*** (0.007)	0.142*** (0.020)	0.157*** (0.031)	0.101*** (0.016)
Percent of Institutions in Carnegie Class Offering Program	0.031*** (0.008)	0.036*** (0.007)	0.064* (0.031)	0.088 (0.051)	0.073** (0.024)
Percent of Institutions in Size Category Offering Program	0.086*** (0.014)	0.036*** (0.007)	0.116*** (0.025)	0.090* (0.035)	0.053** (0.017)
Percent of Institutions in Selectivity Category Offering Program	0.050*** (0.010)	0.027*** (0.009)	0.119** (0.044)	0.144* (0.068)	0.0758*** (0.018)
Cox & Snell R Square	0.403	0.377	0.240	0.133	0.222
Nagelkerke R Square	0.588	0.514	0.493	0.493	0.459

Note: *P < .05; ** P < .01; ***P < .001

The results presented so far suggest that structural peer networks, regional location, and selectivity have the strongest effects on the likelihood of program adoption.

The final set of regression models, presented in Table A.6, incorporate only the 60 cases that comprised the original randomly-selected sample. These 60 colleges and universities were each contacted and asked to provide a self-selected list of colleges and universities that they see as their peers (called "relational peers" in Table A.6). Because the sample size is so small, the models presented in Table A.6 draw only on the relational peers variable and the two strongest variables from the prior analyses, the percentage of colleges and universities in the same state that offer a program and the selectivity of the college or university. While the overall effect size of these regressions is the strongest of all of those presented here, the only variable that is significant is the percentage of relational peers offering a program, and then only for women's studies.

The results presented in this Appendix are only a summary of the larger quantitative project, which remains ongoing as of this writing. These results are presented in order to provide some larger context for the case studies that make up the bulk of the book. So far, the quantitative project suggests that peers and

Table A.6   Regression Coefficients (and Standard Errors) for Peer Models

Variable	Women's Studies	Women's Studies Major	Asian American Studies	Queer Studies
Percent of Relational Peers Offering Program	0.090* (0.042)	0.112** (0.036)	0.050 (0.038)	0.049 (0.043)
Percent of Institutions in State Offering Program	0.033 (0.052)	0.024 (0.020)	0.061 (0.059)	0.154 (0.096)
Selectivity	0.143 (0.081)	-0.003 (0.041)	0.055 (0.081)	0.528 (0.528)
Cox & Snell R Square	0.437	0.468	0.137	0.338
Nagelkerke R Square	0.787	0.626	0.321	0.707

Note: *P < .05; ** P < .01; ***P < .001

networks, particularly the peers a college or university self-selects, play a stronger role in curricular change than do structural or organizational variables. However, even relational peers play a limited role in explaining curricular change decisions; they are significant only for women's studies, the oldest and most institutionalized of the fields of study considered in this book. Therefore, it is likely that networks and neoinstitutional factors play a role only for more institutionalized fields, and that the contentious politics explanation developed in this book is a better explanation for much of curricular change, particularly programs that emerge earlier in the trajectory of a new field of study. It is also worth pointing out that neoinstitutional logic is often drawn on by the activists pushing for curricular change, as it was most clearly in the campaigns for women's studies at Promenade University, Sagebrush University, and the College of Assisi and in the campaigns for Asian American studies and queer studies at Sagebrush University. Therefore, the presence of a neoinstitutional effect on curricular change does not tell us whether administrators are making change decisions to keep up with their peers or whether activists are using the presence of programs at peer colleges and universities as a strategic level to increase their influence on the curricular change process.

Bibliography

Abbot, Andrew. 2001. *Chaos of Disciplines*. Chicago, IL: The University of Chicago Press.

Adelman, Clifford. 2004. *The Empirical Curriculum: Changes in Postsecondary Course-Taking, 1972–2000*. Washington, DC: U.S. Department of Education.

Aldridge, Delores P. and Carlene Young, ed. 2000. *Out of the Revolution: The Development of Africana Studies*. Lanham, MD: Lexington Books.

Amenta, Edwin. 2006. *When Movements Matter: The Impact of the Townsend Plan and U.S. Social Spending Challengers*. Princeton, NJ: Princeton University Press.

Amenta, Edwin and Neal Caren. 2004. "The Legislative, Organizational, and Beneficiary Consequences of State-Oriented Challengers." Pp. 461–88 in *The Blackwell Companion to Social Movements*, edited by David A. Snow, Sarah A. Soule, and Hanspeter Kriesi. Malden, MA: Blackwell.

Amenta, Edwin, Neal Caren, Tina Fetner, and Michael P. Young. 2002. "Challengers and States: Toward a Political Sociology of Social Movements." *Research in Political Sociology* 10:47–83.

Amenta, Edwin, Neal Caren, and Sheera Joy Olasky. 2005. "Age for Leisure? Political Mediation and the Impact of the Pension Movement on U.S. Old-Age Policy." *American Sociological Review* 70:516–38.

Amenta, Edwin, Drew Halfmann, and Michael P. Young. 1999. "The Strategies and Contexts of Social Protest: Political Mediation and the Impact of the Townsend Movement in California." *Mobilization* 4:1–24.

Amenta, Edwin and Michael P. Young. 1999a. "Democratic States and Social Movements: Theoretical Arguments and Hypotheses." *Social Problems* 57:153–68.

—. 1999b. "Making an Impact: Conceptual and Methodological Implications of the Collective Goods Criterion." Pp. 22–41 in *How Movements Matter: Theoretical and Comparative Studies on the Consequences of Social Movements*, edited by Marco Guigini, Doug McAdam, and Charles Tilly. Minneapolis, MN: University of Minnesota Press.

Anchita, Angelo. 1998. *Race, Rights, and the Asian American Experience*. New Brunswick, NJ: Rutgers University Press.

Andrews, Kenneth T. 2001. "Social Movements and Policy Implementation: The Mississippi Civil Rights Movement and the War on Poverty, 1965–1971." *American Sociological Review* 66:71–95.

Armstrong, Elizabeth and Mary Bernstein. 2008. "Culture, Power, and Institutions: A Multi-Institutional Politics Approach to Social Movements." *Sociological Theory* 26:74–99.

Arthur, Mikaila Mariel Lemonik. 2008. "Social Movements in Organizations." *Sociology Compass* 2/3:1014–30.

—. 2009. "Thinking Outside the Master's House: New Knowledge Movements and the Emergence of Academic Disciplines." *Social Movement Studies* 8:73–87.

Asregadoo, Edward Dyanand. 2000. "Revolution Interrupted: Chronicling and Comparing Student Protest Movements at Stanford University, San Francisco State College, and the University of California at Berkeley, 1964–1970." Ph.D. Dissertation, American Civilization, University of Pennsylvania, Philadelphia, PA.

Astin, Helen S. and Allison Parelman. 1973. "Women's Studies in American Colleges and Universities." *International Social Science Journal* 25:389–400.

Avery, Christopher, Mark Clickman, Caroline Hoxby, and Andrew Metrick. 2004. "A Revealed Preference Ranking of U.S. Colleges and Universities." Cambridge, MA: National Bureau of Economic Research. NBER Working Paper No. 10803. Retrieved October 17, 2004. (http://www.nber.org/papers/w10803).

Baldridge, J. Victor. 1971. *Power and Conflict in the University: Research in the Sociology of Complex Organizations*. New York: John Wiley & Sons, Inc.

Barlow, William and Peter Shapiro. 1971. *An End to Silence: The San Francisco State College Student Movement in the '60s*. New York: Pegasus.

Bayer, Alan E. 1972. "Institutional Correlates of Faculty Support of Campus Unrest." *Sociology of Education* 45:76–94.

Becher, Tony and Paul R. Trowler. 1989. *Academic Tribes and Territories: Intellectual Enquiry and the Culture of Disciplines*, Second ed. Philadelphia, PA: Open University Press.

Benford, Robert D. and David A. Snow. 2000. "Framing Processes and Social Movements: An Overview and Assessment." *Annual Review of Sociology* 26: 611–39.

Bernstein, Richard. 1994. *Dictatorship of Virtue: Multiculturalism and the Battle for America's Future*. New York: Alfred A. Knopf.

Binder, Amy J. 2002. *Contentious Curricula: Afrocentrism and Creationism in American Public Schools*. Princeton, NJ: Princeton University Press.

Blau, Peter M. 1994. *The Organization of Academic Work*, Second ed. New Brunswick, NJ: Transaction Publishers.

Bok, Derek. 2003. *Universities in the Marketplace: The Commercialization of Higher Education*. Princeton, NJ: Princeton University Press.

Boren, Mark Edelman. 2001. *Student Resistance: A History of the Unruly Subject*. New York: Routledge.

Boxer, Marilyn Jacoby. 1982. "For and about Women: the Theory and Practice of Women's Studies in the United States." *Signs* 7:661–95.

—. 1998. *When Women Ask the Questions: Creating Women's Studies in America*. Baltimore, MD: The Johns Hopkins University Press.

Brewer, Dominic J., Susan M. Gates, and Charles A. Goldman. 2002. *In Pursuit of Prestige: Strategy and Competition in U.S. Higher Education*. New Brunswick, NJ: Transaction Publishers.

Brinker, Paul A. 1960. "Our Illiberal Liberal-Arts Colleges: the Dangers of Undergraduate Overspecialization." *The Journal of Higher Education* 31: 133–8.

Brint, Steven G., Mark Riddle, Lori Turk-Bicakci, and Charles S. Levy. 2005. "From the Liberal Arts to the Practical Arts in American Colleges and Universities: Organizational Analysis and Curricular Change." *The Journal of Higher Education* 76:151–80.

Bryson, Bethany. 2005. *Making Multiculturalism: Boundaries and Meaning in U.S. English Departments*. Stanford, CA: Stanford University Press.

Buhle, Mari Jo. 2000. "Introduction." Pp. xv-xxvi in *The Politics of Women's Studies: Testimony from Thirty Founding Mothers*, edited by Florence Howe. New York: The Feminist Press.

Bull, Chris. 1998. "Theoretical Battles: It's Popular on Campus, but Queer Studies is Under Attack from Both the Right and the Left." *The Advocate*, September 29, 1998, p. 44.

Burstein, Paul, Rachael L. Einwohner, and Jocelyn A. Hollander. 1995. "The Success of Political Movements: A Bargaining Perspective." Pp. 275–95 in *The Politics of Social Protest: Comparative Perspectives on States and Social Movements*, edited by J. Craig Jenkins and Bert Klandermans. Minneapolis, MN: University of Minnesota Press.

Calhoun, Craig. 2006. "Discipline and Hybridity." Paper presented at the 2006 Annual Meetings of the American Sociological Association, Montreal, Canada.

Cantor, Nancy E. and Paul N. Courant. 1997. "Budgets and Budgeting at the University of Michigan—A Work in Progress." *The University Record of the University of Michigan*, November 26, 1997.

—. 2001. *Scrounge We Must: Reflections on the Whys and Wherefores of Higher Education Finance*. Paper presented at the CHERI Conference on Higher Education Finance, Cornell University.

Carnegie Foundation for the Advancement of Teaching. 2001. "The Carnegie Classification of Institutions of Higher Education: 2000 Edition." Carnegie Publications, Menlo Park, CA.

Carr, Joe. 2010. "Kennedy Announces UMaine Academic Reorganization." *UMaine News*. Retrieved May 20, 2010, (http://www.umaine.edu/news/blog/2010/05/04/kennedy-announces-umaine-academic-reorganization/).

Chan, Sucheng. 1991. *Asian Americans: An Interpretive History*. New York: Twayne Publishers.

—. 2005. *In Defense of Asian American Studies: The Politics of Teaching and Program Building*. Chicago, IL: University of Illinois Press.

Chang, Mitchell J. 1999. "Expansion and its Discontents: The Formation of Asian American Studies Programs in the 1990s." *Journal of Asian American Studies* 2:181–206.

Chiang, Mark. 2009. *The Cultural Capital of Asian American Studies: Autonomy and Representation in the University.* New York: NYU Press.

Clark, Burton R. 1996. "Substantive Growth and Innovative Organization: New Categories for Higher Education Research." *Higher Education* 32:417–30.

Clark, Terry N. 1968. "Institutionalization of Innovations in Higher Education: Four Models." *Administrative Science Quarterly* 13:1–25.

Clemens, Elisabeth S. and James M. Cook. 1999. "Politics and Institutionalism: Explaining Durability and Change." *Annual Review of Sociology* 25:441–66.

Cohen, Michael D. and James G. March. 1974. *Leadership and Ambiguity: The American College President.* Boston, MA: Harvard Business School Press.

Cohen, Michael D., James G. March, and Johan P. Olsen. 1972. "A Garbage Can Model of Organizational Choice." *Administrative Science Quarterly* 17:1–25.

CollegeSource, Inc. 2009. "CollegeSource Online." Retrieved May 29, 2009, (http://www.collegesource.org/).

Cook, Stacey Ann. 2001. "Power and Resistance: Berkeley's Third World Liberation Front Strikes." Ed.D. Dissertation, Organization and Leadership Department, University of San Francisco, San Francisco, CA.

Cress, David M. and David A. Snow. 2000. "The Outcomes of Homeless Mobilization: The Influence of Organization, Disruption, Political Mediation, and Framing." *American Journal of Sociology* 105: 1063–1104.

Crowley, Helen. 1999. "Women's Studies: Between a Rock and a Hard Place or Just Another Cell in the Beehive?" *Feminist Review* 61:131–50.

Cruikshank, Margaret. 1992. *The Gay and Lesbian Liberation Movement.* New York: Routledge.

D'Emilio, John. 1974. "Introduction." Pp. 9–20 in *The Universities and the Gay Experience*, edited by the Gay Academic Union. New York: Towne and Country Press.

Damrosch, David. 1995. *We Scholars: Changing the Culture of the University.* Cambridge, MA: Harvard University Press.

Davies, Scott. 1999. "From Moral Duty to Cultural Rights: A Case Study of Political Framing in Education." *Sociology of Education* 72:1–21.

Degroot, Gerard J. 1998. *Student Protest: The Sixties and After.* London: Longman.

Dillon, Sam. 2010. "Marquette Rescinds Offer to Sociologist." *New York Times,* May 7, 2010, p. A16.

DiMaggio, Paul J. and Walter W. Powell. 1983. "The Iron Cage Revisited: Institutional Isomorphism and Collective Rationality in Organizational Fields." *American Sociological Review* 48:147–60.

—. 1991. "The Iron Cage Revisited: Institutional Isomorphism and Collective Rationality in Organizational Fields." Pp. 63–82 in *The New Institutionalism in Organizational Analysis*, edited by Walter W. Powell and Paul J. DiMaggio. Chicago, IL: University of Chicago Press.

Dugger, Ronnie. 2000. "Introduction: The Struggle That Matters the Most." Pp. 17–28 in *Campus, Inc.: Corporate Power in the Ivory Tower*, edited by Geoffry D. White and Flannery C. Hauck. Amherst, NY: Prometheus Books.

Dynes, Wayne R. 1993. "Queer Studies: In Search of a Discipline." *Academic Questions* 7:34–52.

Edelstein, Frederick S. 1973. "The Politics of Ethnic Studies in Higher Education: A Case Study of the Establishment of Ethnic Studies Programs at Four Big Eight Universities." Ph.D. Dissertation, Department of History and Philosophy of Education, University of Nebraska, Lincoln, NE.

Edwards, Bob and John D. McCarthy. 2004. "Resources and Social Movement Mobilization." Pp. 116–52 in *The Blackwell Companion to Social Movements*, edited by Snow, David A., Sarah A. Soule, and Hanspeter Kriesi. London, UK: Blackwell.

Eisenstein, Hester. 1996. *Inside Agitators: Australian Femocrats and the State*. Philadelphia, PA: Temple University Press.

Ellin, Abby. 2006. "Big People on Campus." *New York Times*, November 26, 2006. Retrieved March 25, 2007, (http://www.nytimes.com/2006/11/26/fashion/26fat.html).

Epstein, Steven. 1996. *Impure Science: AIDS, Activism, and the Politics of Knowledge*. Berkeley, CA: University of California Press.

Espenshade, Thomas J. and Alexandria Walton Radford. 2009. *No Longer Separate, Not Yet Equal*. Princeton, NJ: Princeton University Press.

Espiritu, Yen Le. 1992. *Asian American Panethnicity: Bridging Institutions and Identities*. Philadelphia, PA: Temple University Press.

Etzioni, Amitai. 1975. *A Comparative Analysis of Complex Organizations*, Second ed. New York: Free Press.

Feldman, Rochelle Cynthia. 1982. "The Institutionalization of the Women's Movement in American Higher Education." Ph.D. Dissertation, Education. University of Connecticut, Storrs, CT.

Foster, Julian and Durward Long, ed. 1970. *Protest! Student Activism in America*. New York: William Morrow & Company.

Freeman, Jo. 1973. "The Origins of the Women's Liberation Movement." *American Journal of Sociology* 78:792–811.

Frickel, Scott. 2004. *Chemical Consequences: Environmental Mutagens, Scientist Activism, and the Rise of Genetic Toxicology*. New Brunswick, NJ: Rutgers University Press.

Frickel, Scott and Neil Gross. 2005. "A General Theory of Scientific/Intellectual Movements." *American Sociological Review* 70:204–32.

Gammon, Carolyn. 1992. "Lesbian Studies Emerging in Canada." Pp. 137–60 in *Gay and Lesbian Studies*, edited by Henry L. Minton. New York: Haworth Press.

Gamson, Joshua and Dawne Moon. 2004. "The Sociology of Sexualities: Queer and Beyond." *Annual Review of Sociology* 30:47–64.

Gamson, William. 1990. *The Strategy of Social Protest*, Second ed. Belmont, CA: Wadsworth.

Ganz, Marshall Louis. 2000. "Resources and Resourcefulness: Strategic Capacity in the Unionization of California Agriculture, 1959–1966." *American Journal of Sociology* 105:1003–62.

Gardiner, Judith Kegan. 2002. "Rethinking Collectivity: Chicago Feminism, Athenian Democracy, and the Consumer University." Pp. 191–201 in *Women's Studies On Its Own, Next Wave: New Directions in Women's Studies*, edited by Robyn Wiegman. Durham, NC: Duke University Press.

Glazer, Nathan. 1970. *Remembering the Answers: Essays on the American Student Revolt*. New York: Basic Books.

Goodwin, Jeff and James M. Jasper. 1999. "Caught in a Winding, Snarling Vine: The Structural Bias of Political Process Theory." *Sociological Forum* 14:27–54.

Gross, Larry. 2005. "The Past and the Future of Gay, Lesbian, Bisexual, and Transgender Studies." *Journal of Communication* 55:508–28.

Grossman, Frank D. 2005. "Dissent from Within: How Educational Insiders use Protest to Change their Institution." Ph.D. Dissertation, Education, Columbia University, New York.

—. 2010. "Dissent from Within: How Educational Insiders Use Protest to Create Policy Change." *Educational Policy* 24:4, 655–86.

Guigini, Marco and Sakura Yamasaki. 2009. "The Policy Impact of Social Movements: A Replication Through Qualitative Comparative Analysis." *Mobilization* 14:467–84.

Gumport, Patricia J. 2000. "Academic Restructuring: Organizational Change and Institutional Imperatives." *Higher Education* 39:67–91.

Gumport, Patricia J. and Stuart K. Snydman. 2002. "The Formal Organization of Knowledge: An Analysis of Academic Structure." *The Journal of Higher Education* 73:375–408.

Hagan, Shirley and Florence Howe. 1980. "Women's Studies Programs—1980." *Women's Studies Newsletter*, Winter 1980.

Halberstam, Judith. 2003. "Reflections on Queer Studies and Queer Pedagogy." *Journal of Homosexuality* 45:361–4.

Hashem, Mazem. 2002. "Academic Knowledge from Elite Closure to Professional Service: The Rise of High-Growth Fields in American Higher Education." Ph.D. Dissertation, Sociology, University of California Riverside, Riverside, CA.

Hefferlin, J.B. Lon. 1969. *Dynamics of Academic Reform*. San Francisco: Jossey-Bass Publishers.

Hekma, Gert and Theo van der Meer. 1992. "Gay and Lesbian Studies in the Netherlands." Pp. 125–36 in *Gay and Lesbian Studies*, edited by Henry L. Minton. New York: Haworth Press.

Henning, Christoph. 2007. "Institution." In *The Blackwell Encyclopedia of Sociology*, edited by George Ritzer. Malden, MA: Blackwell Reference Online.

Howe, Florence. 1977. "Seven Years Later: Women's Studies Programs in 1976." Report of the National Advisory Council on Women's Educational Programs.

Hoxby, Caroline M. 2000. "The Effects of Geographic Integration and Increasing Competition in the Market for College Education." National Bureau of Economic Research. NBER Working Paper No. 6323.

Hu-DeHart, Evelyn. 1993. "The History, Development, and Future of Ethnic Studies." *Phi Delta Kappan* 75:50–5.

—. 2004. "Ethnic Studies in U.S. Higher Education: History, Development, Goals." Pp. 869–81 in *Handbook of Research on Multicultural Education*, edited by James A. Banks and Cherry A. McGee Banks. San Francisco, CA: Jossey-Bass Publishers.

Hunt, Stephen. 2007. "Organizations." In *The Blackwell Encyclopedia of Sociology*, edited by George Ritzer. Malden, MA: Blackwell Reference Online.

Ijima, Chris. 2001. "Pontifications on the Distinction Between Grains of Sand and Yellow Pearls." Pp. 3–15 in *Asian Americans: The Movements and the Moment*, edited by Steven G. Louie and Glenn K. Omatsu. Los Angeles, CA: UCLA Asian American Studies Center Press.

Jaschik, Scott. 2006. "Affirmative Action for Men." *Inside Higher Ed*, March 27, 2006. Retrieved January 7, 2007, (http://insidehighered.com/news/2006/03/27/admit).

Jenkins, Craig. 1983. "Resource Mobilization Theory and the Study of Social Movements." *Annual Review of Sociology* 9:527–53.

Johnson, Nate. 2009. "What Does a College Degree Cost? Comparing Approaches to Measuring 'Cost Per Degree.'" Delta Cost Project White Paper Series. Retrieved June 3, 2010, (http://www.deltacostproject.org/resources/pdf/johnson3-09_WP.pdf).

Joseph, Miranda. 2002. "Analogy and Complicity: Women's Studies, Lesbian/Gay Studies, and Capitalism." Pp. 267–92 in *Women's Studies On Its Own, Next Wave: New Directions in Women's Studies*, edited by Robyn Wiegman. Durham, NC: Duke University Press.

June, Audrey Williams. 2010. "Scholar Rejected by Marquette Says Her Work Is Noncontroversial at Seattle U." *The Chronicle of Higher Education*, May 11, 2010. Retrieved June 11, 2010, (http://chronicle.com/article/Rejected-by-Marquette-Nonc/65481/).

Karabel, Jerome. 2005. *The Chosen: The Hidden History of Admissions and Exclusion at Harvard, Yale, and Princeton*. New York: Houghton Mifflin.

Katzenstein, Mary Fainsod. 1998. *Faithful and Fearless: Moving Feminist Protest inside the Church and Military*. Princeton, NJ: Princeton University Press.

Keller, George. 1983. *Academic Strategy: The Management Revolution in American Higher Education*. Baltimore, MD: Johns Hopkins University Press.

Kennedy, Jennie. 2000a. "Rejection of AAS Director Candidate Sparks Conflict, Arrests." *The Daily Texan*, November 28, 2000. Retrieved September 15, 2006, (http://tspweb02.tsp.utexas.edu/webarchive/11-28-00/2000112801_s03_Rejection.html).

—. 2000b. "Students' Struggle Marks Beginning of UT AAS Odyssey." *The Daily Texan*, November 27, 2000, p. 59. Retrieved September 15, 2006, (http://tspweb02.tsp.utexas.edu/webarchive/11-27-00/2000112706_s01_.html).

Kerr, Clark. 1995. *The Uses of the University*. Cambridge, MA: Harvard University Press.

Kimura-Walsh, Erin Fukiko. 2009. "Balancing the Values of Ethnic Studies and Academe: Exploring Efforts to Advance the Organizational Stability of

American Indian and Asian American Studies." Ph.D. Dissertation, Education, University of California Los Angeles, Los Angeles, CA.

King, Brayden G. 2008. "A Political Mediation Model of Corporate Response to Social Movement Activism." *Administrative Science Quarterly* 53:395–421.

King, Brayden G. and Nicholas A. Pearce. 2010. "The Contentiousness of Markets: Politics, Social Movements, and Institutional Change in Markets." *Annual Review of Sociology* 36:249–67.

Kirp, David L. 2003. *Shakespeare, Einstein, and the Bottom Line: The Marketing of Higher Education*. Cambridge, MA: Harvard University Press.

Kitschelt, Herbert P. 1986. "Political Opportunity Structure and Political Protest: Anti-Nuclear Movements in Four Democracies." *British Journal of Political Science* 16:57–85.

Klein, Julie Thompson. 1990. *Interdisciplinarity: History, Theory, and Practice*. Detroit, MI: Wayne State University Press.

—. 1996. *Crossing Boundaries: Knowledge, Disciplinarities, and Interdisciplinarities*. Charlottesville, VA: University Press of Virginia.

Kraatz, Matthew S. and Edward J. Zajac. 1996. "Exploring the Limits of the New Institutionalism: The Causes and Consequences of Illegitimate Organizational Change." *American Sociological Review* 61:812–36.

Kriesi, Hanspeter. 2004. "Political Context and Opportunity." Pp. 67–90 in *The Blackwell Companion to Social Movements*, edited by David A. Snow, Sarah A. Soule, and Hanspeter Kriesi. London, UK: Blackwell.

Lattuca, Lisa R. 2001. *Creating Interdisciplinarity: Interdisciplinary Research and Teaching among College and University Faculty*. Nashville, TN: Vanderbilt University Press.

Levin, Miriam R. 2005. *Defining Women's Scientific Enterprise: Mount Holyoke Faculty and the Rise of American Science*. Lebanon, NH: University Press of New England.

Levitt, Cyril. 1984. *Children of Privilege: Student Revolt in the Sixties*. Toronto, Canada: University of Toronto Press.

Lien, Pei-te. 2001. *The Making of Asian America through Political Participation*. Philadelphia, PA: Temple University Press.

Lim, Ji Hyun. 2001. "The State of Asian American Studies in 2001." *Asian Week*, September 6, 2001. Retrieved December 16, 2004, (http://www.asianweek.com/2001_08_31/feature_aastudies.html).

Linders, Anulla. 2004. "Victory and Beyond: A Historical Comparative Analysis of the Outcomes of the Abortion Movements in Sweden and the United States." *Sociological Forum* 19:371–404.

Lipset, Seymour Martin. 1967. *Student Politics*. New York: Basic Books.

—. 1976. *Rebellion in the University*. Chicago, IL: University of Chicago Press.

Lombardi, John V., Diane D. Craig, Elizabeth D. Capaldi, and Denise S. Gater. 2002. "The Top American Research Universities, 1999." TheCenter, Gainesville, FL.

Louie, Steven G. and Glenn K. Omatsu, eds. 2001. *Asian Americans: the Movement and the Moment*. Los Angeles, CA: UCLA Asian American Studies Center Press.

Lounsbury, Michael. 2001. "Institutional Sources of Practice Variation: Staffing College and University Recycling Programs." *Administrative Science Quarterly* 46:29–56.

Maeda, Daryl J. 2009. *Chains of Babylon: The Rise of Asian America*. Minneapolis, MN: University of Minnesota Press.

Maher, Frances. 1993. "Classroom Pedagogy and the New Scholarship on Women." Pp. 565–77 in *Women in Higher Education: A Feminist Perspective*, edited by Judith S. Glazer, Estela M. Bensimon, and Barbara K. Townsend. Needham Heights, MA: Ginn Press.

Mahoney, James. 2003. "Strategies of Causal Assessment in Comparative Historical Analysis." Pp. 337–72 in *Comparative Historical Analysis in the Social Sciences*, edited by James Mahoney and Dietrich Rueschemeyer. Cambridge, UK: Cambridge University Press.

—. 2004. "Comparative-Historical Methodology." *Annual Review of Sociology* 30:81–101.

Martin, Biddy. 2001. "Success and Its Failures." Pp. 353–80 in *Feminist Consequences: Theory for the New Century, Gender and Culture*, edited by Elisabeth Bronfen and Misha Kavka. New York: Columbia University Press.

McAdam, Doug. 1986. "Recruitment to High Risk Activism: The Case of Freedom Summer." *American Journal of Sociology* 92:64–90.

McAdam, Doug, Sidney Tarrow, and Charles Tilly. 2001. *Dynamics of Contention*. New York: Cambridge University Press.

McCarthy, John D. and Mayer N. Zald. 1977. "Resource Mobilization and Social Movements: A Partial Theory." *American Journal of Sociology* 82:1212–41.

—. 2002. "The Enduring Vitality of the Resource Mobilization Theory of Social Movements." Pp. 533–65 in *Handbook of Sociological Theory*, edited by Jonathan Turner. New York: Plenum.

McMartin, Flora Pearle. 1993. "The Institutionalization of Women's Centers and Women's Studies Programs at Three Research Universities." Ed.D. Dissertation, Education, University of California Berkeley, Berkeley, CA.

McPherson, Michael S. and Morton Owen Schapiro. 1999. "The Future Economic Challenges for the Liberal Arts Colleges." *Daedalus* 128:47–75.

Meyer, David S. 1993. "Institutionalizing Dissent: The United States Structure of Political Opportunity and the End of the Nuclear Freeze." *Sociological Forum* 8:157–79.

Meyer, David S. and Debra C. Minkoff. 2004. "Conceptualizing Political Opportunity." *Social Forces* 82:1457–92.

Meyer, John W. 1977. "The Effects of Education as an Institution." *American Journal of Sociology* 83:55–77.

Meyer, John W., Francisco O. Ramirez, David John Frank, and Evan Schofer. 2005. "Higher Education as an Institution." Center on Democracy, Development, and the Rule of Law Working Paper No. 57, Stanford University, Stanford, CA. Retrieved August 11, 2007, (http://iis-db.stanford.edu/pubs/21108/Meyer_No_57.pdf).

Meyerson, Debra E. 2001. *Tempered Radicals: How People Use Difference to Inspire Change at Work*. Boston, MA: Harvard Business School Press.

Meyerson, Debra E. and Maureen A. Scully. 1995. "Tempered Radicalism and the Politics of Ambivalence and Change." *Organization Science* 6:585–600.

—. 1999. "Tempered Radicalism: Changing the Workplace from Within." *Insights: Linking Gender and Organizational Effectiveness* 6:1–4.

Meyerson, Debra E. and Megan Tompkins. 2007. "Tempered Radicals as Institutional Change Agents: The Case of Advancing Gender Equity at University of Michigan." *Harvard Journal of Law and Gender* 30:303–22.

Miller, Frederick D. 1999. "The End of SDS and the Emergence of Weathermen: Demise Through Success." Pp. 303–24 in *Waves of Protest: Social Movements Since the Sixties, People, Passions, and Power*, edited by Jo Freeman and Victoria Johnson. Lanham, MD: Rowman and Littlefield.

Mohr, Richard D. 1989. "Gay Studies as Moral Vision." *Educational Theory* 39:121–32.

Moore, Kelly. 1999. "Political Protest and Institutional Change: The Anti-Vietnam War Movement and American Science." Pp. 97–118 in *How Social Movements Matter*, edited by Marco Guigini, Doug McAdam, and Charles Tilly. Minneapolis, MN: University of Minnesota Press.

Mora-Ninci, Carlos Oswaldo. 1999. "The Chicano/a Student Movement in Southern California in the 1990s." Ph.D. Dissertation, Department of Education, University of California Los Angeles, Los Angeles, CA.

Morrill, Calvin, Mayer N. Zald, and Hayagreeva Rao. 2003. "Covert Political Conflict in Organizations: Challenges from Below." *Annual Review of Sociology* 29:391–415.

Naples, Nancy A. 2002. "Negotiating the Politics of Experiential Learning in Women's Studies: Lessons from the Community Action Project." Pp. 383–415 in *Women's Studies On Its Own, Next Wave: New Directions in Women's Studies*, edited by Robyn Wiegman. Durham, NC: Duke University Press.

National Center for Education Statistics. 2008. "The Condition of Education." Washington, DC: U.S. Department of Education. Retrieved June 24, 2010, (http://nces.ed.gov/programs/coe/).

—. 2010. "IPEDS Data Center." Washington, DC: U.S. Department of Education. Retrieved June 14, 2010, (http://nces.ed.gov/ipeds/datacenter/Default.aspx).

Nomura, Gail M. and Russell Endo, ed. 1989. Pullman, WA: Washington State University Press.

Nussbaum, Martha C. 1997. *Cultivating Humanity: A Classical Defense of Reform in Liberal Education*. Cambridge, MA: Harvard University Press.

O'Connell, Sean P. 2004. "Telling Tales in School: A Queer Response to the Heterosexist Narrative Structure of Higher Education." *Journal of Homosexuality* 47:79–93.

Ocamb, Karen. 1990. "Gay Studies Makes the Grade." *The Advocate*, October 9, 1990, p. 40.

Oliver, Christine. 1988. "The Collective Strategy Framework: An Application to Competing Predictions of Isomorphism." *Administrative Science Quarterly* 33:543–61.

Omatsu, Glenn. 2010. "Freedom Schooling: Reconceptualizing Asian American Studies for Our Communities." Pp. 498–514 in *Asian American Studies Now: A Critical Reader*, edited by Jean Yu-wen Shen Wu and Thomas C. Chen. New Brunswick, NJ: Rutgers University Press.

Park, Robert Ezra. 1950. *Race and Culture*. Glencoe, IL: Free Press.

Patai, Daphne and Noretta Koertge. 2003. *Professing Feminism: Education and Indoctrination in Women's Studies*. Lanham, MD: Lexington Books.

Peterson, Valarie V. 2009. "Against Interdisciplinarity." *Women and Language* 31:42–50.

Powell, Walter W. and Paul J. DiMaggio, ed. 1991. *The New Institutionalism in Organizational Analysis*. Chicago, IL: University of Chicago Press.

Raeburn, Nicole C. 2004. *Changing Corporate America from the Inside Out: Lesbian and Gay Workplace Rights*. Minneapolis, MN: University of Minnesota Press.

Rao, Hayagreeva. 2009. *Market Rebels: How Activists Make or Break Radical Innovations*. Princeton, NJ: Princeton University Press.

Rao, Hayagreeva and Kumar Sivakumar. 1999. "Institutional Sources of Boundary-Spanning Structures: The Establishment of Investor Relations Departments in the Fortune 500 Industrials." *Organization Science* 10:27–42.

Readings, Bill. 1996. *The University in Ruins*. Cambridge, MA: Harvard University Press.

Renda, Mary A. and the Gender Studies Advisory Group. 2005. "Proposal for a Department of Gender Studies." Mount Holyoke College, South Hadley, MA. Unpublished document on file with author.

Riesman, David. 1973. "Commentary and Epilogue." Pp. 409–74 in *Academic Transformation: Seventeen Institutions Under Pressure, Carnegie Commission on Higher Education Sponsored Research Series*, edited by David Riesman and Verne A. Statdtman. New York: McGraw Hill.

Rojas, Fabio. 2006. "Social Movement Tactics, Organizational Change, and the Spread of African-American Studies." *Social Forces* 84:2147–66.

—. 2007. *From Black Power to Black Studies: How a Radical Social Movement Became an Academic Discipline*. Baltimore, MD: Johns Hopkins University Press.

Rudolph, Frederick. 1989. *Curriculum: A History of the American Undergraduate Course of Study Since 1636*. San Francisco: Jossey-Bass Publishers.

Santa Cruz, Nicole. 2010. "Arizona Bill Targeting Ethnic Studies Signed Into Law." *Los Angeles Times*, May 12, 2010. Retrieved June 11, 2010, (http://articles.latimes.com/2010/may/12/nation/la-na-ethnic-studies-20100512).

Santoro, Wayne A. and Gail M. McGuire. 1997. "Social Movement Insiders: The Impact of Institutional Activists on Affirmative Action and Comparable Worth Policies." *Social Problems* 44:503–19.

Saslow, James M. 1991. "Lavender Academia Debates its Role: Gay and Lesbian Studies Programs Experience Growing Pains." *The Advocate*, September 24, 1991, pp. 66–9.

Schmitz, Betty, Beverly Guy-Sheftall, Johnella E. Butler, and Deborah Rosenfelt. 2004. "Women's Studies and Curriculum Transformation in the United States." Pp. 882–905 in *Handbook of Research on Multicultural Education*, edited by James A. Banks and Cherry A. McGee Banks. San Francisco: Jossey-Bass Publishers.

Shircliffe, Barbara Joseph. 1996. "The History of a Student-Run Women's Studies Program, 1971–1985." Ph.D. Dissertation, Philosophy, State University of New York at Buffalo, Buffalo, NY.

Silbergeld, Diana. 2001. "Students Kiss for Queer Studies." *The Wesleyan News*, March 7, 2001. Retrieved September 15, 2006, (http://www.wesleyan.edu/argus/mar0701/n1.html).

Skrentny, John D. 2002. *The Minority Rights Revolution*. Cambridge, MA: Harvard University Press.

Slaughter, Shelia. 1997. "Class, Race, and Gender and the Construction of Post-Secondary Curricula in the United States: Social Movement, Professionalization and Political Economic Theories of Curricular Change." *Journal of Curriculum Studies* 29:1–30.

Slaughter, Shelia and Larry L. Leslie. 2001. "Expanding and Elaborating the Concept of Academic Capitalism." *Organization* 8:145–61.

Slaughter, Shelia and Gary Rhoades. 2005. "Markets in Higher Education: Students in the Seventies, Patents in the Eighties, Copyrights in the Nineties." Pp. 486–516 in *American Higher Education in the Twenty-First Century: Social, Political, and Economic Challenges*, edited by Philip C. Altbach, Robert O. Berdhal, and Patricia J. Gumport. Baltimore, MD: Johns Hopkins University Press.

Small, Mario. 1999. "Departmental Conditions and the Emergence of New Disciplines: Two Cases in the Legitimation of African-American Studies." *Theory and Society* 28:659–707.

Smelser, Neil. 1963. *Theory of Collective Behavior*. New York: Free Press.

Smith, G. Kerry, ed. 1970. *The Troubled Campus*. San Francisco, CA: Jossey-Bass Publishers.

Snow, David A. E., Burke Rochford, Jr., Steven K. Worden, and Robert D. Benford. 1986. "Frame Alignment Processes, Micromobilization, and Movement Participation." *American Sociological Review* 51:464–81.

Snow, David A., Sarah A. Soule, and Hanspeter Kriesi. 2004. "Mapping the Terrain." Pp. 3–16 in *The Blackwell Companion to Social Movements*, edited by David A. Snow, Sarah A. Soule, and Hanspeter Kriesi. Malden, MA: Blackwell.

Spalter-Roth, Roberta M., Norman L. Fortenberry, and Barbara Lovitts. 2007. "What Sociologists Know About the Acceptance and Diffusion of Innovation: The Case of Engineering Education." American Sociological Association, Washington, DC. Retrieved August 25, 2007, (http://www.asanet.org/images/research/docs/pdf/Acceptance%20and%20Diffusion%20of%20Innovation.pdf)

Stevens, Mitchell L., Elizabeth Armstrong, and Richard Arum. 2006. "A Report to the American Sociological Association on the Conference 'A New Research Agenda for the Sociology of Education.'" Unpublished paper.

Strobel, Margaret. 2000. "Collective Practice and Multicultural Focus." Pp. 155–69 in *The Politics of Women's Studies: Testimony from Thirty Founding Mothers*, edited by Florence Howe. New York: The Feminist Press.

Sumida, Stephen H. 1998. "East of California: Points of Origin in Asian American Studies." *Journal of Asian American Studies* 1:83–100.

Takaki, Ronald. 1989. *Strangers from a Different Shore: A History of Asian Americans*. Boston, MA: Back Bay Books.

Tarrow, Sidney. 1998. *Power in Movement: Social Movements, Collective Action, and Politics*, Second ed. Cambridge, UK: Cambridge University Press.

Taylor, Catherine G. 1998. "Teaching for a Freer Future in Troubled Times." Pp. 15–30 in *Inside the Academy and Out: Lesbian/Gay/Queer Studies and Social Action*, edited by Janice L. Ristock and Catherine G. Taylor. Toronto, Canada: University of Toronto Press.

Taylor, Verta and Nicole C. Raeburn. 1995. "Identity Politics as High-Risk Activism: Career Consequences for Lesbian, Gay, and Bisexual Sociologists." *Social Problems* 42:252–73.

Teraguchi, Daniel Hiroyuki. 2002. "An Examination of the Ways in Which Contextual Conditions Influence the Sustainability of an Asian American Studies Program at an Urban Public University in the Northeast of the United States." Ed.D. Dissertation, Education, Idaho State University, Pocatello, ID.

Tierny, William. 1989. *Curricular Landscapes, Democratic Vistas: Transformative Leadership in Higher Education*. New York: Praeger.

—. 2008. *The Impact of Culture on Organizational Decision-Making: Theory and Practice in Higher Education*. Sterling, VA: Stylus.

Tilly, Charles. 1999. "Regimes and Contention." New York: Columbia International Affairs Online Working Papers Series. Retrieved February 28, 2007, (http://www.ciaonet.org/wps/tic09/).

Turner, Stephen. 2000. "What are Disciplines? And How is Interdisciplinarity Different?" Pp. 46–65 in *Practising Interdisciplinarity*, edited by Peter Weingart and Nico Stehr. Toronto, Canada: University of Toronto Press.

U.S. Census Bureau. 2010a. "Race Data." Washington, DC: Racial Statistics Branch, Population Division, U.S. Census Bureau. Retrieved June 23, 2010, (http://www.census.gov/population/www/socdemo/race.html).

—. 2010b. " Years of School Completed by People 25 Years and Over, by Age and Sex: Selected Years 1940 to 2009." Washington, DC: Retrieved June 23, 2010, (http://www.census.gov/population/socdemo/education/cps2009/tabA-1.xls).

—. n.d. "Census Regions and Divisions of the United States." U.S. Department of Commerce, Economics and Statistics Administration. Retrieved May 24, 2010, (http://www.census.gov/geo/www/us_regdiv.pdf).

Valenzuela, J. Samuel. 1998. "Macro Comparisons without the Pitfalls: A Protocol for Comparative Research." Pp. 237–66 in *Politics, Society, and Democracy: Latin America*, edited by Scott Mainwaring and Arturo Valenzuela. Boulder, CO: Westview Press.

Van Dyke, Nella, Sarah A. Soule, and Verta A. Taylor. 2004. "The Targets of Social Movements: Beyond a Focus on the State." *Research in Social Movements, Conflicts, and Change* 25:27–51.

Walker, Alice. 1983. *In Search of Our Mothers' Gardens: Womanist Prose.* Orlando, FL: Harcourt Brace Jovanovich.

Walker, Edward T., Andrew W. Martin, and John D. McCarthy. 2008. "Confronting the State, the Corporation, and the Academy: The Influence of Institutional Targets on Social Movement Repertoires." *American Journal of Sociology* 114:35–76.

Wei, William. 1993. *The Asian American Movement.* Philadelphia, PA: Temple University Press.

Weick, Karl E. 1976. "Educational Organizations as Loosely Coupled Systems." *Administrative Science Quarterly* 21:1–19.

Wiegman, Robyn. 2002. "The Progress of Gender: Whither "Women"?" Pp. 106–40 in *Women's Studies On Its Own, Next Wave: New Directions in Women's Studies*, edited by Robyn Wiegman. Durham, NC: Duke University Press.

Weingart, Peter. 2000. "Interdisciplinarity: The Paradoxical Discourse." Pp. 25–42 in *Practising Interdisciplinarity*, edited by Peter Weingart and Nico Stehr. Toronto, Canada: University of Toronto Press.

Wilde, Melissa J. 2004. "How Culture Mattered at Vatican II: Collegiality Trumps Authority in the Council's Social Movement Organizations." *American Sociological Review* 69:576–602.

Winston, Gordon C. 1999. "Subsidies, Hierarchy and Peers: The Awkward Economics of Higher Education." *The Journal of Economic Perspectives* 13:13–36.

WMST-L. 2009. "Archives of WMST-L@LISTSERV.UMD.EDU." University of Maryland. Retrieved June 15, 2009, (https://listserv.umd.edu/archives/wmst-l.html).

Wood, Donna Jean. 1979. "Women's Studies Programs in American Colleges and Universities: A Case of Organizational Innovation." Ph.D. Dissertation, Sociology, Vanderbilt University, Nashville, TN.

Wotipka, Christine, Francisco O. Ramírez, and Capitolina Diaz Martínez. 2007. "Un Análisis Trasnacional del Surgimiento e Institucionalización de los Planes Académicos de los Estudios de las Mujeres." (In Spanish). *Revista Española de Investigaciones Sociológicas* 117:35–59.

Yamane, David. 2001. *Student Movements for Multiculturalism: Challenging the Curricular Color Line in Higher Education.* Baltimore, MD: The Johns Hopkins University Press.

Yoshimura, Evelyn. 1971. "G.I.s and Asian Women." Pp. 27–9 in *Roots: An Asian American Reader*, edited by Amy Tachiki, Eddie Wong, Franklin Odo, and Buck Wong. Los Angeles, CA: UCLA Asian American Studies Center Press.

Yoshino, Kenji. 2006. *Covering: The Hidden Assault on Our Civil Rights*. New York: Random House.

Zald, Mayer N. and John D McCarthy, ed. 1979. *The Dynamics of Social Movements: Resource Mobilization, Social Control, and Tactics*. Cambridge, MA: Winthrop.

Index